Local Area Networks

Data Communications and Networks Series

Consulting Editor: Dr C. Smythe, Surrey University

Selected titles

X400 Message Handling: Standards, Interworking, Applications
  B. Plattner, C. Lanz, H. Lubich, M. Müller and T. Walter

Network Management: Problems, Standards and Strategies
  Franz-Joachim Kauffels

Token Ring: Principles, perspectives and strategies
  Hans-Georg Göhring and Franz-Joachim Kauffels

Local Area Networks

Making the Right Choices

Philip Hunter

▲▼ **ADDISON-WESLEY**

Harlow, England • Reading, Massachusetts • Menlo Park, California
New York • Don Mills, Ontario • Amsterdam • Bonn • Sydney • Singapore
Tokyo • Madrid • San Juan • Milan • Mexico City • Seoul • Taipei

© 1993 Addison-Wesley Publishers Ltd
© 1993 Addison-Wesley Publishing Company Inc.

The programs in this book have been included for their instructional value. They have been tested with care but are not guaranteed for any particular purpose. The publisher does not offer any warranties or representations, nor does it accept any liabilities with respect to the programs.

Many of the designations used by manufacturers and sellers used to distinguish their products are claimed as trademarks. Addison-Wesley has made every attempt to supply trademark information about manufacturers and their products mentioned in this book. A list of trademark designations and their owners appears below.

Cover designed by Designers & Partners of Oxford
and printed by Ethedo Press, High Wycombe, Bucks
Typeset by Colset Pte Ltd, Singapore
in 11¼/13 point Baskerville
Printed and bound in Great Britain by Biddles Ltd, Guildford and King's Lynn

First printed 1993
Reprinted 1994, 1997

ISBN 0-201-62763-9

British Library Cataloguing in Publication Data
A catalogue record for this book is available from the British Library

Library of Congress Cataloging in Publication Data

Trademark notice

NetWare, IPX, NetWare 3.11, NetWare 4.0, NetWare SFT, NetWare management system, NetWare Lite, NetWare 286, NetWare 386, DR-DOS, Unix, UnixWare and LAN workplace are trademarks of Novell Inc.

Systimax, Unified Network Management architecture are trademarks of AT&T.

LAN Manager, Windows 3, Windows NT, Windows for Workgroups and MS Mail are trademarks of Microsoft Corporation.

Expressnet hub is a trademark of David Systems.

System 7 for Apple Macintosh is a trademark of Apple Computer Inc.

Netview, System network architecture, System application architecture, LAN Server and IBM AT are trademarks of International Business Machines Corporation.

VINES is a trademark of Banyan Systems Inc.

Xerox Network Systems is a trademark of Xerox Corporation.

PowerLAN is a trademark of Performance Technology.

DECnet is a trademark of Digital Equipment Corporation.

LANtastic is a trademark of Artisoft.

10Net is a trademark of Sitka.

SmartCAU is a trademark of Madge Networks.

Contents

Chapter 7

How do I choose my own LAN?   **175**

Chapter 8

How do I design my network so that it will last and can be easily extended?   **203**

Chapter 9

What is an open system and is it important to me and my network?   **226**

Chapter 10

How do I manage and maintain my network?   **253**

Introduction

The LAN (local area network) is fast becoming indispensable for small and medium sized businesses for sharing information, applications and resources such as printers. Without a LAN, it is difficult or impossible for companies to exploit information technology efficiently or competitively, given recent trends in computing. Yet many smaller businesses still do not have LANs and many that do have made poor choices of technology that make it difficult to expand or adopt superior computing technologies as they emerge.

The aim of this book is to help you choose LAN systems that are compatible with your business objectives and that best exploit the current technological opportunities. This includes the technical components of the LAN itself but perhaps more important embraces issues such as choice of supplier and how much help to obtain in implementing the LAN. The book also addresses the skills needed to manage a LAN effectively, which is a factor that needs to be considered in calculating how much a LAN will cost. But at the same time the potential savings of a LAN need to be considered, compared with alternative options. Such issues are discussed in detail in Chapter 1, which answers the fundamental question: when do I know that I need a local area network?

Subsequent chapters deal with the different components or aspects of a LAN and issues that arise as the network expands. Running through the whole book is a twin theme: the LAN must solve your current problems while at the same time keeping future options as open as possible. The latter is important because both technology and business needs change at an ever increasing rate and successful companies in the 1990s will be those that are able to react most quickly to these.

In the rest of this introduction we explain first of all why LANs are becoming so important for almost all companies with more than a handful of employees, and then outline the main components of a LAN, thus setting the scene for subsequent chapters.

The fundamental *raison d'être* of LANs is that they enable businesses to derive maximum benefit from their existing computer systems. In effect they do this by combining the best of the new and old worlds of computing in a cost effective and flexible way.

In the old world, by which I mean in particular the period from 1960 up to around 1985, major organizations had large centralized computers enabling information, software applications and facilities such as printers to be shared by many users. However, in the old world only specialist programmers and hardware engineers had direct access to computing facilities. Until 1978 or so, most users had to submit their applications on punched cards and often had to wait several hours for the result. Furthermore, worthwhile applications typically took months if not years to develop, which tended to stifle innovation in the field.

In the new world, ushered in by the personal computer (PC) during the early 1980s, computing became far more accessible to ordinary users. They now had a desktop machine directly under their control, encouraging greater use of computers to solve problems and save valuable time through applications such as word processing and financial modelling. But the very success of PCs in taking computing to the people introduced a new problem. As PCs proliferated there was a growing need to share common information and facilities between them. Clearly if there were ten PCs in an office it made sense to share one or perhaps two printers between them rather than, for example, give one to each user.

This led to the introduction of LANs, which within larger organizations spread rapidly from 1986 onwards. They enabled the advantages of the PC, such as ease of use and constant availability to its user, to be combined with the information and resource sharing capabilities of the traditional centralized computers. LANs can therefore be regarded as a sharing mechanism, enabling individual users with PCs to access common information and resources. LANs also allow computer applications to be shared where appropriate, for example where there are tasks that require a powerful expensive computer to execute. In such cases it makes sense to provide users with common access to just one central machine via a LAN rather than giving such a machine to each user. This is just another form of resource sharing.

Essentially both information and the applications that process that information can reside either in the desktop PC, or in central servers, or in a combination of both. Information or software applications used by just one person may be best held in a single PC. On the other hand, information that is shared by or needs to be accessed by a number of users may be best held on a central machine. However, this issue of splitting information and applications between central servers and desktop PCs may not be relevant for many small businesses.

In fact there does not have to be any central store of data or applications at all (Figure I.1). LANs make it possible for each PC to access every other computer on the network. This means that the data and applications held in every single PC attached to the LAN can be made available to users of all other PCs on that LAN. Networks that provide this ability to share each other's PCs are often called peer-to-peer and are described in Chapter 4.

Apart from accessing data and applications, the other key feature of LANs is their support for communication between users themselves via electronic mail. This may not count for much when, as sometimes happens, all users of a LAN reside within one room. But it can be effective when users are scattered throughout a building, or, as increasingly happens within larger organizations, when a variety of LANs are linked together into a bigger enterprise-wide network. Then the ability to deliver memoranda and text messages instantly to any number of recipients can speed up decision making and problem solving.

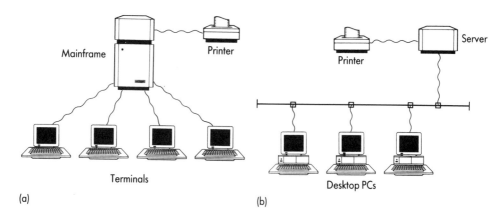

Figure I.1 Comparing old centralized mainframe computer with modern LAN. (a) Centralized host computer supporting dumb terminals. Resources such as printers are attached to mainframe, or host, computer and shared out among users of dumb terminals. (b) LAN, with PCs sharing server that provides access to shared data such as printer.

Components of a LAN

The principal feature of a LAN underpinning the benefits we have already touched on is that it enables PCs and other types of computer to communicate both with each other and with devices such as printers that are shared between some or all users of the network. There is also the caveat implicit in the name, which is that the LAN only allows such communication within a limited area.

To achieve this we identify two fundamental categories of components: physical ones, such as cabling which can be seen, and logical ones implemented in software that control access to the network and its resources. Together these comprise a complete LAN which delivers the required features and benefits. These two categories in fact overlap. For example, PCs are usually attached to the physical cabling by cards, called network interface cards (NICs), in an expansion slot at the back of the PC (Figure I.2). This device is physical but it also contains the software code that enables programs in the PC to access the LAN.

An important point to note is that the components of LANs are not fixed in stone but are constantly changing. The major development during the early 1990s was the emergence of the hub. This originally served as a focal point for cabling but has since evolved to provide additional facilities such as network management and the ability to access other networks. The hub is described in Chapter 3, with more discussion of its role in management in Chapter 10.

Another key related development has been the ability to implement LANs on progressively cheaper and thinner cable. The most

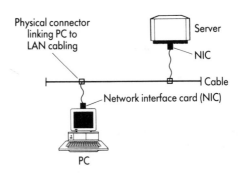

Figure I.2   Illustrating general structure of a LAN.

popular type of LAN, commonly called Ethernet, is now generally implemented over telephone-type cabling, which is cheaper and easier to install. However, such cabling has a more limited range, which has led to changes in the physical design of Ethernet LANs. Originally Ethernet was laid out in a tree-and-branch structure called a bus, with a maximum span between any two attached nodes of 500 metres, although this could be extended to 2500 metres with the use of repeaters that boost the electrical signal. Over the lower-cost telephone wiring, called twisted pair, the maximum distance allowed between a pair of devices connected by this cable using Ethernet protocols was 100 metres.

To cover the original distances of up to 2500 metres, hubs are used in which a number of nodes are attached in a star-shaped formation using the lower-cost twisted pair cable. None of these devices can be more than 100 metres from the hub, which is sometimes called a concentrator. To span greater distances the hubs themselves must be connected together with higher-grade cable. This arrangement enables the network to be clustered around workgroups in little constellations and minimizes the amount of expensive cable.

Can components be installed separately?

LANs can be installed as complete packages but it is also possible to purchase them piecemeal in their various components. In many cases setting up the most suitable LAN for a given situation requires careful matching of the various components. For this reason the different components are all discussed in detail in this book.

Relationship between LAN components and the standard international model specifying how networks should be built

LANs are designed in layers conforming to an internationally agreed seven layer model which defines how computers should communicate across any network. This model is described in Chapter 9. A complete LAN including PCs and applications spans all seven layers but the basic communications are covered just by the bottom two. The bottom physical layer specifies the communications medium, which for LANs usually is some type of cable. We look at cabling in Chapter 3. The second layer then deals with how data is transmitted over that cable – and it is at this level that the various types of LAN, such as Ethernet or token ring, are distinguished. We compare Ethernet and token ring in Chapter 2.

The other essential component of a LAN is some type of operating system for controlling access to data and to shared resources across the network. In this sense a LAN is rather like a single large computer that supports a number of users. Traditional large computers were accessed by users via simple terminals that provided just a keyboard and screen with shared access to data, printers and other facilities. A LAN can do just the same, except that now users have a more intelligent device on their desktop, a PC, which enables them to perform tasks without reference to any other system. LAN operating systems are discussed in Chapter 4.

A non-essential component but one that is becoming increasingly important for all but the smallest networks, is some management system. For users of smaller networks adequate management facilities will usually be provided within the network operating system. This may include security features that can, for example, prevent some users from accessing certain types of information or stop them accessing some zones of the LAN.

For larger networks, however, there will usually be additional management systems dedicated to specific parts of the network, providing facilities such as fault detection and management. Management issues in general are discussed in Chapter 10.

Another non-essential but increasingly common element of modern LANs is a central cabling hub, which can also provide network management and other LAN functions. The general structure of a hub-based LAN is shown in Figure I.3.

Having defined LANs and outlined the areas we are covering, it is worth noting two related fields that this book does not cover. It does not tackle wide area networks (WANs) spanning larger distances than LANs cover. WANs utilize telecommunications links to interconnect LANs and other computer systems over large distances, for example between the national branches of a major company. However, we do touch on the use of telecommunications links to connect two or more remote LANs in Chapters 6 and 8.

The other significant area this book does not address is the use of LANs in manufacturing and process control, which involves real time control of equipment such as machine tools and robots.

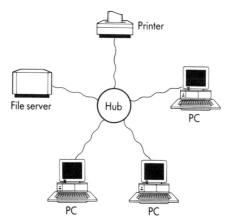

Figure I.3 Structure of a hub-based LAN. All devices, including PCs, printer and server, are connected to a central cabling hub. This hub can also provide management and other functions, such as access to other LANs and remote telecommunications links.

1

How do I know when I need a local area network?

CHAPTER CONTENTS

CHAPTER OBJECTIVES

This chapter is primarily for businesses that are contemplating their first LAN and want a sketch of the basic options. It tackles the following questions or issues:

1

Need to share and exchange information

For a local area network (LAN) to be necessary or at least highly desirable within a small business, or within a department of a larger one, two principal conditions need to be met. First, there have to be at least three people using some kind of desktop PC (you can have a LAN with just two users but the advantages normally only begin to be realized with three or more). Second, these people must need either to communicate with other computer users or to share information or computing resources such as a printer with them. For small businesses the most common devices to be shared are a printer and a file server. The latter in turn holds the information to be shared between users.

The ability to share data is particularly important for popular small business applications such as accounting, as this enables peaks of activity to be handled. For example, when annual accounts need to be submitted, staff can be assigned to the task if it is possible to provide common access to the application and relevant data. The LAN is fast becoming the most popular way of fulfilling this requirement. Later in the chapter we examine the criteria for needing a LAN in detail but first let us consider the principal alternative, the minicomputer.

What is the main alternative to a LAN?

The principal alternative to the LAN for small businesses is the traditional minicomputer, in which applications and data reside centrally on a single computer. The differences between a minicomputer and a LAN have begun to blur in recent years but they still present two distinct alternatives for many small businesses. The mini comprises a single central computer that users access through dumb terminals, which generally lack the ability to execute computer programs on their own without the help of the central mini. This is illustrated in the Introduction in Figure I.1(a).

LANs distribute computing power

Many LANs also have a central machine, usually called a server, but the difference is that users are more likely to have PCs that are small computers in their own right, that is, able to execute applications without the help of a server. However, as we shall explain in Chapter 4, there is a growing body of applications, called client/server applications, in which the PCs cooperate with servers. It is this development that is leading to some convergence between minicomputers and LANs on larger networks. In fact minicomputers are often attached to a LAN, accessed by terminals also linked to the LAN, as explained later in this chapter.

However, many small LANs do not have a dedicated central server. Such LANs, often called peer-to-peer LANs, consist solely of interconnected desktop PCs with no central machine. Peer-to-peer LANs are discussed further in Chapter 4.

Why small businesses prefer LANs to minicomputers

For small businesses, LANs are generally preferred to dedicated minicomputers, for two main reasons. First, they are more flexible, with greater potential for future growth and change as we shall explain further in Chapter 8. Second, LANs tend to cost less for a given application. PCs have fallen steadily in price over recent years, eroding previous cost arguments in favour of using dumb terminals linked to a single computer. Suppose, for example, a business has six active computer users. There could be a LAN comprising six PCs and perhaps a further dedicated server machine. Alternatively there could be a minicomputer and six dumb terminals. Until recently the terminals would cost substantially less, typically about 20 % of the price of the PC. So, given the extra cost of the minicomputer the LAN might have worked out more expensive. But recently the cost of PCs and the LAN components has fallen dramatically, eroding any cost argument in favour of the minicomputer. We consider the pros and cons of minis and LANs in more detail at the end of Chapter 8.

But the LAN is not always the best solution

As we shall see later in the chapter, there are some small business applications where a LAN may not be the best solution, even when the two conditions stated at the beginning of the chapter are met. But, as we shall make clear, this is to some extent hair splitting because some form of network will still be required – it is just that it does not happen to be the traditional LAN solution.

Defining the LAN in brief

In many cases, though, the LAN satisfies the above two requirements by providing a network enabling PCs to communicate with each other and with any shared resources. It needs three components to achieve this. First, there is a communications cable providing the electrical link connecting the PCs with each other and with any other computing devices. Second, there has to be some method of controlling access to the cable by the PCs and other devices. This second component comprises both the physical mechanism of attaching a PC or device to the cable of the LAN and a technique for controlling access from each PC to the LAN. The latter is required because generally only one device can be transmitting data at any instant. In most cases, as explained further in Chapter 2, this is provided by a card, called a network interface card or NIC, that fits into a slot in the back of a standard PC. This card then attaches to the main LAN cable via an adaptor. Third, there has to be some software controlling the overall operation of a LAN: handling tasks such as printing and exchanging data files. This component, called a network operating system, works in a similar way to PC operating systems such as the well-known MS-DOS. The difference is that whereas MS-DOS controls the operation of devices attached to just one PC, such as its disk drive and keyboard, the networking operating system does the same job for the LAN as a whole. Figure 1.1 illustrates how these three basic functions interact on a typical LAN.

These three components are each dealt with in detail in Chapters 2 to 4. In this chapter we consider the LAN as a whole, the service it provides and the situations where it is needed.

Within most large organizations, LANs are already well established. In such cases the first criterion, that there have to be at least three users, will be satisfied many times over, often in many different departments. Here too the original requirements were to share

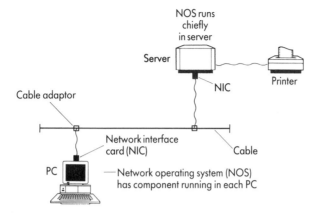

Figure 1.1 How the basic components of the LAN (cabling system, network interface card (NIC) and network operating system (NOS)) fit together. Note that some LANs do not have a dedicated server. In that case, the NOS is installed in all PCs attached to the network. Some of the PCs may be configured to act as non-dedicated servers on behalf of others. Non-dedicated servers also function as desktop PCs under control of a single user.

information and resources, and often to exchange messages and data, with other people working in the same team or department.

Within an accounts department, for example, it is clearly a good idea for all staff to have access to the same bought ledger files, which pertain to goods or services that have been purchased from suppliers. Then, if a supplier telephones with an enquiry about an invoice that has not been paid, any member of the department taking the call can obtain consistent up-to-date information about the status of that order.

Alternatively, an automobile engineer may want to send a computerized drawing of a car design to a colleague somewhere else in the building. The drawing has been produced on a desktop workstation, which is essentially a powerful PC, using a computer-aided design package. Without a LAN the data defining this drawing would have to be saved on a computer disk and carried to the destination for loading into the workstation of the recipient engineer. With a LAN, the drawing could be transmitted electronically between the two workstations.

At this point you may stop and ask: why do you need a LAN to accomplish these tasks? Could you not just connect the relevant computers directly together with a piece of cable? Is there no alternative method?

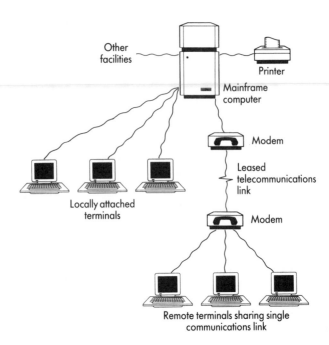

Figure 1.2 Traditional centralized mainframe supporting terminals via point-to-point links. Terminals could be at a remote site, where several terminals might share a single link.

The answer to the last two questions is yes. When there is a requirement to do no more than transmit data between two computers then a direct link between them would be the best solution. We look at some low-cost alternatives to LANs later in the chapter.

In the pre-LAN era, resources and data were shared in a different way, with a single mainframe computer occupying a whole room linked by point-to-point links via dumb terminals, as illustrated in Figure 1.2.

Such centralized systems still exist of course, particularly for large-scale applications like running the payroll of a big company, or controlling the cash dispensing machines of a major bank. However, for smaller-scale operations the LAN is steadily taking over because it can do the job for less money and with other advantages, such as the ability to expand the network at an even pace rather than having to grow in large steps. For smaller organizations, at which this book is primarily aimed, the advantages of LANs are particularly overwhelming, as should become clearer during this chapter.

How LANs evolved from traditional centralized computer systems

LANs in fact combine the advantages of the old centralized approach to computing and the more recently introduced world of desktop PCs. Under the old approach all the computer processing and all the data was held on a central machine, often housed in a dedicated machine room. Users accessed this machine remotely from dumb terminals that just provided a screen and keyboard with no computing power of their own, or from now obsolete devices such as card readers. The advantage of this approach was that expensive resources and information could be shared and properly controlled. The disadvantage was that it was not responsive to users' needs. It discouraged innovative use of computers because applications were under the control of central information technology departments and the majority of staff had no direct access to the computer.

How LANs helped solve new problems brought by proliferating PCs

The PC changed all this, bringing computing to the people, but introduced new problems that did not exist under the old centralized regime. One major problem was that a number of PCs might each have their own printer, involving unnecessary costs as the amount of usage did not justify each user having one. PCs also encouraged the proliferation of different sources of data, often overlapping but not consistent with each other. Generally there was an upwelling of anarchy, with no central control over an increasingly important piece of the overall information technology jigsaw.

The LAN emerged as a solution to these mounting problems. Since then it has become the dominant method of networking computers and other devices together at local level within offices, buildings or small companies. This dominance has reinforced itself because it has encouraged the whole computer industry to develop products for it. Therefore, for a company starting out today there is really no alternative to the LAN for networking computers at local level, although as we shall see in Chapter 7 there is a range of options at different prices.

In the early days of the PC, however, it was not so obvious which way the computer industry would go. Many larger organizations already had medium-scale departmental computers, often called mini-computers. For them one option was to connect the PCs to these minicomputers on a point-to-point basis to access existing devices and data, as shown in Figure 1.3. In this case the PC is seen by the minicomputer as a dumb terminal. However, the PC is not like a terminal in that it can extract data from the central machine and use it within applications on the desktop. It responds faster than a dumb terminal linked to a central machine and provides a much richer vein of facilities.

However, although it appears also to combine the advantages of the PC and central machine, this arrangement ultimately proved cumbersome and expensive. PCs improved more quickly than mini-computers in terms of power and sophistication and provided a much more cost effective solution for the smaller business. Today it is unlikely that a start-up company would contemplate a small centralized system with dumb terminals rather than a network of PCs (although we describe some situations where they might at the end of the chapter).

A detailed look at the criteria for needing a LAN

A LAN may be installed either to connect existing PCs and computing equipment within an office or as part of a complete IT (information technology) purchase starting from scratch. The same selection criteria apply in either case. The difference is that in the latter case everything can be matched together to obtain the best overall fit for the business, whereas in the former the LAN has to be suitable for the equipment already installed.

We identify six fundamental criteria for needing a LAN, with a pre-condition that there have to be at least three people with a PC, or immediate plans to have at least three people with a PC, all within one location. The criteria then are:

Figure 1.3 PCs serving users directly for applications such as word processing, but also linked to a departmental minicomputer for shared applications. To do this, the PCs mimic, or emulate, the screen and keyboard functions of dumb terminals. But unlike a dumb terminal, the PC can extract data from the minicomputer and manipulate it within independent desktop applications such as spreadsheets.

(1) When these users, at least three, need to share expensive computing facilities such as printers or have shared access to some other computing service.

(2) When users need to share information in the form of computer data.

(3) When three or more people use the same applications software, such as word processing.

(4) When there is a need to exchange data between PCs within a business or department.

(5) When central supervision of computing resources such as PCs is needed.

(6) When new applications require cooperation between two or more PCs to perform their function.

This sixth criterion issue has only emerged recently and is less likely to be relevant for the typical small business but we include it because it is likely to grow in importance over the coming five years.

When users need to share expensive computing facilities, such as printers

The way LANs allow resources to be shared is shown in outline in Figure 1.4. The most common resource to be shared on a LAN, apart

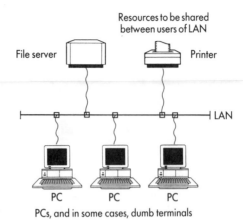

Figure 1.4   On a LAN, users have access to a common network to which shared resources are attached.

from file servers for sharing data which comes under our second criterion, is the printer. Typically one printer is capable of serving a group of up to 20 people depending on the application, although a LAN can equally allow several printers to be shared. The point is that when there are more than two users it becomes time consuming and messy to share the printer by swopping cables between desktop PCs.

LANs were originally introduced largely for resource sharing in the early 1980s. Nowadays this is rarely the only criterion for needing a LAN. Where the main need is just to share resources there are a number of low-cost LAN solutions around but, as we shall discuss further in Chapter 8, these may preclude significant extension of the network in future. Some low-cost suppliers of LANs will be described in Chapter 7.

Print spooling

One point to note is that printing on a LAN requires a technique called spooling, which is explained in more detail in Chapter 5. Spooling allows a succession of print jobs to be stacked up. PC applications and users do not then need to wait for a printer to become free before submitting work to be printed. Jobs can be sent to a print queue and the PC is then free to continue other work such as word processing. Spooling is usually handled by a server computer. However, there are now some printers that support spooling and can be attached directly to the network. In the former case, which is more common, the printer is not attached to the LAN directly but instead is linked by a cable to a file server. These two possible arrangements for printer attachment are shown in Figure 1.5.

Spooling is less important if users on the network have PCs that support multitasking, which is the ability to perform more than one task at once. Such PCs can run applications like word processing and at the same time attempt to submit jobs for printing in the background. However, even with multitasking PCs it is more efficient and orderly to be able to submit jobs automatically to a central queue. Otherwise the order with which jobs are printed will tend to be rather random, with jobs jumping the queue if they happen to be submitted at a given time.

Another point to note is that it is possible to have more than one printer on a LAN. There could, for example, be a laser printer for high-quality output using colour and a basic high-speed text printer.

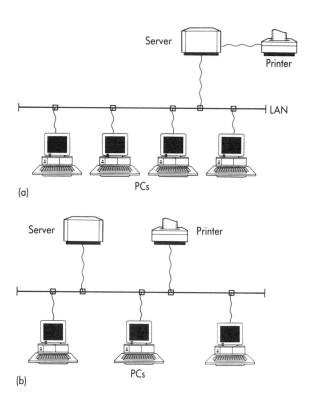

Figure 1.5 (a) Printer attached to a LAN via a server. This is the most common arrangement. (b) Printer attached directly to the LAN. To do this, the printers need to have their own memory and processor to support queuing, as explained in Chapter 5.

Each printer has a unique address which enables users and applications to route output to the one appropriate for a particular job.

Apart from printers, there is a growing range of other hardware that may be shared on a LAN. Increasingly common are image scanners, which turn any form of hard copy – including photographs, diagrams and printed text – into digital data that can be stored and reproduced in its original form. A small press cuttings agency, for example, might use such a scanner on a LAN to capture images of press clippings each day. These would be stored on a suitable file server, perhaps using an optical disk drive, so that they could be retrieved on screen. There might also be a shared laser printer for reproducing images of the cuttings on demand. A LAN providing these facilities is shown in Figure 1.6.

Another important class of resource that can be shared on a LAN is the communications server. This can take a variety of forms. It can be a PC or other type of small computer programmed to perform tasks that enable users to access computing services via the LAN. Alternatively it can be a means of sharing devices such as modems that otherwise would be required by each PC, just as printers can be shared. A special kind of communications server is the fax server, which enables facsimile transmissions to be sent and sometimes also received without using a dedicated fax machine.

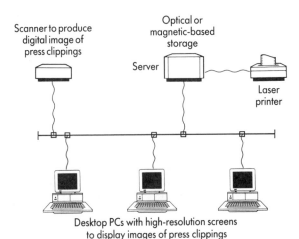

Figure 1.6 A LAN that could be used by a press clippings agency. A single server computer could control high-capacity storage for images of the clippings and a laser printer to print such images. PCs would need high-resolution screens to view images.

Terminal servers

One class of communications device that can be shared is the terminal server. This enables dumb terminals rather than PCs to access a large computer designed to serve a number of users rather than just one (Figure 1.7). Such computers are often called host computers because they play 'host' to a variety of users, holding all the data and applications software. This is the traditional centralized computing world, where all the intelligence resides in the host machine with users accessing applications from relatively dumb terminals or from PCs that are acting in this case as dumb terminals. Terminal servers are discussed in Chapter 5, which looks at the full range of devices that can be attached to a LAN and the issues that arise.

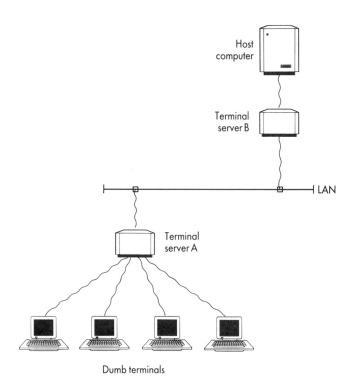

Dumb terminals

Figure 1.7   Use of a LAN to connect dumb terminals to a host computer via terminal servers. The host expects to have each dumb terminal attached via separate point-to-point connections. The function of terminal server A at the terminal end is to funnel all of these connections into a single communications channel along the LAN. This process is called 'multiplexing'. The function of terminal server B at the host end is to unravel the single channel and identify the messages coming from the terminal.

Linking PCs to host systems

LANs may also be used to connect PCs to host systems. Traditional dumb terminals provide access to host systems with data stored and processed in the central host computer. Then as PCs grew popular during the mid 1980s, more and more people needed both a PC and a dumb terminal on their desks.

This did not leave much room for other desktop artefacts like paper, telephones and coffee cups. Users began to ask why not make the PC behave like a dumb terminal sometimes? Then they could do away with their dumb terminals and clear their desks.

This led to the development of PC-to-host connectivity software, in which the PC mimicked the behaviour of the dumb terminal. Such software was installed in the PC and required a cable running from the PC to some terminal server or other device attaching directly to the host system.

But when LANs came along, and we are chiefly talking here of larger organizations during the latter half of the 1980s, a further improvement became possible. If LANs were there anyway, it made sense to use them to connect PCs to host systems via a single device sometimes called a host server. This is akin to a terminal server, except that this time it handles PCs. It avoided the need for a separate cable running from each PC. It also meant that the terminal emulation software, that enabled each PC to work like a dumb terminal, could now reside in just one place. Such an arrangement also makes change easier to handle. If, for example, a new PC needs access to a host it is necessary just to connect the PC to the LAN and then reconfigure the host server to recognize the extra PC.

For the average small business, the second type of communications server, enabling devices to be shared, will probably be of greater interest than terminal and host servers. The commonest communications device shared in this way is the modem but there are growing requirements for servers that enable users to share fax services and ISDN (integrated service digital network) links.

Shared modems

Modems enable PCs and other computers to communicate with each other and with services such as online databases via standard telephone lines. Traditionally PCs have modems attached directly on a one-to-one basis, but they typically only utilize them for a small proportion of the time. Once again it can make economic sense to share modems across a LAN. Figure 1.8 illustrates the two possibilities,

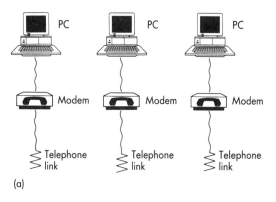

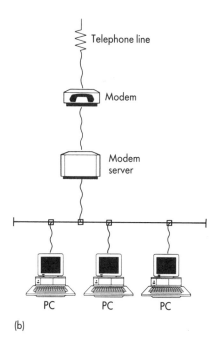

Figure 1.8 (a) PCs attached to a LAN, each having their own modem and needing separate telephone connections. (b) PCs sharing a single modem and telephone line via a modem server attached to a LAN.

showing how a modem server enables several users to share a modem and telephone line. When only occasional use is made of modem communications, a single modem shared between a small group of LAN users, as shown in Figure 1.9(b), will almost certainly be sufficient.

However, if there is a significant amount of usage a second modem can be provided. Indeed, it is possible with some systems to increase the number of modems attached to a LAN one at a time as demand rises. The number of modems will always be less than the number of users, just as on a private telephone exchange there never needs to be as many external lines as there are internal telephone handsets. Therefore the use of a LAN to share modems should always result in cost savings. With more than one modem, it is possible to configure each one differently to match particular communication requirements. Consider, for example, a business selling an online information service, whose customers dial in from their computers. It would make sense to ensure that at least some of the modems are kept free for incoming calls only but on the same network there could be one or more modems set just for outgoing calls.

Shared fax service

LANs can also be used to provide a shared facsimile service, allowing fax transmissions to be sent and received directly from PCs without use of a fax machine. This is achieved by use of fax cards which, like the LAN attachment cards described earlier in this chapter, usually slot into the back of PCs. These cards enable text and in some cases diagrams and photographic images to be transmitted to a remote fax machine directly from a PC, without having to be printed out and then sent via a fax machine. This saves time because there is no need to print out material generated within the PC for transmission by a fax machine. It also results in better quality hard copy at the receiving end because it bypasses the fax scanning process during which some of the image detail is always lost. Furthermore, it saves time waiting by a fax machine. If the destination number is engaged, the transmission can be retried automatically and faxes can be stacked up for transmission at a specified time, possibly to take advantage of lower call charges.

Dedicated fax servers can also receive faxed documents but this does not usually work as well as fax transmission. One problem with receiving faxes on a PC rather than a standard machine is the amount of memory on the hard disk drive that a fax uses. A few long faxes will consume a significant proportion of a typical PC's entire disk drive, impairing the performance of other applications. It is much better to store incoming faxes on a dedicated machine, where sufficient hard disk storage capacity can be provided more economically and alert users when a fax has come for them. However, on smaller networks this is not likely to be a cost effective option.

Shared ISDN (integrated services digital network) link

ISDN is the successor to the standard public switched telephone network (PSTN), providing digital rather than analog communications. It is usually accessed from PCs by ISDN terminal adaptors, just as modems connect PCs to the standard telephone network. Like modems, ISDN adaptors can be shared over a LAN. ISDN is discussed in more detail in Appendix 1.

When users need to share data

We have already mentioned how LANs were initially installed to share computing resources, especially printers, among a number of PCs. As the use of PCs increased, there was a growing need to share information and in particular to have single consistent sources of data within workgroups and departments. This led to the birth of the file server. Figure 1.9 shows how LANs enabled users to share disk drives. Figure 1.9(a) illustrates how in a single stand-alone PC the processor communicates directly with its own internal hard disk drive. Figure 1.9(b) shows how a basic file server acts as a 'virtual' disk drive shared by several PCs. It is called virtual because to each PC it appears as a directly attached drive not shared by other users.

Growth of the file server

Initially file servers were standard low-power PCs that any user on the LAN could access and update. Now file servers are usually top-end PCs, having greater processing power and memory than are needed for desktop applications. In a sense they are a reinvention of part of the centralized computer, as they provide similar data management features. In addition to supporting centralized data, they provide the means to share other resources, just as host computers do. For example, they can often support print spooling so that a printer can be attached to a LAN via the server. The difference is that while traditional host machines do all the processing involved in an application the file server performs only tasks involved in accessing and managing the data on behalf of PCs on desktops – that is why they are called servers. The specific processing required for each application is now done in the PC on the desktop.

The use of file servers to manage data is a crucial development for users of LANs. Originally file servers created as many problems

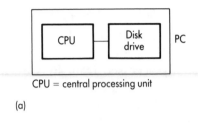

CPU = central processing unit

(a)

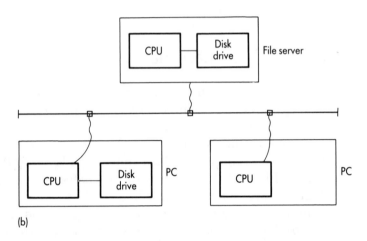

(b)

Figure 1.9   (a) Single PC processor communicating directly with internal hard disk drive on which permanent data and programs are stored. (b) How several PCs can share a disk drive on a LAN. Each PC shares the disk drive of the file server, which it accesses via the file server's CPU. Each PC usually has its own disk drive for storing private data. However, shared information pertaining to the whole business would be held on the server's disk drive.

as they solved, partly because they encouraged the proliferation of data that was increasingly vital to a company's business but which was poorly protected from accidental corruption and access from unauthorized users. There was also a performance problem resulting from the way data was accessed by the growing number of databases running in desktop machines.

To understand this problem and how it is now being solved, we need to look briefly at how a database works. Most databases are now based on the relational model, in which data is represented in various files that in turn hold individual records, such as a name and address. The structure of a typical simple database is shown in Figure 1.10. Here details of a firm's customers are held in two files one containing addresses as individual records, the other listing the products or services they have purchased. Records in turn comprise fields that

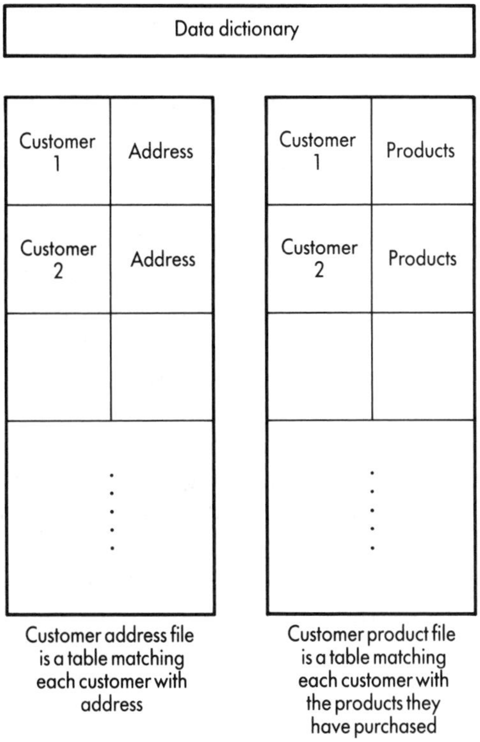

Figure 1.10 Structure of a simple database of a firm's customers. Both tables are based on the same customer list. There could be other customer files, such as a list of credit status.

describe individual elements, such as a street name in the case of the address record in our example. Access to these files is controlled via a data dictionary, which provides indexes to the entries in each table.

A typical PC application will access these files one record at a time. For example, if the application is looking for all customers who live in a particular town, it will access each name and address record in turn, bringing the record into its main processor to examine the field. This is satisfactory when the data is stored on the disk drive of the PC running the application but when the records are held instead on a file server on a LAN, this process involves fetching a record across the LAN to the PC to perform each comparison. When a number of users start running such applications on a very large customer file the LAN starts to become congested and performance starts to deteriorate and become unpredictable.

Client/server computing

This led to the application of a technique, often called client/server computing, to improve performance of such applications across a LAN. The idea is that by dividing an application into two parts where each is run on different computers, it is possible to provide faster response times and also manage the all-important data better. Each application is divided into two parts: a client part, which will often run on a desktop PC, and a server part, which runs on a central machine shared by all users of the LAN. Typically a server will be more powerful than the desktop clients. The idea is that the server performs functions relating to shared data and resources, while the clients run specific applications that require access to these data and resources. Note, however, that servers can handle tasks other than data management, although on a typical business LAN the server's main functions will usually be data management, along with provision of print services.

In the case of our example involving searching for customers who live in a particular town, the client/server principle works simply. The database management system is now located on the central server machine rather than in each desktop PC. Figure 1.11 illustrates client/server computing schematically, compared to the old file server approach.

With client/server computing, instead of pulling each record in sequence across the LAN to examine the field relating to town in the PC, the application sends a request to the server to obtain just the records of those customers who live in the relevant town. So instead of every record in the customer address file being transmitted across the LAN, only the records required by that application come across. This cuts down on LAN traffic and also speeds up the search process because it is all handled on a single machine designed for the task, rather than involving a constant shuffling of records across the LAN.

In fact it may be possible to make further improvements, depending on the particular application requirements. Suppose that having obtained records of customers living in a particular town, the user wants to know the names and addresses of those who have purchased a particular product. This information may be contained in a separate file in the customer database, which is also held on the server. Therefore the whole search process can be performed on the server. First the names of customers living in the required town are located on the address file and then these are cross-referenced with the file of products purchased. The names and addresses of the people who come under both categories are sent across the LAN. The desktop PC

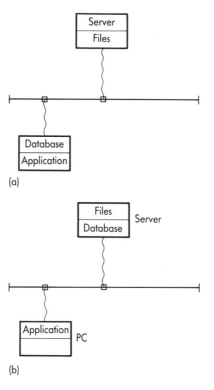

Figure 1.11 (a) Old file server approach, where database software resides in PC but files are held in a separate server machine. Searching for particular records can generate heavy traffic on the LAN. (b) Client/server approach, where database and the files reside in same server, now called the database server. Searching for records now generates only minimal traffic on the LAN.

may then need to do no more than display the relevant names and addresses, or it may want to find out other information from the customer base and display it graphically. The point is that this division of labour enables all data management to be performed centrally where it can be supervised properly and performance is maximized.

This is just as relevant on a small LAN as on a large one because as soon as data needs to be shared, it makes sense to consolidate it on a single machine and manage it properly to ensure that updates are performed consistently. However, on a small LAN, as we shall explain further in Chapter 7, it may be neither necessary nor affordable to have a computer dedicated as a server. We shall explain how it is possible to have a desktop PC double up as a server, to avoid having to buy a separate server machine.

When three or more people use the same applications software, such as word processing

Many vendors of application software packages for PCs, such as spreadsheets and word processing products, sell networked versions for operation across a LAN. These usually work out less expensive than buying the equivalent number of individual versions of the same software for each PC. This can therefore provide an economic argument for a LAN, quite apart from other advantages such as sharing of data and resources.

There are three major aspects to networked software packages. One is the economic argument already mentioned. Then there are the technical issues relating to the types of LAN, the software supports and use of techniques such as client/server computing. Finally, there is the management issue, relating to control of use of applications.

(1)   Economic. Packages may cost less because users buy a licence entitling a given number of users to load the software across the network and run it on their PC at a given time. Licences can be obtained for just five users or 100 or more users. A licence for five users, say, should cost less than buying five single copies of the package for desktop PCs.

The software will be held on a server computer, and then loaded across the LAN to individual PCs where it is run. There may be some counter mechanism to limit the number of users that can load the software at any given time. This is to reduce the risk of licences being abused. The idea is that if a company with a licence for only five users wants six people to be able to run the application at any one time, the licence has to be upgraded for an additional payment.

(2)   Technical. In some cases the LAN may just be used to share software between users, delivering it from a file server to a PC on demand. However, the software may also exploit the LAN and techniques such as client/server computing to provide other advantages such as faster performance and greater data security. Or yet again, applications written originally for PCs may now run almost entirely on the server. This is the case with some database management packages, which are now available both for stand-alone PCs and for servers operating on a LAN.

Applications that are split up across the LAN will be

designed to work with certain LAN operating systems. As will be discussed in Chapter 4, some form of operating system is required to control access to resources across the LAN, including the server.

(3)   Management. By holding application software on a server accessed via a LAN rather than it residing permanently in desktop PCs, use can be controlled. The alternative is for users to have their own copies of applications. This can lead to a proliferation of different versions of software. When software is administered via the LAN, it is possible to ensure that all users have a clean consistent version of each software product. Another advantage is that users can be given access only to the software they need. This in turn feeds back to the economic issue. Money can be saved by minimizing the number of users specified on each licence.

Some organizations have installed LANs with diskless PCs. Such PCs have no means of storing software or data themselves and therefore are totally dependent on the LAN. The advantage is that use of PCs is much more tightly controlled. Users cannot load their own software, and their activities can be centrally monitored. Software vendors also like this arrangement because it makes it harder for users to copy their products to pass on to colleagues or friends.

When there is a need to exchange data and messages between PCs within a business or department

Users of PCs within a workgroup may want to exchange data, files and messages between themselves as well as accessing shared information and facilities. For a small company this may not alone be a sufficient reason for installing a LAN because it may be just as easy to transfer data manually by exchanging floppy disks and there is no need for electronic mail when people are all within a single room anyway. However, if a LAN is installed for one or more of the other reasons listed, it is quite likely that it will then be found a useful vehicle at least for file and data transfer.

We can identify three situations where the ability to transfer data, files and messages becomes a primary motive for installing a LAN.

(1) For larger networks with, say, at least 20 PCs attached where there is also some need to exchange files. This could be, for example, the editorial office of a magazine, where there is a need to pass copies of an article between staff at different stages of preparation. In such cases it becomes tedious to exchange the files on floppy disk.

(2) Where large files that may be too big for a single floppy disk need to be exchanged. An example could be computer-aided design, where large graphical designs may need to be exchanged between engineers at desktop workstations.

(3) Where the network extends over quite a large area, such as a multi-building site. Here the LAN becomes a useful vehicle for exchanging text, data and electronic mail.

A LAN provides the basic mechanism for file and data transfer, but additional software is also required. As is explained further in Chapter 9, which looks at open systems, the basic LAN provides just the bottom layers of communication required to support an application. To exchange files or data between computers, software operating at a higher level is required.

Most LANs now come complete with an operating system and also software to support such facilities as file transfer. We shall look at this further in Chapter 7 where we discuss the issues involved in deciding who to buy your LAN from.

In Chapter 9 we discuss the standards that enable applications on different systems attached to a LAN to work together. It is worth noting here that there is a wide range of packages available to support functions like electronic mail and file transfer for companies that already have LANs without such facilities.

When central supervision is needed of computing resources such as PCs

This is more relevant for larger networks that have PCs scattered across several offices. Then a LAN allows use of computing resources to be monitored and controlled from a single point. Users can still run their own applications on PCs but any access to shared resources such as printers and file servers can be controlled. In Chapter 10 we discuss the role of LANs in overall network management.

When new applications require cooperation between two or more computers to perform their function

This is generally only relevant for larger organizations running more complex applications. Essentially cooperative processing involves interaction between two or more applications residing on different computers. It goes beyond straightforward client/server computing where a single application is split into two parts, each of which is processed on different machines. Cooperative processing is discussed further in Appendix 3.

Situations where a LAN may not be the answer

We end this first chapter by identifying situations where a LAN may not provide the best solution. This is not as illogical as it seems in a book about LANs because in these situations a network will still be required containing many of the same ingredients as a LAN. For example, it will still require some form of cabling system. Some form of operating system will also be needed and indeed most other issues discussed in following chapters will still be relevant. Only two chapters will not be relevant to users of alternatives to LANs. One is Chapter 2, which deals with the differences between the main types of LAN: Ethernet and token ring. The other is Chapter 4, which deals with network operating systems.

Why have a LAN if there is a cheaper way of doing things?

Essentially a LAN may not be the best solution when some other type of computing platform provides the required applications at a lower cost. Or in some cases the required application software may not run on a LAN at all. An important consideration, however, is that the solution must not constrain future growth of the network – issues relating to future development are discussed in Chapter 8.

The principal alternative to the LAN is a centralized computer serving a group of users, accessed either by dumb terminals, or by desktop PCs acting as dumb terminals. The latter is called terminal emulation because the PC 'emulates' the actions of a dumb terminal.

This is essentially the data processing set-up of large companies in the pre-LAN era. The difference now is that such solutions can be suitable for smaller companies running the same sort of traditional applications, such as payroll and accounting. Another important difference is that the central computer can now itself be a souped-up desktop PC, based on the same standard microprocessor technology, just as the servers on LANs are that we discussed earlier. In fact the only real difference between this and a LAN is that whereas in the latter there can be active cooperation between the desktop PC and the central server, with this alternative solution the desktop PC acts as a passive terminal. Its main function is to provide a window into the centralized system, although, unlike real dumb terminals, it can drive the graphics on the screen to make the application easier and more attractive to use. Centralized systems also allow printers and data to be shared, although not with the same degree of flexibility as a LAN. Factors to consider when choosing between centralized systems and LAN based client/server systems are summarized in Table 1.1.

The centralized solution may be appropriate for a small business that expects just to run shared applications, along perhaps with some word processing on the desktop but where there is little need for sharing of data between users. In a way it is suitable for applications serving a business's financial requirements, rather than those serving workgroups.

Another situation where the centralized solution may be appropriate occurs when staff dealing with customers over the telephone need to access computer-based information. For example, sales staff taking orders over the telephone could want first to check that relevant items are in stock and then take details of the order.

Again, sales staff within a department usually need the same applications, which may be accessed most efficiently and also with fastest response times with a centralized system and dumb terminals. Response time is after all critical when customers are waiting on the telephone.

It should be emphasized however that a centralized solution does not, and should not, preclude the addition of a LAN at some future time. Indeed, a centralized system can be implemented on a LAN, although without exploiting the LAN's full potential.

Table 1.1 Factors to consider in choosing between centralized computer and distributed client/server LAN.

1 Need to share information. This is fairly neutral, as it can equally well be satisfied with a LAN or a centralized computer supporting dumb terminals.

2 Need to share applications. This favours the centralized computer approach, although it can be satisfied quite well on a LAN.

3 Need for a variety of different desktop applications. Much better suited for a LAN supporting PCs rather than dumb terminals.

4 Need to exchange messages. Better suited to a LAN, but can be supported adequately on a centralized system with dumb terminals.

Increasingly, the differences are academic and it comes down to mixing and matching appropriate technologies on a given infrastructure of cabling and computers. The best advice is to seek quotes from a variety of suppliers based on the applications you need to run. Then different solutions can be compared on price, flexibility and support for future expansion or change. These issues are expanded in Chapters 7 and 8.

Other low-cost alternatives for very small businesses

For a very small business with two users, for example, a sole proprietor and secretary, even a small low-cost LAN may be neither cost justifiable nor necessary. If the requirement is just for occasional exchange of files between the two machines, there may be no need at all for any communications link. In that case, files can be exchanged between the two PCs on floppy disk. This is a time consuming process if files are large or need to be exchanged frequently. However, there are various *ad hoc* solutions that facilitate direct communications between two machines.

It is possible to link the two PCs via their serial or parallel ports with a standard piece of cable. Then a suitable software product needs to be installed to allow each PC to access the other's hard disk. There are products that allow two PCs to share each other's files directly without need for transfer, rather like a miniature peer-to-peer LAN as described in Chapter 4.

It is also possible to link two PCs remotely either via a modem over a standard dial-up telephone connection, or over the ISDN network (see Appendix 1 for a description of ISDN). There are several popular software packages that facilitate this, which your local dealer should be able to supply.

There are also products that allow two PCs to share a printer, sometimes in addition to accessing each other's files and/or exchanging messages. Increasingly a low-cost Ethernet solution may be adopted, given the falling cost of network interface cards. But there are still some low-cost switches worth considering. Essentially these provide a port, or outlet, for a printer and two ports for PCs.

Summary

By now you will have a basic idea of whether you need a LAN. You should have a sketchy knowledge of the alternatives, and whether they are right for you. In Chapter 2 we home in on the fundamental choices of LAN.

2

Ethernet or token ring?

CHAPTER CONTENTS

CHAPTER OBJECTIVES

This chapter sets out to prepare you to decide what type of
LAN you need. Unlike Chapter 1, this is worth reading by
people who already have one type of LAN and are contemplating either replacing it, or installing another at that
site. Basic questions and issues tackled are:

29

Choice comes down to cost, flexibility and compatibility with any existing networks

Ethernet and token ring are the two most popular underlying technologies for LANs. As Figure 2.1 shows, the dominance of these two LAN types is still increasing.

As can be seen, the two main types of LAN for smaller companies are still going to be token ring and Ethernet in the immediate future. The two operate in fundamentally different ways and each has pros and cons which we discuss later in this chapter. Technical differences are less important than factors such as cost, ease of cabling and ability to support current and future applications.

The fact is that most users of computers are not going to notice whether their LAN is token ring or Ethernet and are not likely to care. They will, however, care whether they can access the applications and information they need from their desktop PCs and whether they are able to do this quickly and easily. Users may also want their data to be protected from unauthorized access across the network.

Market share for Ethernet and TR in 1992:

Ethernet	TR
5.7 million nodes[†] shipped in the year	2.2 million nodes shipped

out of a total market of 9.6 million in 1992

Estimate for 1996:

Ethernet	TR
7.9 million nodes shipped	2.6 million nodes shipped

out of a total market of 12.4 million

[†] Note: A node is a device such as a PC or printer attached to the LAN.

Figures supplied by IDC (International Data Corporation)

Figure 2.1   Market shares of token ring and Ethernet (and FDDI).

These key requirements can be satisfied equally well by either Ethernet or token ring. However, they need other essential components as well as the basic LAN structure defined by the IEEE 802.3 and IEEE 802.5 standards, which respectively describe the operation of Ethernet and token ring.

In Chapter 1 we defined these basic components: cabling, the LAN operating system, and support for communication between users and applications at the level required. All these components are now largely independent of whether the basic LAN structure is Ethernet or token ring.

In principle, therefore, complete LAN solutions can now be provided equally easily on either token ring or Ethernet. We shall see in Chapter 3, for example, how both can now operate over the same cabling systems.

Ethernet remains the favourite for small LANs

Small LANs are more likely to be based on Ethernet, largely because solutions based on it tend to cost less. Also, partly because it has been in the market several years longer, there are more complete LAN solutions at the bottom end of the market based on Ethernet than on token ring.

It is worth stressing though that there are no longer any technical reasons not to start up with a token ring LAN even if there are just two or three users on it and although Ethernet is still cheaper, the cost differential has diminished.

Five factors to consider when choosing between Ethernet and token ring

Ethernet still costs less to implement than token ring but all network operating systems and most applications will now run over either Ethernet or token ring LANs. Furthermore, as we shall see in the next chapter, both Ethernet and token ring can now be implemented over the same cabling infrastructure.

However, there remain significant distinguishing factors between Ethernet and token ring. These relate to the following factors:

(1) The size of LAN or LANs you have or are planning to install.

(2) The type of applications you support or plan to support across the LAN.

(3) The number of users on the LAN.

(4) The nature of other systems you need to connect your LAN to.

(5) Anticipated future development of your overall network.

Consideration of these five factors together should help you decide whether token ring or Ethernet will be more suitable for your network. However, we emphasize that either can work well for most network requirements, and decisions will often swing on personal preferences or slight cost differences.

Relating these five factors to Ethernet and token ring

To establish a basis for examining the two types of LAN in the light of these five factors, we need first to describe the mechanism of each in more detail. Readers familiar with the basic workings of Ethernet and token ring will get nothing new from this section, and can move on to the comparative discussion. Ethernet and token ring, although dominant for smaller networks, are not the only types of LAN so we shall end the chapter by discussing the other two significant types: FDDI (fibre distributed data interface) and Arcnet.

FDDI is growing in popularity as a backbone network for linking a number of LANs, and where high transmission speeds are required. It is currently too expensive for small business LANs but may be important in future as your network grows in size and carries more data traffic.

Arcnet is an alternative to Ethernet and token ring and, although not widely used in the UK, is more popular in the USA. However, a recently announced high-speed version of Arcnet overcomes some of the earlier performance limitations. So it looks as if Arcnet will retain a significant if declining presence in the LAN market, especially in the US.

Brief history of Ethernet

Ethernet has been established for several years longer than token ring and as a result has a greater number of users world-wide, being particularly predominant for small LANs supporting fewer than 12 users. Since first developed by Xerox, Intel and Digital Equipment in the 1970s, Ethernet has evolved in various ways. The most significant recent developments have centred on cabling requirements, with additions to the IEEE 802.3 standard to cater for these. All the standards mentioned in this book are defined in the glossary.

Originally Ethernet required thick coaxial cable which was very expensive. Then in the mid 1980s it became possible to run Ethernet on cheaper thin coaxial cable. Now it can run on standard twisted pair telephone-type wiring for short distances. Equally important is that Ethernet can now be supported over more flexible structured cabling arrangements, although this is also true of token ring. Cabling issues are discussed in more detail in Chapter 3.

How Ethernet works

Through all these developments, the essential features of Ethernet have remained unchanged. These are the speed at which data is transmitted across the LAN and the method used by attached computers to send data onto the network, known as CSMA/CD (carrier sense with multiple access/collision detection). Readers who would like a full discussion of the CSMA/CD method should turn to Appendix 2. Essentially, each device on the LAN monitors the network. When a device wants to transmit a data packet, it does so if no other transmission can be detected at the time. If during the time between deciding to start transmitting a data packet and actually placing it onto the network, some other device also starts transmitting, a collision occurs. Both devices detect that collision and back off. Each starts again after a random time interval which usually ensures that the collision is not repeated. One problem is that as loading of the network increases, the number of collisions and the resulting delays can cause performance to deteriorate sharply.

Token ring

Token ring LANs arrived on the market several years after Ethernet. It was an attempt to avoid the performance limitations of Ethernet discussed in Appendix 2, although it introduced some new problems. It is a two-speed LAN: there are versions operating at 4 Mbit/s and 16 Mbit/s, although the latter is increasingly predominant. Note that the two speeds cannot be mixed. A single token ring LAN operates either at one speed or the other.

Brief token ring history

Token ring has been identified closely with IBM, which introduced it in 1985 as its strategic method of creating PC workgroups and linking them to larger centralized computer systems. Because of IBM's strong influence in the industry, token ring has gained a reasonable foothold, accounting for 23 % of the world market in 1992, measured in total number of nodes installed that year. Partly for the same reason, token ring has become an international standard of comparable importance to Ethernet. Like Ethernet it has become possible to run token ring over structured cabling systems and on lower-grade cable than was originally envisaged.

How token ring works

As with Ethernet, only one computer at a time can transmit data across a token ring LAN. A major design aim was to avoid the collisions when devices try to transmit at the same time. An Ethernet LAN is idle, with no data transmission taking place at all, while collisions are being resolved. The designers of token ring wanted a method which kept the LAN operating all the time to improve performance.

The solution that emerged was based on a closed loop, or ring, shown in Figure 2.2, to which all devices are attached in a circle. This contrasts with the original structure of Ethernet, which was a straight line, called a bus, in which data transmissions are broadcast along the cable to all devices.

With token ring, the transmission of data is controlled by a token that circulates continuously around the ring passing in turn through each device attached to it. The idea is that computing devices can only transmit data when they possess the token. This ensures that only one device can transmit at a time because only one can have the token

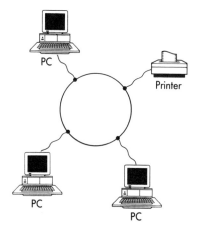

Figure 2.2 Original token ring structure. Devices were connected directly to a cable ring.

at any time. A more detailed discussion of token ring and some recent developments to improve performance can be found in Appendix 2.

Token ring reliability

In its original form, the token ring method was unreliable, although this has largely been solved and turned to advantage. This springs from the fact that each device attached to the ring is required to regenerate the signal and pass the token back onto the ring, as explained in Appendix 2. This means that token ring LANs as originally conceived required the active participation of all devices on them to continue operation. If any device on the LAN failed, the ring was broken and no other devices could communicate on it.

Clearly this was unacceptable because on a large network the probability of a device failing would be quite significant. The network would therefore be highly unreliable. Some way of bypassing faulty nodes on the network was needed.

Introducing token ring's multi-station access units (MAU)

The solution adopted by IBM in its first version of token ring was to build the ring from a star-based cabling system. Provided the LAN is arranged so that data can flow sequentially from one device to another, eventually returning to its starting point – in other words in a logical ring – it does not matter what the underlying physical cabling structure looks like.

IBM's arrangement was to have devices connected in star clusters to wiring concentrators called multi-station access units (MAUs). The MAUs themselves are connected in a ring. Therefore, the network had already condensed from being a simple ring to an inner ring supporting a sequence of star-shaped subnetworks. Figure 2.3 shows how this arrangement maintains the logical form of a ring, while introducing a more flexible and reliable physical layout.

In Chapter 3 we see how IBM and others have gone further by introducing central concentrators that act as hubs for the whole network, taking out the physical ring altogether, while still preserving the logical structure so that the same token ring communication technique can be used.

The MAU makes the network as a whole more reliable because it isolates it from individual devices, as shown in Figure 2.4. Now if

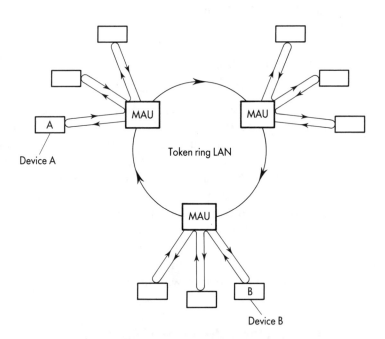

Figure 2.3 Illustrating use of media access unit (MAU) in a token ring LAN. If device A transmits a data packet to device B, the route taken would follow the arrows. Note this route follows a logical ring structure spanning the intermediate devices attached to the network.

a device fails, the MAU automatically bypasses it, maintaining a continuous ring. Furthermore a secondary ring is provided, so that if a link between MAUs fails, a continuous loop can again be restored by switching from the normal primary ring, as is also shown in Figure 2.4.

This technique turns a weakness into an actual advantage. It avoids each device becoming a point of failure. Furthermore, because action has to be taken, the token ring management system knows at once that a fault has occurred. With earlier Ethernet networks, there is no inbuilt mechanism for detecting faults on attached devices because the network may not be immediately affected by them. However, Ethernet has now caught up on this count in the increasingly predominant version for small networks called 10Base-T. As 10Base-T networks implement Ethernet in a star-shaped network, it is possible to isolate individual faults without bringing down the whole of the network. 10Base-T is discussed further in Chapter 3.

Comparative discussion of Ethernet versus token ring performance

We have already touched on some of the issues in describing Ethernet and token ring separately. Remember we identified five factors relating to your installation that could influence whether one or the other would be more suitable for your network. We now match Ethernet and token ring up against each of them.

The size of LAN or LANs you have or are planning to install

Whether you use token ring or Ethernet, large networks operate more efficiently when broken up into segments by local bridges, as we discuss in Chapter 10. In general, token ring, particularly the 16 Mbit/s version, performs best on networks with relatively small numbers of attached computers but where each makes heavy use of the network. Ethernet is definitely best at the opposite extreme, for

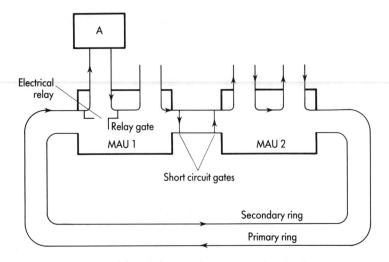

Figure 2.4   How MAU protects network from failure of devices attached to it, and also from a fault on the physical cable. Normally data flows through all attached devices. But if, for example, device A failed, the relay gate indicated by an arrow would close, creating a short circuit that would bypass device A. Similarly if the primary ring failed between MAU 1 and MAU 2, for example, the ring is maintained by creating short circuits at the two short circuit gates shown. The primary ring therefore switches to the secondary ring to bypass the fault.

networks with large numbers of attached computers making just occasional use of the network. With Ethernet, performance is not affected by the number of devices attached to it. Performance is only affected when devices start transmitting data onto the network and collisions start to occur. Token ring on the other hand is affected just by having devices attached to it, even when they are doing nothing.

Ethernet, as we have discussed, tends to keel over when loading of the network exceeds a critical point, usually about 20 % of its theoretical data transmission capacity. However, the critical point is higher when relatively few users are transmitting large amounts of data than when many users are transmitting small amounts of ata. This is because more collisions will occur if many users are vying for access to send small batches of data. The ideal situation for Ethernet is in supporting large numbers of users where only a few want access to the network at any time, sending big files of data when they do.

Token ring's ideal hunting ground is in supporting a small number of highly active users that have applications generating frequent data transmissions onto the network. It too operates more efficiently when there are relatively few large transmissions of data than when there are many small ones. It handles numerous small transmissions more efficiently than Ethernet because there are no collisions. Token ring also has the advantage that its performance degrades smoothly and predictably as loading on the network increases. Unlike Ethernet, there is no sudden crunch, which means there is more time to redress a deterioration in performance. Token ring provides much more predictable performance for a given number of users because under normal conditions, transmission speed is governed by the rate at which data packets circulate round the ring. This depends on the number of users on the ring and their degree of activity but not so much on the amount of data being transmitted, provided there is enough capacity on the ring. Performance of Ethernet, on the other hand, starts to degrade sharply long before the network is saturated because of the collision bottleneck as devices contend for access.

We look at measures such as local bridging that can be taken to improve performance, or stop it getting worse, in Chapter 10.

The type of applications you support or plan to support across the LAN

We have already discussed some of the strengths and weaknesses of Ethernet and token ring with regard to performance. To determine whether the strong or weak points will predominate, it is necessary to consider the applications running on the network.

Applications favouring Ethernet

There is one situation, albeit a rare one, where Ethernet is perfect. This is when there are a large number of users working most of the time on their own PCs in stand-alone mode, without needing access to data or computing facilities located elsewhere, but who need just occasional access to a network. In this case Ethernet is the ideal solution because, unlike token ring, it is not affected by the number of devices attached to it, provided they are not actually transmitting data. Even if a few devices are transmitting, Ethernet is not much affected.

Ethernet also performs relatively well when handling a few large batches of data rather than numerous small ones, although here token ring does not suffer from any particular disadvantage. Therefore, Ethernet is quite well suited for applications generating large amounts of data, such as computer-aided design and high-resolution graphics in general. This also applies to the increasingly popular image processing applications, in which scanners are used to digitize documents and diagrams so that they can be stored and retrieved electronically. The falling cost of computers and data storage in real terms is making it viable even for small companies to use imaging systems for applications like storing and retrieving newspaper clippings or correspondence with customers. Both Ethernet and token ring are suitable for this type of application.

Where Ethernet is less suitable

Ethernet is less suitable for applications where many users make frequent short calls upon the network. This could be the case, for example, in a large travel reservations company where agents need to access a database across a LAN, first to check whether holidays, flights or hotel rooms are available, and then to make bookings. The actual database could be located remotely at some central location, with access from the travel agency being made via a communications server on a LAN.

Such an application in a large agency involves frequent calls of short duration on the network. With Ethernet this can lead to fluctuating levels of performance. With token ring response time to requests from users would be more predictable for an application of this type. Yet in practice Ethernet is often used in this type of application. The performance problem is often solved by dividing the total Ethernet LAN into segments, as we have already indicated and describe in Chapter 10. However this involves extra cost that could be avoided by using token ring.

However, just to emphasize that the LAN world is constantly changing, it is worth pointing out that this is becoming less of an issue as the availability of intelligent hubs with filtering enables Ethernet to be used without the same performance handicap. The performance implications of LAN hubs are discussed further in Chapter 3.

For the typical small business, the main applications of LANs are for office applications like word processing and to automate traditional accounting procedures. In the first case the LAN is used to access central file servers to store documents, and to exchange messages and data with other users. In the second case the LAN is used to access a central database pertaining to the business. Small business accounting systems themselves may also be centralized, with users accessing them from PCs across the LAN. In these cases it probably does not matter whether Ethernet or token ring is used. However, for small low-cost LANs, there is a greater number of products based on Ethernet than token ring, as we noted earlier, and Ethernet is still somewhat cheaper.

The number of users on the LAN

We have largely covered this point in earlier discussions. We have identified the one general type of network where token ring is distinctly inferior to Ethernet. This is where there is a large number of occasional network users that do not access the LAN very often. Ethernet, on the other hand, is inferior where there is a substantial number of users making frequent, but short, calls on the LAN. For small numbers of users, less than ten for example, there is little to choose between Ethernet and token ring, except when very large files are being transmitted. Then Ethernet may be slightly superior to 4 Mbit/s token ring but inferior to 16 Mbit/s token ring.

The nature of other systems you need to connect your LAN to

The relevance of this depends largely on the size and structure of your company or organization. For small businesses, with fewer than about 40 employees, all computers and devices may well be connected to a single LAN. There may be no need to access systems outside the company, or there may just be a need to dial into external information services. In this case there are no real issues that affect any choice between token ring and Ethernet.

However, in slightly larger organizations there probably will be other systems inside the company that you want to be able to access from your own LAN. Increasingly, business efficiency demands that staff should be able to gain access to information and computer resources from all buildings and offices. This means that all computing resources have to be linked together in some way.

Essentially there are two types of connection that may need to be made from your LAN: direct links to existing host computers; and links to other LANs, to which host computers and other PCs may in turn be attached.

Connecting to other LANs

The issue of connecting to other LANs is given thorough treatment in Chapter 6. The main point to note here is that if you require a LAN for your workgroup or department, it may make sense to install the same type of LAN that is used elsewhere in your organization. For example, if there are already two Ethernet LANs in different buildings within your company, there would have to be a good reason not to continue with Ethernet in your case. This is because it is still easier and less costly to connect together two existing LANs of the same type than different types.

However, as we shall see in Chapters 3 and 6, it is becoming easier to interconnect Ethernet and token ring LANs.

Factors likely to precipitate replacement of one LAN type with another

There is a small but increasing number of organizations that have decided to switch from one type of LAN to the other. Usually the swing is from Ethernet to token ring but it can be the other way round. One reason for switching from Ethernet to token ring seems to be to exploit the more reliable performance and greater resilience of token ring. Reliability factors are discussed later in the section following this one. However a switch from Ethernet to token ring is more likely to be brought about by the need to be compatible with or connect to IBM systems in your organization.

While researching this book, I found two organizations that planned to switch from Ethernet to token ring. Both cited similar reasons, having just purchased a host computer from IBM. Although IBM supports Ethernet, it encourages its customers to use token ring. The support of IBM has been, as we have already observed, a major factor in propelling token ring into the market against an entrenched base of Ethernet users and applications. Organizations with substantial numbers of IBM computers are still more likely to install token ring than Ethernet.

On the other hand, organizations that have host computers from a vendor that has promoted Ethernet, such as Digital Equipment, are less likely to implement token ring. There are examples of organizations, although not many, that have switched from token ring to Ethernet after replacing IBM host computers with those from other vendors. Ethernet is still widely regarded as the best choice of LAN for organizations that want to provide access from desktop PCs and terminals to a wide variety of different host computers. Figure 2.5 shows an Ethernet LAN providing access to a range of different systems.

2

We can now summarize the token ring versus Ethernet issue as it is affected by the type of existing host computers that need to be accessed. Token ring is preferred where IBM computers other than PCs are installed largely to the exclusion of others. Ethernet is preferred where there is a wide range of different host systems, or where the predominant vendor strongly prefers Ethernet.

This last part of the discussion is more likely to be relevant to readers in large rather than small organizations. However, the issue of host connectivity may be a point to consider for smaller organizations contemplating the purchase of a LAN and host computer at the same time.

Anticipated future development of your overall network

The issue of designing a network capable of expansion to meet future needs is discussed in detail in Chapter 8. The general trend is toward cabling systems based around wiring hubs that will equally support Ethernet or token ring. Therefore organizations that install soundly structured cabling systems should be able to migrate relatively easily from Ethernet to token ring or vice versa in future if required. However many of the low-cost hubs are designed solely for one or the other type of LAN, so there is a danger of having to replace hubs in future to move from Ethernet to token ring, for example.

The token ring versus Ethernet issue as it relates to future development of your network is more likely to be relevant in a department of a larger organization than in a small business. It is not so much a matter of performance but of what type of computers and networks are already in place elsewhere in the organization. It may be that the LAN will initially serve an isolated workgroup but it should be remembered that in future it may need to connect to systems elsewhere in the organization. The issues of interconnecting LANs are discussed in Chapter 6. The main point to note here is that the initial choice of LAN may, indeed should, be influenced not just by

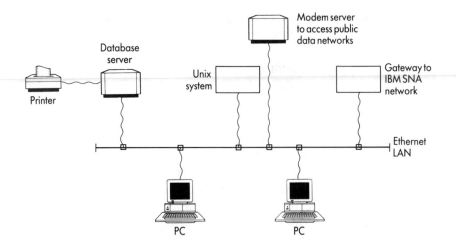

Figure 2.5   Ethernet LAN providing a range of systems.

short-term requirements but also by the possibility that it may need to hook up to other parts of the organization.

The other issue relating more directly to performance is that the LAN may need to support increasing numbers of users and carry more data in future. Note that when we refer here to a LAN system, we mean the central hub, the cabling connecting the hub to computing devices such as PCs on the LAN, and the adaptor cards or NICs that slot into the computers, to which the cable is attached directly. It is primarily the hub that determines the size of the LAN and its expansion capability, as we explain further in Chapter 3.

Many of the cheap and cheerful LAN systems available have a maximum number of users they can support. You then need to balance the immediate cost savings of a less sophisticated product against the future likelihood that you may need to invest in a more expensive product anyway. It may be that it is worthwhile starting with a simple solution if it looks likely that the cost can be written off before it needs to be replaced. If it looks as if use of the LAN will expand quickly – which often happens – then it may be worth looking for a modular solution that lets you start with a small network and then expand.

Reliability factors

The main differences between token ring and Ethernet are in performance rather than reliability. This is increasingly true as Ethernet and token ring are supported over the same cabling systems, which means that they are subject to the same kinds of faults at the physical level. Both Ethernet and token ring LANs are commonly implemented now over point-to-point links between computers and central hubs. Reliability therefore depends on the way the cable is laid out and on the resilience built into the hubs.

However, the original designs of token ring and Ethernet did differ in their approach to reliability. These are worth describing briefly because there are still a large number of Ethernet and token ring networks based on the traditional cable layout.

For Ethernet, the traditional layout was an open-ended bus which can have branches, and for token ring, a closed loop, as we described earlier. Data is broadcast to all devices simultaneously in the case of Ethernet, while for token ring it travels sequentially around the ring in a given direction. Ethernet's structure appears at first sight to be more resilient against cable breaks. If the cable is cut on an Ethernet LAN, the LAN is effectively broken in two. All devices on one side of the break can still communicate with each other and the same applies to those on the other side, as shown in Figure 2.6. However, errors would be more likely to occur.

With token ring as it was initially conceived, a break would stop all data transmission as the token could no longer return to its starting point as required in the specification. To get round this, a self-healing facility was built into most implementations of token ring. Earlier in

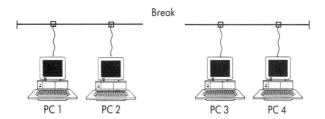

Figure 2.6 Ethernet LAN severed into halves. PCs 1 and 2 and PCs 3 and 4 are still within reach of each other if the LAN is broken where indicated. However, errors would be likely to occur.

the chapter we described IBM's MAU, which is really a halfway house between the original ring to which devices are attached directly, and the star-based hub structure that we describe in the next chapter. When MAUs were added, token ring networks became more resilient to cabling faults than Ethernet. Again it must be stressed that distinctions between them on reliability grounds are fading.

Fibre distributed data interface (FDDI)

This is a more recent kind of LAN, offering higher transmission speeds, enabling more computers to be attached and covering greater distances. Indeed with a maximum circumference of 200 km it is not really a 'local' network at all, as it could span all of an organization's sites within a large metropolitan area. London Underground, for example, has an FDDI network linking its stations and offices with cables running through the tunnels.

FDDI is based on the same token passing technique as token ring. But it is a more sophisticated implementation, with timing devices enabling data to be transmitted at much higher speeds. The bandwidth is 100 Mbit/s, which is ten times greater than Ethernet.

A detailed description of how FDDI works is beyond the scope of this book. Currently it is too expensive for most LANs, owing to the cost of the hardware needed to support it. However, costs are coming down and over the next few years it will become increasingly viable for applications that need to transmit data particularly quickly. This might apply to some applications of high-resolution graphics such as molecular modelling. In such cases the FDDI network would come right up to desktop computers, just as Ethernet or token ring does at present. An important point to note here is that FDDI no longer requires fibre optic cable to run right up to the desk. The standard was originally developed for fibre optic cable, as the name suggests, but recent advances in data transmission technology enable the full speed of FDDI to be sustained over standard twisted pair copper cabling over short distances, up to 100 metres. The CDDI (copper data distributed interface) supports FDDI for 100 metres over shielded twisted pair cable. A standard for FDDI over unshielded cable is expected to follow, although there may be problems meeting electro-

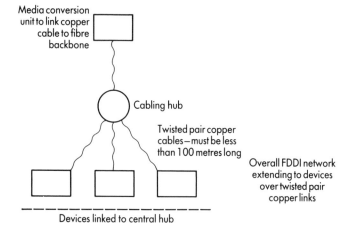

Media conversion
unit to link copper
cable to fibre
backbone

Cabling hub

Twisted pair copper
cables – must be less
than 100 metres long

Overall FDDI network
extending to devices
over twisted pair
copper links

Devices linked to central hub

Figure 2.7 Backbone FDDI network. Devices connected directly to an FDDI network over existing twisted pair cabling connected to a hub.

magnetic emissions standards, as is explained further in Chapter 3.

The aim is to enable desktop computers to attach directly over existing copper cabling to a backbone FDDI network, as shown in Figure 2.7. However, in the immediate future it is as a backbone network that FDDI will be mainly used, connecting different LANs together within a large building, or a site such as a university campus. For this situation it offers several distinct advantages over token ring and Ethernet LANs. Essentially these come under two headings: performance and reliability.

Performance

The extra speed enables more data to be carried but, more importantly, FDDI has techniques that enable large numbers of devices to exploit the extra transmission speed. It supports multiple tokens, which means that many different packets of data can be transmitted over the LAN simultaneously (Figure 2.8). This is in addition to a technique similar but superior to the early token release method which is now available in 16 Mbit/s token ring, and which we describe in Appendix 2.

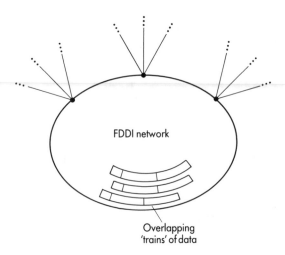

Overlapping
'trains' of data

Figure 2.8 FDDI allows the network to carry multiple 'trains' of data simultaneously.

Reliability

Firstly, FDDI is implemented over a pair of rings: a primary and a secondary ring. Data flows in opposite directions along each ring, although during normal operation in the absence of faults, the secondary ring remains unused. Devices or LANs can be attached either to one or both rings, via FDDI nodes. In the latter case the node can heal itself if the primary cable fails. Then even if both cables are severed a loop embracing the two nodes either side of the break can be recreated using the secondary ring. Such nodes are called dual attached nodes because they are connected to both rings. The disadvantage of this is that an extra fibre optic interface is required and this is a substantial fraction of the overall cost.

The alternative is the single attached node connected to just one of the rings, which is cheaper but does not offer the same protection against cable faults. A cable break could isolate the node from the network, rendering it unable to communicate with other nodes on the network.

When individual computers or lower-speed LANs are connected to the FDDI ring in single attached mode, a concentrator is required. This converts between the dual ring and the single ring used by attached LANs. Like Ethernet and token ring LANs, FDDI will in some cases be implemented within central hubs: then reliability will depend on the way such hubs are designed.

FDDI backbone networks are also more reliable in some circumstances for another reason. The fact that FDDI runs on fibre rather than copper cable means that it is immune from electrical interference. This is useful in electrically noisy environments such as factory floors, where copper-based networks can suffer interference from high-power equipment. London Underground again is a good example. Interference from high-voltage cable and track in its tunnels meant that copper cable was not a viable option for data transmission.

Arcnet

Like token ring, Arcnet uses a token passing method, but like Ethernet the network has a logical bus structure with each node receiving all data packets at virtually the same instant. In effect Arcnet operates similarly to token ring in the way that PCs and other devices gain access to the network but like Ethernet in the way that data is sent and received once access has been gained.

As with token ring, a token circulates round the network when no transmissions are taking place and is then seized by the first device that wants to send data. There is, however, a difference in that whereas in a token ring LAN the token circulates round a ring, in Arcnet it passes from node to node in descending order of network identifier. In other words, after leaving one node it passes to the node with the next higher identifier.

When a device has taken the token, it broadcasts packets like Ethernet. However, there is again a difference. With Ethernet, there is just one method in which data packets are transmitted. All nodes except the one to which the packet is addressed ignore it. Arcnet on the other hand offers two modes of transmission. One is called acknowledged data, in which packets are sent addressed to a single destination node. All other nodes ignore the packet, like Ethernet, but the destination node replies with an acknowledgement packet. The idea is to provide an efficient way of guaranteed delivery of data. The other method is broadcast data, in which data is actually sent to all nodes that are enabled to receive. This time there is no acknowledgement, the idea being to achieve the greatest possible throughput of network traffic.

Arcnet speed and range

Until 1992 Arcnet operated just at 2.4 Mbit/s, slower than both token ring and Ethernet, although the efficient operation of the protocol meant that in some circumstances it actually performed better. In 1992 a new high-performance version called Arcnet Plus was announced by Datapoint, the company that developed the LAN. Arcnet Plus leapfrogs Ethernet and token ring in raw performance, operating at 20 Mbit/s. It represents an attempt to restore Arcnet's dwindling share of the LAN market. However, most Arcnet observers thought that Arcnet Plus was too expensive and that while it was good news for existing users, it would be unlikely to attract many new customers.

Arcnet is also at a disadvantage, particularly in the UK, in that it does not enjoy the same level of support and investment from the networking industry in general. There are fewer suppliers, and consequently a poorer vein of facilities. For example, there is less choice when it comes to devices that interconnect Arcnet LANs.

Nonetheless, when it comes to range, Arcnet offers considerable advantages over Ethernet. It allows up to 255 nodes on the network, but distances can be up to 6.5 km (4 miles). The network can be configured around a hub, as with Ethernet and token ring.

Summary

By now we have set out the basic choices between the main types of LAN. We have seen that on the whole Ethernet is preferable for small networks, but that token ring is still predominant among IBM's customers. FDDI, or more particularly CDDI, is worth considering for applications where large amounts of data need to be transmitted between powerful desktop machines across a LAN. This still leaves the important matter of the underlying cabling, required whatever type of LAN you have. In the next chapter we look at the cabling issues and relate them to other choices you need to make.

3

Should I go for a structured cabling system?

CHAPTER CONTENTS

CHAPTER OBJECTIVES

This chapter sets out the basic choices to be made when installing or replacing a cable network. This is partly related to the choice of supplier, which is discussed in Chapter 7. Questions or issues tackled in this chapter are:

Introduction

For most small businesses, the most suitable cable now is unshielded twisted pair copper, increasingly, although not necessarily, within some form of structured cabling system. We therefore begin this chapter with a discussion of structured cabling systems and how these relate to the two principal LAN types: Ethernet and token ring. Then we proceed to discuss the different types of cable available – essentially fibre optic and several types of copper. In Appendix 4, we examine the costing of a low-end LAN solution, including cabling. It is worth noting at this point though, that a formal structured cabling system is not always essential for small networks. Later in the chapter we identify one type of solution, the PC hub card, suitable for unstructured cabling systems.

Finally, at the end of the chapter, the main points are drawn together to focus on the cabling issues that should be considered when installing a network.

Structured cabling systems

Structured cabling systems based around centralized hubs have become increasingly popular. They make the cable network easier to manage, more supportive of shuffling of personnel and computers within offices, and provide better insurance against the future. Although a small business may not need a cabling system conforming to one of the main industry standards for structured cabling, it will almost certainly benefit from a system carefully laid out with a view to the future. Flexibility is the key: whatever the size of a business, the labour costs of installing cabling are considerable and can equal the combined cost of other networking equipment. It is therefore vital to install a cable network that has as long a life as possible and that will not need alterations to cope with expansion or changes.

To understand current cabling products, it is worth considering briefly how cabling systems have evolved over the last ten years. The key theme has been one of convergence, in that both Ethernet and token ring LANs can now be supported over the same cabling system, to which most or all of an organization's computers can be attached.

Originally cabling was an integral part of both token ring and Ethernet LANs, which both specified a particular layout. Ethernet requires an open-ended network in a tree-and-branch bus structure. There must not be a closed loop, because Ethernet uses a broadcast technology in which data transmitted by a particular device travels in both directions along the network until it reaches both ends. If there were a loop, data would circulate endlessly, because there is no mechanism for removing data from the network. Originally Ethernet was implemented over a cable network that conformed religiously to this tree-and-branch structure. However, it gradually dawned on LAN designers that the basic Ethernet structure could in fact be supported over a cable network that looked nothing like the original tree-and-branch arrangement. It could, for example, be implemented over a star-shaped network provided there was some device at the centre to transmit the electrical signals along each spur of the star. This meant Ethernet could be supported over more convenient manageable cable networks based on central wiring closets. Cables could then radiate out from the closets to PCs and other devices on the office floor.

Token ring cabling followed a similar path. Token ring, as we recall from Chapter 2, requires a closed loop, in which data travels in sequence round the ring from one device to the next. Unlike Ethernet, nodes on the network have the ability to remove data from the ring, which avoids having data packets circulating endlessly. As explained in Appendix 2, data transmitted by one device circulates round the ring until it reaches its destination device, which copies it. The data, now containing an acknowledgement, returns to the device that sent it, which strips it off the ring. Therefore, every item of data completes one circuit of the ring.

This is the established logical wiring pattern for token ring and Ethernet LANs. By logical we mean how the LAN appears to the computers on it – as a closed ring for token ring and as an open bus for Ethernet. As we have just explained in the case of Ethernet, this does not require the cable to be laid out physically in this way. Indeed, as we explain, it is possible to support both Ethernet and token ring on the same cable layout, even though the network must appear to be different in each case. This is accomplished through the electrical characteristics of the devices used to attach computers to the network. We will show how it is now possible to lay a cable network that can support either token ring or Ethernet. Note that, at present at least, it is impossible for a given portion of the cable network to support both token ring and Ethernet at the same time because different connection equipment is needed for each. It is possible, though, and has been done by a number of organizations, to have Ethernet and token ring LANs running on different parts of the same cable network, communicating with each other. In Chapter 6 we examine the issues of connecting Ethernet and token ring LANs together.

First we recap briefly on the evolution of Ethernet and token ring cabling in turn, which we described in Chapter 2, showing how they have converged.

Token ring

It was quickly apparent that the original concept of devices linked serially in a ring would not be sufficiently reliable. The failure of any one device would bring the network down as would any single break in the cable. Apart from being exposed to failure, it would not always be convenient to install cabling in a physical ring structure.

The token ring MAU (multi-station access unit)

To counter these problems, the multi-station access unit (MAU) was invented. The idea was that this device, built specially for reliability, would have devices attached to it in star-shaped clusters. MAUs in turn would be connected together in a ring. The network as a whole then comprises star-shaped clusters connected in an inner ring.

The MAU prevents failure or removal of a node, or a break in the links between MAUs and attached devices, from bringing down the whole network. The MAU does this by monitoring each device and healing the wiring, should a fault occur, by wrapping round the fault.

The network still functions logically as a single ring because data still flows in sequence around the network, up and down the spurs of each MAU, and then from MAU to MAU. The flow of data in an MAU-based token ring and also the way the MAU wraps round fault devices to maintain continuity is illustrated in Figure 2.7 in Chapter 2.

MAUs are available from a number of token ring system vendors, including IBM, but they do not solve the whole problem. For example, the network is still exposed to faults in the cables of the inner ring connecting the MAUs together. So the question arose: why have a physical ring at all? Provided each spur could be sufficiently long to reach all users, why not condense the network down into a single star with just one MAU acting as a central hub?

The token ring CAU (controlled access unit)

This led to the token ring concentrator or hub (with parallel developments for Ethernet as we shall see in the next section). These three stages of evolution of token ring cable layout are shown in Figure 3.1.

Such token ring hubs are called concentrator access units (CAUs). IBM announced its CAU in 1990, setting the standards for token ring hubs. Other vendors subsequently introduced hubs compatible with the IBM CAU but with additional functions. An example is Madge Network's SmartCAU. The compatibility with IBM's CAU means the products can interoperate in a single network and can be controlled with a common network management system.

IBM's CAU allows up to 80 PCs or other devices to be attached on lengths of cable via pluggable lobe attachment modules (LAMs). These LAMs attach directly to the CAU. There can be up to four LAMs, each capable of attaching up to 20 PCs.

The maximum length of each spur of cable running from the LAM to attached devices of the star depends on whether the network supports 4 or 16 Mbit/s (these being the two speeds supported by token ring). If IBM's shielded cable is used, each spur can be up to 375 metres long at 4 Mbit/s, or 145 metres at 16 Mbit/s. If unshielded cable is used, the maximum limit is 100 metres for 4 Mbit/s. Standards to support 16 Mbit/s over unshielded cable were being finalized at the time of writing.

A number of CAUs, including IBM's own, are designed just for token ring LANs. As we shall see, there are now a growing number of sophisticated hubs for large networks that support both Ethernet and token ring in the same box. However, for smaller networks hubs still tend to support just one or the other.

Ethernet cabling developments

The story of Ethernet's evolution from bus to hub began with the repeater. With token ring every node on the network is a repeater. Ethernet does not need this, but separate repeaters are necessary to extend the network beyond its normal limits.

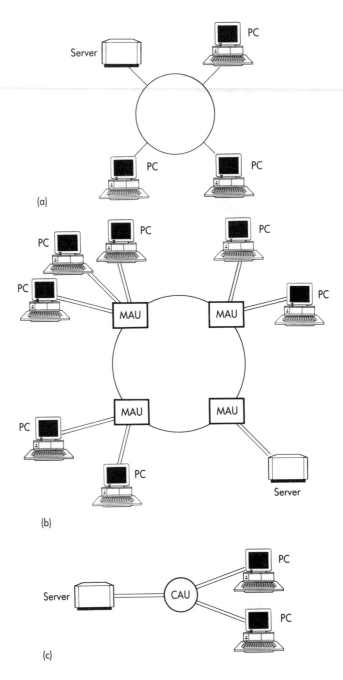

Figure 3.1 Three stages of token ring development. (a) Simple ring. (b) Ring of media access units (MAUs) supporting star-shaped clusters. (c) Token ring supported in single star-shaped cluster from central concentrator access unit (CAU). Note that the CAU can also be linked to MAUs, which in turn support clusters of PCs or other devices.

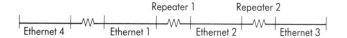

Figure 3.2 A number of Ethernet segments connected by repeaters. Note: a maximum of five repeaters is allowed between any two devices on an Ethernet network.

3

The original version of Ethernet over coaxial cable was limited in length to 500 metres. To create networks covering greater distances, repeaters were devised to regenerate or amplify the signal, to avoid it degrading too far before reaching the end of the network. Each portion of the Ethernet LAN connected by a repeater was then termed a segment. We have already used the term loosely to describe the local portion of a LAN within a floor or small building.

A number of segments can be created within a single overall Ethernet network based on thick coaxial cable using repeaters, but there is a maximum of five repeaters allowed between any two points of the network, as shown in Figure 3.2. This makes the maximum span of a continuous Ethernet network 2500 metres. This limit is imposed by the collision detect (CD) mechanism of Ethernet, which is described in Chapter 2.

However, it is possible to span a greater distance than 2500 metres using a pair of half-repeaters at either end of an extension link that is not part of the continuous network. A pair of Ethernet segments joined by such a link is shown in Figure 3.3. More intelligent devices called bridges or routers are now more often used to extend Ethernet LANs in this way, as we explain further in Chapter 6.

In these early networks, each repeater had two ports, one each for the two segments it was joining. The idea was to increase the maximum length of the network to cover greater distances in a large site and to enable more devices to be supported. However, repeaters did not solve the problem of growing network traffic congestion. This required local bridges, as described in Chapter 10.

As far as cabling was concerned, the significant developments

Figure 3.3 Two Ethernet segments joined by a pair of half repeaters each side of an extended link.

came with repeaters. First, multiport repeaters were developed, which meant that more than two segments could be connected through a single repeater box, simplifying cabling and network design. A more significant development came with the ability to run an Ethernet LAN over unshielded twisted pair cable, which was cheaper, easier to install and much more flexible.

The 10Base-T revolution

The 10Base-T standard was developed to support transmission of data at 10 Mbit/s using Ethernet's CSMA/CD transmission method over unshielded twisted pair cable. The standard, approved in 1990 by the IEEE committee responsible for Ethernet LANs, was a significant breakthrough because it allowed networks to become more flexible, reliable and easier to manage. The only real disadvantage, compared to traditional LANs based on coaxial cable, is that 10Base-T networks require a hub, which is an additional cost, although as we shall see this can be more than offset by savings in cabling and network management.

The main alternative to 10Base-T for smaller Ethernet networks is an earlier standard called 10Base-2. This supports a thin type of coaxial cable which is cheaper and less bulky than thick coax. 10Base-2 is similar to the original Ethernet specification (called 10Base-5) except that distances and the number of devices it can support are reduced. The maximum span of a 10Base-2 segment is 185 metres, compared with 500 metres for traditional 10Base-5 based on thick coax, and the total number of devices that can be supported is 30 instead of 100. As with 10Base-5, the range and size of the LAN can be increased by use of repeaters, and also by bridges or routers, as described in Chapter 6.

With 10Base-T the situation is rather different. Unlike traditional coax-based networks, devices are attached to a central hub in a point-to-point star formation, as shown in Figure 3.4. Typically devices are connected to the cable via NICs (network interface cards) through an RJ45 connector, which is a standard device. The hub functions as a repeater, regenerating the signals transmitted to it along spurs of the star. Although this looks quite different from a traditional Ethernet network, it is based on the same CSMA/CD method. Data packets are still broadcast to all devices attached to the network.

There are, however, rather different limitations. The maximum number of devices, 1024, that can theoretically be connected to a

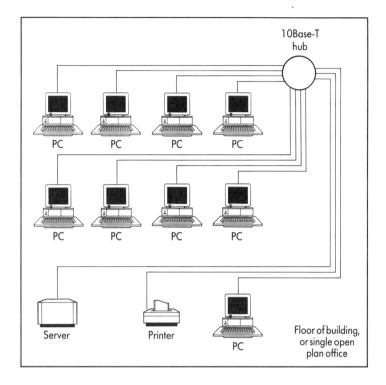

Figure 3.4 10Base-T network. Each device is attached to the hub via an unshielded twisted pair cable, which must be less than 100 metres long. Although the network is physically star-shaped, it functions logically like a bus, with data broadcast to all attached devices.

10Base-T network is greater than for traditional Ethernets. Distances are reduced compared with thick coax, although comparable with 10Base-2 over thin coax: the maximum distance between a hub and attached devices is 100 metres, although greater distances can be achieved using low-loss cable. In general, however, this makes the maximum span of the network 200 metres.

It is possible to extend the network by connecting two or more hubs together with a segment of the network. This can be done even when the hubs being connected come from different vendors because no signalling is required between the hubs, which are just acting as repeaters.

However, the hubs themselves cannot be more than 100 metres apart because this is the most allowed by 10Base-T. Therefore, to extend the network over larger distances, some other cable is required, usually either fibre or coaxial. In fact most 10Base-T hubs have a port for coaxial cable. This enables them to be connected together over distances greater than 100 metres with a coaxial cable, as shown in Figure 3.5.

Advantages of 10Base-T

10Base-T has several advantages over traditional Ethernet networks based on coaxial cable.

(1)   It is more flexible, capable of supporting change and expansion more easily. Adding or removing users to or from the network is less expensive than with coaxial cables.

(2)   The cable itself costs less and is easier to install.

(3)   The cable network is easier to manage and requires less staff resources. The centralized hub makes it easier for problems, to do with transmission errors, for example, to be identified before they bring the network down.

(4)   The 10Base-T standard reduces compatibility problems. Previously some Ethernet products would not work with others because of differences in the way they implemented the protocols but products supporting 10Base-T are more likely to interoperate.

(5)   The network as a whole is more reliable, with less average downtime.

Against these is the added expense of the hub. This may be offset by savings in cabling and even if it does not, the less visible cost advantages, through improved reliability and less staff time spent on troubleshooting, will often swing the balance in favour of 10Base-T.

Another possible objection to 10Base-T is the fact that unshielded twisted pair cable is susceptible to electrical interference. In a typical business office, however, the level of electrical noise is sufficiently low for this not to be a problem. Even so, some 10Base-T products are designed to mitigate the effects of interference, and some work with shielded twisted pair cable, which is much less prone to this problem (10Base-T will operate on shielded twisted pair and indeed on coaxial cable as well, but then some of the advantages are lost). It is true, though, that in environments with a lot of electrical interference, such as a factory floor, 10Base-T is not recommended.

Although the hubs are an added cost, they provide useful focal

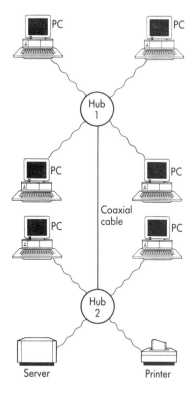

3

Figure 3.5 10Base-T hubs interconnected by coax cable. In this way, individual 10Base-T networks serving workgroups can be connected together into a larger network.

points for control and management of the network. In fact hubs have evolved rapidly to provide a range of management facilities and communication functions far beyond the original simple repeater. We will look at their role as local nodes for building interconnected networks in Chapter 6, at how they impact the design of future-proof networks in Chapter 8, and their role in management in Chapter 10.

It is also worth remembering that not all organizations have the luxury of starting from scratch with an empty building or office to cable. Many already have coaxial cable networks and want to migrate toward twisted pair but cannot afford to do so at a stroke. In such cases the old coaxial network can be retained, at least for a time, while introducing 10Base-T hubs into selected workgroups. The coaxial cable can then act as a backbone, carrying data between 10Base-T local networks over distances that exceed the 100-metre limit. The eventual plan will often be to replace the coaxial with fibre for the backbone cabling.

Low-cost and PC-based hubs

A welcome innovation for small businesses has been the development of low-cost hubs designed for networks with less than 12 users. Well-known vendors in the networking field such as Hewlett Packard and 3 Com have introduced hubs designed for small networks at prices that work out around £50 per port, that is, for each device supported. Bear in mind that prices quoted by vendors assume that all the ports provided are used to connect devices. In practice hubs tend to come in multiples of four or eight, so investment in such networks often has to increase in quite large steps. However, there are some hubs that come in multiples of two ports, which is more practical for small networks.

An alternative to stand-alone hubs at this end of the market is the PC-based hub card, which slots into the back of a standard PC-based LAN server (Figure 3.6). The advantage of this is that it avoids the need for a separate hub but it means that expansion slots in the back of a server are occupied by hub cards taking up space that could be used to provide other functions. For this reason PC-based cards are generally only recommended for small networks of at most 20 users, without a structured cabling system. For small networks where substantial growth in number of users is not anticipitated within a particular business or workgroup, then PC LAN cards are an attractive option.

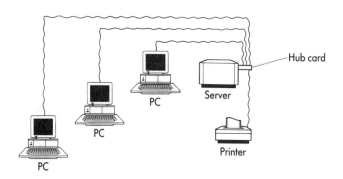

Figure 3.6   Server functioning as a hub.

In general a disadvantage of low-cost hubs is that they offer no expansion path beyond a certain point. This means that an organization starting with, say, six users on the network may never be able to expand beyond 12 or 24 users without ditching the original hub and moving into a more sophisticated and more expensive range. This constraint may not matter if you are certain your network is never going to grow much but past experience shows that most networks do grow more quickly than their users anticipated.

This issue of expandability is explored more thoroughly in Chapter 8.

3

The universal cable network has arrived

We have now shown how Ethernet and token ring have converged from a cabling perspective. Both can now run over twisted pair, either shielded or unshielded, or over fibre. Both can be supported on hub networks. Both therefore can now have the same physical shape, with the difference lying in how data is transmitted.

At first hubs were dedicated to either token ring or Ethernet, and this remains true for the low-cost products for small networks. However, it was not long before hubs began to support both token ring and Ethernet. This does not mean that Ethernet and token ring could run simultaneously over the same cable, which is impossible at present but it does mean that a star-shaped network linked to a single hub could have some spokes running token ring and others running Ethernet. Data traffic from both LANs passes through the hub, although this does not necessarily mean that the Ethernet and token ring LANs communicate with each other. It is quite possible to have two totally independent LANs, one Ethernet and one token ring, supported from the same hub, as shown in Figure 3.7.

Most organizations, though, want to connect their networks together, to make their applications and data as widely available as possible. Clearly a hub provides a convenient point to implement the connection between networks. We shall see in Chapter 6 how bridges and routers can now be installed inside hubs to connect LANs together.

Hubs also provide a convenient point to monitor the network and obtain information about traffic levels and faults. Many hubs now offer management facilities that help keep the network running efficiently and plan for future growth. In Chapter 10 we shall examine the role of hubs in network management.

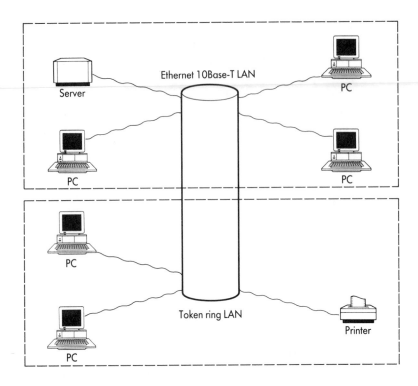

Figure 3.7 Single hub supporting both token ring and Ethernet LANs.

The main point to emphasize is that support for both Ethernet and token ring as options is fast becoming standard for hubs in the middle and upper reaches of the market.

It is also now possible to purchase single network interface cards that will connect PCs directly to either token ring or Ethernet networks. So now that both Ethernet and token ring will run over a common cabling system, the next step will be to establish a network which can be switched from Ethernet to token ring operation without having to make any hardware changes. The network would be reconfigured from a screen just by changing settings in the software running the hub and PC. However, this was not possible at the time this book was published; products to support simultaneous Ethernet/token ring operation are likely to arrive in 1995.

In practice, few small businesses will want to run both Ethernet and token ring. In larger organizations, it is common to find both types of LAN, and there is a growing requirement for LAN systems capable of being configured to support either Ethernet or token ring.

Overall standards for structured cabling within a building

We have already seen how hubs have grown in popularity as centralized points of focus for cabling within a local area. We have also highlighted the rise of universal cabling systems capable of meeting all of an organizations' data communication needs.

All of this, however, needs to be related to the physical structure of the building in which the cable is laid. Structured cabling systems were introduced during the mid 1980s to provide a coherent way of establishing a universal cabling system capable of satisfying a wide range of data transmission requirements, while fitting in with the physical structure of buildings.

This meant that cabling systems had to consist of two physical layers within buildings: vertical risers, interconnecting different floors, and horizontal cabling linking the risers with computers on each floor. Typically the vertical risers correspond to the backbone network, while the horizontal cabling supports individual LANs which may be based on hubs. There could be a hub on each floor interconnected by a backbone network. Figure 3.8 shows how this could be done.

There is often also a third element of a structured cabling system, the access to external services. Organizations that need to provide access to remote computers or IT services will need to connect their internal network to long-distance telecommunication services. This could be via the public telephone network, via ISDN, or via leased lines.

Two major types of structured cabling system

Two major standards for structured cabling emerged: AT&T's Premised Distribution System (PDS), which is now called Systimax, and the IBM cabling system. These specify a range of cable types and equipment and rules for laying out the cable. PDS requires cable to be laid out in a star-shaped arrangement on each floor, linked back to wiring centres. It can be used for any type of LAN, although it has been associated particularly with Ethernet. Systimax also specifies either unshielded twisted pair cable or fibre optic. The IBM cabling system allows a range of cable types including unshielded twisted pair but in most cases comprises either shielded twisted pair, or fibre, or a combination of both.

Small businesses may not require a cabling system with the

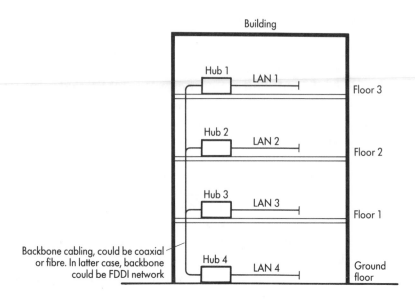

Figure 3.8 Showing hubs interconnected by vertical backbone cabling. This is really an extension of the network shown in Figure 3.5, in which two hubs were linked together. Backbone cabling can be fibre optic or coaxial cable.

official seal of IBM or AT&T but it is well worth following the basic rules because then they will have a cabling system that can expand in an orderly way without requiring continual replacement. The cable system then becomes a long-lasting business asset that can be expanded if necessary, but which may have a life expectancy almost as long as the building itself. More typically, though, the cable network will last about a third as long as a commercial building, around 20 years.

Different types of cable

We now proceed to discuss the different types of cable that can be used within a structured system. The first decision is whether to use fibre or copper, and then to decide which options to go for within these groups. However, it is worth stressing that for most small networks, fibre looks like being too expensive in the immediate future.

Fibre and copper compared

Put simply, the three factors that shape the choice between fibre and copper cabling are cost, performance and network size. Fibre costs more to install but the main additional expense is on the devices for connecting computers to the cable. On the other hand, it offers higher potential performance and supports larger networks both in terms of the number of computing devices that can be attached and the distance between them. Another major advantage in electrically noisy environments such as factory floors is fibre's immunity from electromagnetic interference.

The balance between these factors is changing all the time, with the cost of fibre networks coming down and copper offering ever greater performance, at least over short distances. This means that the number of situations where fibre can be cost justified is increasing. However, it also means that organizations with existing copper-based networks can extract greater performance and therefore may not need to consider moving to fibre in the near future.

Fibre too expensive and not necessary for many small businesses

For many small businesses the debate between fibre and copper is academic, especially when all the computers they need to connect are in one office. In this case fibre would almost certainly be an expensive overkill, with the best solution probably being one of the low-cost copper-based LAN solutions. We look at such solutions in Appendix 4.

Note that fibre on its own does not increase the throughput of data. For example, Ethernet can be implemented over fibre cable, but the speed is still 10 Mbit/s. The point is that fibre offers greater potential, but this potential is only realized when it is combined with an appropriate method for transmitting data, such as FDDI. In fact even FDDI comes nowhere near exploiting the full power of fibre.

Copper and fibre can coexist

Copper and fibre are not mutually exclusive, and in a growing number of larger networks they complement each other. A key point to note about fibre is that it is the cost of connecting computing devices to it that is expensive rather than the purchase and installation of the cable itself. This means that while fibre optic works out expensive for networking individual desktop PCs within an office, it can be cost effective as a backbone network interconnecting different LANs. This arrangement is suitable for larger sites such as university campuses or factory complexes where there is a need to provide a common communications backbone for all users.

Individual workgroups or departments would still have single LANs running on copper cable, with these being interconnected by the fibre backbone, as shown in Figure 3.9. In this way the number of expensive connections onto the fibre backbone is minimized. It also exploits the advantages of fibre in covering larger distances and providing extra data transmission capacity, enabling it to serve all users within a large site. In this arrangement the backbone fibre network itself operates as a high-speed LAN supporting lower-speed Ethernet and token ring LANs as nodes. In Chapter 2 we describe FDDI, the international standard for such fibre backbone LANs.

The use of fibre for interconnecting LANs is discussed further in Chapter 6, while the issue of using fibre to ensure a network can be extended in the future is covered in Chapter 8. Later in this chapter we describe the physical layout of hybrid fibre/copper networks and the devices needed to connect computers to a fibre network.

Role of fibre in future proofing

Before making a detailed assessment of copper and fibre in the context of your network, two factors need to be considered. One is your business plan or longer-term strategy, which determines the kind of applications the network will need to support and how it is likely to evolve. The other is the relative merits of fibre and copper given the network you have now and in the future. We have already seen that the best solution for organizations with distributed sites or large single buildings may comprise a number of distinct copper-based networks within offices interconnected by a fibre backbone. It is still quite rare to find fibre used throughout a network including the final links to desktop computers. However a few organizations with plenty of money to spend on information technology have decided to install such 'fibre to the desk' solutions even though their present levels of data traffic do not require it. The argument is that using fibre 'future proofs' the network, ensuring that it will be able to support computer applications that generate much larger flows of data than present ones.

The future-proofing argument comes down to data transmission capacity. Both fibre and copper are established standards and will

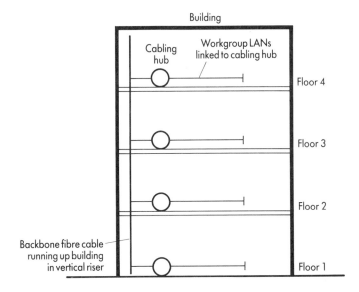

Figure 3.9 Use of fibre backbone to interconnect local workgroup LANs. The fibre backbone could be FDDI, although it does not have to be. The fibre could carry normal Ethernet or token ring traffic over longer distances than are possible using twisted copper pair cable.

continue to enjoy widespread support. Fibre will always support higher transmission speeds because of its intrinsic carrier mechanism based on light rather than electrical signals. However, advances in technology have led to great increases in the amount of data that can be squeezed down relatively standard twisted copper pairs similar to telephone wiring. As a result copper cable will continue to provide enough capacity for standard business applications, and most others for that matter, at the local networking level.

We shall look at the developments that enable copper to support high transmission rates at distances up to 100 metres later in the chapter. First we describe the basic differences between fibre and copper.

What is fibre cabling?

Optical fibre uses light rather than electrical signals to carry information. The light is transmitted down a continuous strand of glass or plastic surrounded by reinforcing material to protect the fibre. A complete cable comprises a number of these individual fibres enclosed in an outer sheath, as shown in Figure 3.10. As each fibre is very narrow, a complete multicore bundle is still small considering the large amount of data it can carry.

As data is initially generated by computers in electrical form, it has to be converted into light signals. This can be done by opto-electrical couplers, in which the electrical signals issued by computers are used directly to generate pulses of light representing the same information. The couplers perform the reverse operation at the receiving end.

There are several different types of fibre cabling that vary in their physical dimensions and in their potential data transmission capacity.

Advantages of fibre

Use of fibre optic confers four distinct advantages. Performance and support for larger networks with more users and spanning greater distances have already been mentioned. The other two advantages relate to security and both follow from the fact that light is used rather than electricity. Fibre networks are immune to electromagnetic interference, which means that data will not be lost because of lightning strikes or proximity to electrical equipment. By the same token, fibre does not emit electromagnetic radiation, which makes it impossible to eavesdrop electronically on data transmitted across the network. It is possible using equipment of the type used in TV detector vans to pick up the electromagnetic signals issued from copper cable and reconstruct the data signals.

Fibre is therefore often preferred in electrically noisy factory environments where interference from machine tools could be a problem with copper cable. It is also preferred where sensitive or confidential data is transmitted, to reduce the risk of electronic eavesdropping, for example in defence establishments.

Disadvantages of fibre

The cost of fibre itself has fallen steadily to the point where it is not much greater than copper. The disadvantages follow from the complexity of connecting devices to the cable. This makes connection to the network expensive and also a potential source of unreliability. Over time a slight movement of the cable in the connectors can cause signal loss resulting in data corruption. This is not a problem if the cable network is maintained regularly but the fact is that fibre, even in its protected sheath, is more fragile than copper and needs to be installed carefully and protected from physical shock afterwards. The cable is useless if it suffers a minor fracture.

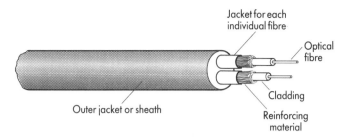

Jacket for each
individual fibre

Optical
fibre

Cladding

Outer jacket or sheath

Reinforcing
material

Figure 3.10 Fibre optic cable.

3

Later in this chapter we will weigh up the pros and cons of both copper and fibre, and consider the best solutions for different types of network. First we describe the different types of copper cable and then establish the basic techniques for building cable networks.

Copper cable

The story of copper cable for data communications is one of increasing transmission rates over wires of decreasing diameter. The improvements have come from use of better techniques for reducing the effect of electromagnetic interference.

Telecommunications for voice began with just one type of cable, comprising twisted pairs of copper. A pair of wires was needed to support two-way communication and they were twisted to reduce crosstalk by cancelling out interference between the two wires.

Data transmission is less tolerant of signal loss and distortion than voice. The onset of data communications in the 1960s therefore spawned a variety of new cabling types to meet increasing requirement for both high reliability and transmission capacity.

Coaxial cable

The first Ethernet LANs in the early 1980s used a thick coaxial cable which was required to provide the capacity of 10 Mbit/s over a distance of 500 metres. It comprised four layers to minimize electrical interference from nearby power cables or appliances with electric motors. In the middle is a central copper conductor surrounded in turn by an insulating layer, then a copper braid and finally a protective outer sheath, as shown in Figure 3.11.

This had two major limitations: it was expensive and it was thick,

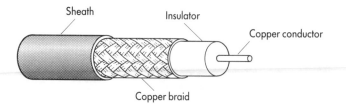

Figure 3.11 Coaxial copper cable.

making it inflexible and hard to fit into small ducts. A thinner, cheaper version of the coaxial cable which was more able to run round tight bends in buildings was introduced for Ethernet LANs in 1985. However, it still suffered from the same problems on a lesser scale and could not support as many computing devices as thick coaxial.

Coaxial of both types is still widely used and supported by makers of LAN equipment, but thick coax is rarely chosen now for new networks.

As LANs became more widely used, efforts increased to make use of thinner, less expensive cable. From the mid 1980s, LANs started to make use of twisted pair cable similar to that used for telephone wiring.

Twisted pair cable

Twisted pair cable consists of pairs of copper wires, each clad in plastic and then twisted together. The pair of plastic covered wires is then encased in an outer sheath. In fact several pairs are usually encased together in a single sheath. Normally there are at least two pairs, or four wires, per sheath, as this is the minimum required by telephone systems.

The first token ring LANs installed by IBM in the mid 1980s used a twisted pair cable specially shielded from external electrical interference, shown in Figure 3.12. This comprised twisted pairs all clad together in a metal outer screen that protects even from severe levels of external radiation. This provided great reliability and data transmission capacity but was only a small improvement on the dimensions and cost of coaxial cable.

Since then it has become possible to run first Ethernet and more recently token ring LANs over unshielded twisted pair cables, shown in Figure 3.13. In the UK this still requires a higher grade of cable than the wires used for telephones, but ditching the protective metal

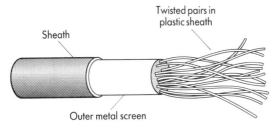

Figure 3.12 Shielded twisted pair cable. Note: some shielded twisted pair cables comprise wires that are each screened individually as well as having an overall outer screen, as shown in the diagram.

sheath brings down both the cost and the bulk considerably. However, it is worth noting that there are different grades of unshielded twisted pair. The most expensive unshielded twisted pair cable actually costs more than some types of shielded twisted pair (stp) cable, although they are still slimmer, making them easier to install in buildings with restricted ducting space. The difference between the various types of unshielded cable lies partly in the degree of twisting and the care taken in its manufacture. The highest-grade unshielded cable is very tightly twisted, which makes it more expensive to manufacture, but can sustain greater data rates because it is more immune to interference.

For Ethernet LANs, unshielded twisted pair (utp) has become the standard transmission medium within offices, workgroups and small businesses. Where the LAN needs to cover larger distances, either coaxial cable or fibre needs to be used. Although utp cable does support Ethernet, it cannot cover as great a distance as coaxial cable. For

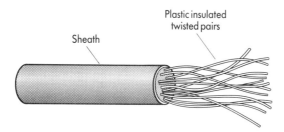

Figure 3.13 Unshielded twisted pair. Note: unshielded twisted pair comes in various grades, which differ in the degree of twisting of the wires. More twisting means greater immunity from electrical interference, and consequently a higher potential transmission capacity.

this reason it cannot be used for backbone networks linking offices or different floors of a building. Coaxial cable still has a role for backbone cabling, although fibre is taking over because it offers far greater capacity and is virtually guaranteed to meet future networking requirements. Coaxial will be a bit like vinyl audio records – gradually it will be phased out as vendors of networking connection equipment cease to support it.

Fibre or copper: do you have to make a choice?

We have already seen how fibre is increasingly often used in buildings as a backbone network, which may run vertically in ducting behind outer walls, while copper is used for individual LANs on each floor. Equally, on a site comprising more than one building, fibre could be used to transport data between LANs in each one.

Fibre and copper can therefore complement each other. However it is possible to use either fibre or copper for the entire network, so it is worth considering the pros and cons at each stage.

We consider the fibre versus copper issue in two stages: for individual workgroup LANs, typically running on cabling on each floor right up to the desk; and for backbone cabling, which may run between floors or between buildings. In fact, as there are different types of copper, we broaden the discussion to consider the relative merits of these for each situation.

Fibre versus copper issues for floor level cabling

For cabling to the desk there is a bewildering choice of options, coming in four basic categories: fibre and the three types of copper (coaxial, unshielded twisted pair and shielded twisted pair). There are different grades of cable in each of these categories, but the differences between each of these grades does not affect the overall choice. Having decided which broad category to go for, you can only determine which grade is most appropriate by a detailed appraisal of the requirements and costs.

We have already pointed out that unshielded twisted pair cabling will be preferable for most single Ethernet LAN segments connecting devices that are relatively close together. We shall see later in the chapter how such LANs based on utp are increasingly based on central wiring hubs. There is also some drift towards utp for token ring LANs.

Shielded twisted pair remains the dominant cabling type for token ring because this is still preferred by IBM. About 80% of organizations that have installed token ring LANs have done so because of encouragement from IBM. For several years token ring required shielded twisted pair, and IBM still recommends stp. However in 1990 some other vendors introduced token ring systems based on unshielded twisted pair suitable for smaller networks. IBM itself subsequently recognized the huge drift towards utp in general, and now supports utp for customers who want to run token ring networks on it.

Both Ethernet and token ring will of course run quite happily on fibre, although as we have said the cost of connecting devices to the physical cable is higher. The main reason currently for running individual token ring or Ethernet LAN segments over fibre to the desk would be in anticipation of needing to carry much greater levels of traffic right to each desktop system in future.

Where copper has already been installed as the cabling within offices, we can say emphatically that there are hardly any circumstances where it is necessary at present to rip this out and replace it with fibre to the desk for LAN segments. We can be so categorical because of startling progress made at extracting high bandwidth over copper cable, both shielded and unshielded, for short distances. An example of this is the new CDDI (copper distributed data interface) standard for shielded twisted pair (stp) copper. This allows an FDDI network running at 100 Mbit/s to be delivered to desktop systems over segments of stp copper cable. The maximum length of the copper segment is 100 metres, but this is sufficient to allow devices to be connected to fibre backbone networks via copper cabling that may already be installed beneath floors. In this way a combination of new fibre backbone cabling and existing copper networks enables a high-speed FDDI network to be built right up to each desk, providing sufficient capacity for all applications in the foreseeable future.

It is also possible, though slightly more difficult, to extend an FDDI network over unshielded twisted pair cable but there is a problem, which we shall explain in a minute, relating to electromagnetic emissions.

It is true that fibre has much greater potential capacity than twisted pair copper cable, which at 100 Mbit/s is running close to its maximum potential speed. However, there will be very few applications requiring more than 100 Mbit/s to the desk until the next century, so the CDDI standard will preclude the need for running fibre to the desk where copper has already been installed, at any rate where this is shielded copper.

This leaves the choice between shielded and unshielded twisted pair copper cable for the local LAN segments. Here there is even less reason to replace one with the other if there is an existing cable network. For new networks, shielded may be preferred if token ring is chosen, but it almost certainly will not be if Ethernet is. However, if it looks likely that 100 Mbit/s to the desk will be needed in the next few years, then shielded may be preferred. Shielded cable costs around 20% more than most unshielded cable, although this depends on the grades used, but it avoids the problem of high-frequency electromagnetic emissions, which cause interference with nearby electronic equipment.

Shielded twisted pair cable provides greater immunity from radiation

When very high data rates, such as 100 Mbit/s, are provided over unshielded cable, a considerable amount of high-frequency radiation is produced. This can interfere with other cabling nearby, or possibly with computing devices such as PCs. Shielded cable is largely immune from this. The outer metal sheath stops much radiation being emitted just as it protects the cable from external interference. Organizations that have already installed shielded cable can therefore feel confident their network will cater for their applications until the end of the century at least.

But organizations with unshielded cable do not need to tear their hair, or networks, out in panic. The use of filters enables token ring LANs at 16 Mbit/s to run over unshielded twisted pair. This enables the cable to conform with European Commission regulations governing emissions. In 1992 there were no filters that would enable a network of unshielded copper cable running at 100 Mbit/s to comply with the EC rules, but networking companies have been working on the problem. It is probable that it will be safe to run 100 Mbit/s over unshielded cable, but shielded is certainly a safer hedge against growing network demand in the future. It is also worth pointing out that emissions are less of a problem with high-grade unshielded cable but such cable may actually cost more than shielded anyway.

Consultants and suppliers of networking systems can provide more detailed advice on this and other aspects of cabling. We look at the issue of commissioning a network in Chapter 7.

Fibre versus copper issue for backbone cabling

We have already alluded to the advantages of fibre for backbone cabling. Fibre is ideally suited because a backbone network usually needs to be capable of higher data rates than local LAN segments since it is the trunk of an organization's onsite network. A telephone trunk circuit between two major cities needs more capacity than local spurs serving a street, and the same argument pertains to data networks. Furthermore, backbone cabling is often close to mains electrical cabling, rendering it vulnerable to electromagnetic interference if copper is used.

As we saw in Chapter 2, fibre also supports the greater distances that a backbone network may need to cover. The FDDI standard over fibre supports rings of total perimeter up to 200 km, with up to 2 km between each network node. A node could be a single computer, or a link supporting a local LAN segment to which in turn a number of devices are attached. This arrangement is ideally suited to a number of large sites such as ports, university campuses or city council headquarters where there is a need to connect a variety of computers distributed over a metropolitan-scale distance in a single coherent network.

And even the specifications of FDDI are a long way from the performance limit of fibre. An existing fibre network would be capable of supporting even higher data rates in future, certainly allowing a tenfold increase to 1 Gbit/s (one billion bit/s) over the same distances. Currently, however, desktop computers are not capable of transmitting data onto the network from their internal communication buses fast enough to make use of such speeds.

The change in performance would be effected not by changing the cable but by replacing the devices attaching computers and LAN segments to it. A properly installed cable network should survive several generations of connection equipment and provide ever increasing performance to satisfy evolving applications and growing numbers of users. This applies equally to copper – as we have seen it is now possible to run FDDI over copper for short distances up to 100 metres.

Twisted pair cable unsuitable for high-speed backbone networks

Twisted pair cable, whether shielded or unshielded, is unsuitable for backbone networks, however, because it cannot sustain high data transmission rates for a sufficient distance. The principal alternative to fibre therefore is thick coaxial copper cable. Some sites have installed broadband backbone networks using cable TV transmission technology over coaxial cable. This provides sufficient bandwidth but is not the way the world is going, which is towards fibre. The thickness of coaxial cable may also be a disadvantage on the parts of a backbone network contained within building walls. Furthermore, the cost of fibre cable is falling in relation to coaxial.

Cabling issues summarized

There are four basic questions that have to be answered with regard to cabling.

(1)   What type of cabling to go for.

(2)   Whether to have a hub and if so what type.

(3)   Whether or not to have a formal structured cabling system.

(4)   Who to go to for installation and subsequent maintenance.

The last of these issues is discussed in Chapter 7. The others hinge on other decisions you may have taken with regard to the structure of the LAN, and also to the size of the network and any requirements for connectivity with other networks.

For networks with 25 users or less, the answer to question (1) is almost certain to be unshielded twisted pair (utp). Now that token ring as well as Ethernet can run over utp, there is little reason for a small site to choose the more expensive option.

The only possible exception is where there is heavy use of high-resolution graphics applications that generate large amounts of network traffic. Then the use of shielded twisted pair cable would provide slightly greater potential for future implementation of faster types of LAN, such as CDDI, as explained earlier in the chapter. However, fibre is the only option if you anticipate needing to be close to the leading edge of transmission speeds.

On the hub front, costs have fallen to the point where the convenience of having a focal point of cabling is worth paying for even on small networks. Where the network has less than 20 users, PC hub cards are certainly worth considering, while stand-alone unmanaged hubs may be used for slightly larger networks with stacking. However, where sustained network growth is anticipated, it is worth going for a managed modular hub that offers greater room for expansion. At this level the answer to question (3) changes from a possible no to a definite yes. Only a structured cabling system allows a network to expand beyond the 12- or 15-user mark without ever increasing disruption each time a new device is added. Again at this point a system to manage the cable network becomes increasingly necessary.

On larger sites, where interoperability between different types of LAN is required, with possible access to wide area networks, smart hubs are required. These are really a different category of product from the 'single-LAN' hubs described in this chapter. Whereas the latter only support one type of LAN, although they can usually inter-connect different cable types, smart hubs allow different LANs to coexist.

Smart hubs are not relevant for most small businesses. But their potential as a focal point of interconnection for multiple LANs is discussed briefly in Chapter 6. Then in Chapter 8 the role of smart hubs in overall network expandability is also discussed briefly.

3

Summary

We have now covered the main cabling issues and options, looking at cable types, structured cabling systems, and hubs. The next chapter takes the subject further by moving up the protocol layers to look at the software controlling operation of your network.

4

What is a network operating system and do I need one?

CHAPTER CONTENTS

CHAPTER OBJECTIVES

Now we discuss the network operating system (NOS) that provides the software base for applications running over your LAN. Basic issues or questions tackled are:

Introduction

All computers require an operating system to perform their function, which is to run applications such as word processing for their users. This applies equally to desktop PCs serving just one user and large water-cooled mainframe computers serving 1000 users. The operating system is needed to coordinate the key functional parts of the computer such as the keyboard, screen, central processing unit, main memory and magnetic disk drive. It also provides a framework for applications and users to manipulate these resources. The best-known and most widely used operating system is MS-DOS, which has been the dominant PC operating system for ten years. The way a basic operating system such as MS-DOS enables an application to run on a single machine is shown schematically in Figure 4.1.

4

What applies to computers is equally true of LANs. The LAN can be regarded as an extended computer, with resources such as disk drives and printers distributed across a network, rather than confined in a discrete stand-alone unit.

What does a NOS do that a PC operating system does not?

When seen in this way, it becomes clear that a LAN requires a network operating system (NOS) just as a single computer requires an operating system. Many of the requirements are the same but additional functions need to be provided when compared with MS-DOS for example. A NOS needs to support sharing of data and resources which an operating system for a single PC such as MS-DOS does not.

Support for sharing of data and resources is of course nothing new because large central, or host, computers have been doing it since the 1960s. In some ways the NOS is a reinvention of traditional multi-user operating systems for large computers, but it does require an important additional ingredient.

The new requirement is support for distributed computing across

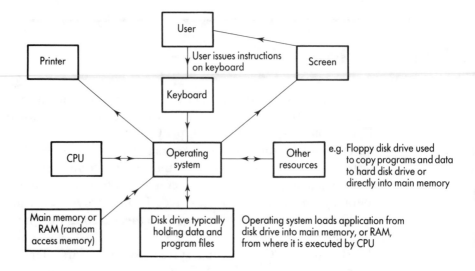

Figure 4.1   How an operating system controls an application on a single computer.

a LAN, where the software running applications may reside partly on desktop PCs and partly on server computers shared across the network. On traditional multi-user systems, all software for applications was in the same place as the data and other resources, in the central system. Users accessed them via dumb terminals that provided a window into the computer. The operating system did not extend its influence beyond the boundaries of the computer room, except to accept input from keyboards or other devices, and to drive the dumb screens.

Are all NOSs essentially the same?

NOSs vary in their scope. Some provide better support for large-scale computing structures. Others are designed specifically for the needs of small networks, supporting the use of existing desktop PCs as shared file storage systems. Such peer-to-peer network operating systems are described later in the chapter.

First we need to describe the essential functions that all NOSs must perform, and then look at the differentiating factors that decide which products are most suitable for a given network. Factors to consider include support for existing computers, applications and net-working protocols. Another is cost, not just of the NOS itself but also the kind of network needed to run it. Then the ability to support future change and growth probably should be considered.

One way of distinguishing NOSs is by their ancestry. Some, such as Novell's NetWare, were designed specifically as LAN operating systems in the early 1980s, and have subsequently extended their range in terms of the type and size of networks they support. On the other hand, BSD (Berkeley Software Distribution) Unix, which is not of itself a NOS, evolved from a centralized multi-user operating system, with support for some NOS type facilities being bolted on later. Yet others, such as Microsoft LAN Manager, were originally extensions of a single-user PC operating system to embrace LANs. More recently there have been efforts to create single operating plat-forms, perhaps embracing two or more different operating systems, that embrace the whole network including the computers it connects.

Before discussing this further, we need to clarify the basic func-tions of a NOS and its relationship with the underlying LAN mechanism, whether this is Ethernet or token ring.

Essential functions

Essentially, a NOS extends the functions provided by basic PC operating systems such as MS-DOS, to embrace resources available on the LAN as well as those directly attached to the PC. NOSs were originally developed to make resources on a LAN appear to each PC as if they were attached directly to it. Figure 4.2 illustrates this schematically. Figure 4.2(a) shows a stand-alone PC complete with printer and disk drive. Figure 4.2(b) shows the same PC attached to a LAN, with the difference that it is now sharing the printer and disk drive with other users. The basic requirement of the NOS is to extend the PC's operating system to allow these resources to be shared as effi-ciently as possible.

But to set the scene, let us consider the fundamental requirements of any traditional computer operating system. There are four broad elements that an operating system needs to control: input, output, management of data files and directories, and execution of programs. On a PC, input usually comes from the keyboard, while output is nor-mally either to the screen or printer.

In general, the NOS is not concerned with direct input from users, as it is driven by applications in the PC. By the same token,

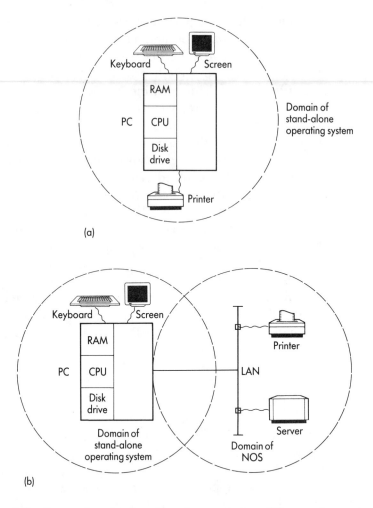

(a)

(b)

Figure 4.2 Comparing the domains of a stand-alone PC operating system like DOS, and a NOS. (a) Stand-alone operating system. (b) NOS.

it is not concerned with running application programs, as this also is under the control of the user's PC. However, as we shall see later, the role of the NOS has had to keep pace with increasingly sophisticated networked applications, in which a number of different systems may cooperate on a given overall task. For example the NOS has to support the growing number of so-called client/server applications, in which tasks are split up between desktop 'client' computers and central server machines.

The NOS has three fundamental functions

To qualify as a NOS only three basic functions need to be provided: file management across the network; print services; and management of communications between devices linked by the LAN. These are the bread and butter of NOS operation, and formed the basis of early versions of NetWare. The aim was to provide these functions as efficiently as possible.

Although the NOS appears only to perform a subset of the overall operating system functions, the fact that it operates over a network makes the tasks more complicated. With printing, the NOS has to be able to queue and prioritize output from different users on the LAN, and make status information available to all. File management is the trickiest task because different users are now contending for access to the same data. This means that file locking has to be supported, so that two users cannot update data at the same time, without slowing down performance unduly.

Performance of this task is critical: if it is slow, response of the whole network is sluggish as almost every application involves accessing, reading and writing data. Apart from strong marketing, the success of NetWare derives from the fact that it was designed in the first instance as a fast network file system.

NOS must support PC operating systems

Another key aspect of the NOS is the number of leading desktop operating systems it supports. The leading ones are MS-DOS, Unix, OS/2, System/7 for the Apple Macintosh, and Windows 3 (which is based on DOS). Another emerging significant desktop operating system is Microsoft's Windows NT, which is a sequel to Windows 3 but more comparable with OS/2 in its level of sophistication.

If a NOS is to allow a single network to support PCs running different operating systems, it must imitate the filing protocols of each one. To do this, a NOS has two parts. The main central part runs in a server, while each desktop PC has a component which intercepts calls from applications to the normal PC operating system. If such calls require action from resources located on the LAN, they are routed to the server. Such calls will emulate filing protocols specific to the desktop operating system. Therefore, the central part of the NOS running in the server has to emulate the relevant filing protocol. In particular, it must support the file and directory structures of each. By doing so, the NOS enables the network's file server to appear to all PC users as part of their system.

For some smaller low-cost NOSs, support for different desktop operating systems is not essential. Some, for example, are designed just for PCs running MS-DOS. But clearly such products restrict your freedom of choice and are not likely to appeal for larger networks where there may already be a range of desktop operating systems within the organization.

Another consequence of operating over a network rather than within a single computer is the need to provide a data transport mechanism. In Chapter 2 we saw that the LAN itself provides a mechanism for carrying data packets and delivering them to the correct node on that LAN. This is a necessary foundation, but not sufficient for applications to operate across a network.

A NOS may have its own data transport protocol, an example being Novell's IPX, for use on LANs it supports. But with the increasing interconnection of different types of LAN, which may not have the same NOS, it helps if there is a common data transport protocol to facilitate communication between applications. Figure 4.3 shows an Ethernet and token ring network running different NOSs but with communication facilitated by a common type of data transport, in this case the popular TCP/IP protocols.

In Chapter 6 we will elaborate on the role of data transport protocols in providing universal communications across interconnected LANs.

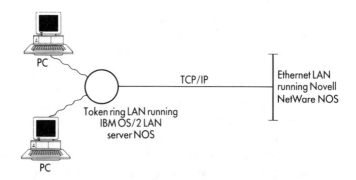

Figure 4.3 Ethernet and token ring LANs running different NOSs communicating via TCP/IP.

Optional features

Many of the features we describe here as optional will be considered compulsory by many network users, particularly those at larger sites. These optional features are mostly concerned with security and management of the network, which grow in importance with the size of the network. However, they will often also be important for small workgroups or departments that have access to a larger enterprise-wide network.

Five major classes of feature can be identified, all of which are optional in the sense that not every single LAN user needs them now, and in any case may not be the sole responsibility of the NOS. Some of these classes overlap. They are: security, fault tolerance/recovery, network management, support for key industry communication standards and support for interconnection with other LANs.

The major NOSs now provide all of these at least in the more sophisticated and expensive versions of their products.

Security

This embraces protection of data and resources from unauthorized attempts to access or sabotage it. The NOS is only part of this picture, but as it controls the flow of data across the network between PCs and central file or database servers, it has the potential to control access to confidential information.

The leading NOSs have the ability to assign security levels to individual files stored on the central server, so that only users with the correct authorization level can access it.

However, this sort of protection is of little value if users can then access the server either physically, or, by loading appropriate applications, change their level of priority. The NOS can help with the latter by preventing users from loading applications without the consent of somebody else, such as the network supervisor.

The NOS cannot help with physical security. It is up to users to ensure that LAN servers holding critical data or applications can only be accessed by authorized personnel. There is a tendency to be more lax about the physical security of LANs than large central computer systems. Yet increasingly LANs are supporting the kind of critical business applications that used to be the preserve of mainframes. Where this is the case it is important that security is improved accordingly.

For small businesses, where there are only a few users and

everybody knows each other, physical security will probably be sufficient. But for larger organizations there is one other security risk to consider where the NOS can help out. This is the risk of tapping into the cable to detect user passwords as they are transmitted across the network. Some NOSs encrypt passwords, making it much harder to gain access to data by tapping into the network. This does not stop someone eavesdropping electronically on the data itself using suitable reception equipment, but this is not a significant threat for most organizations. The expense of encrypting all data on a LAN is only worth incurring if the data is so sensitive that even a slight risk of eavesdropping cannot be contemplated.

Fault tolerance/recovery

This is closely allied to security because failure to cater for it can have similarly disastrous results for a business. In either case critical data may be lost or corrupted. The twin goals are to minimize the risk of the network being unavailable at any time, and maximize the speed of recovery if it does go down. It is impossible to avoid faults occurring in any complex system but the aim is to make the overall network as tolerant of them as possible. The first line of defence is to prevent a fault from actually stopping the network, or at any rate to limit the number of users affected by it. This is done wherever possible by avoiding a single point of failure in the network.

The second aim is to bring the network back up as quickly as possible in the event of it failing altogether. This involves building as much redundancy as possible into the network, making it possible to reconfigure it to avoid failed links or computing devices. Ideally, the network would reconfigure itself automatically immediately the fault occurs but in practice this does not often happen. So at least if the potential is there to re-route traffic around failed links, service can be restored relatively quickly after appropriate intervention by network administrators.

As with security, the NOS itself cannot provide all aspects of fault tolerance, many of which are a matter of good network design. Figure 4.4 shows a network of interconnected LANs, where no single cable break can prevent each individual LAN from communicating with any of the other three. This is because there are two paths between any two of the LANs. In Chapter 6 we explain how a technique called Spanning Tree bridging has been developed to support such a network for Ethernet LANs, given that the network we show appears to violate the Ethernet rule against having a closed network. Ethernet

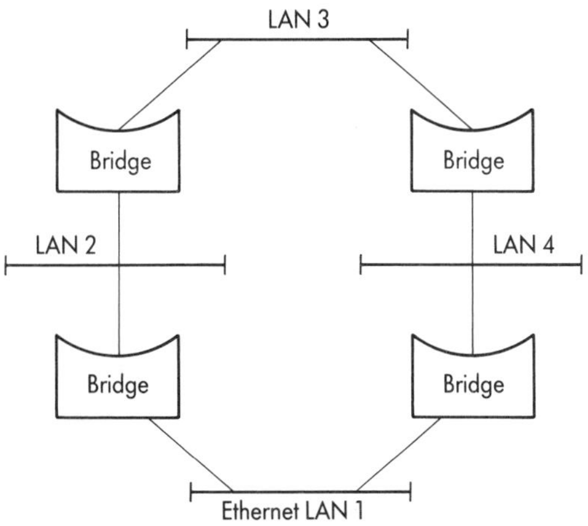

Figure 4.4 A network of interconnected LANs with no single point of failure on the links between the LANs. Here the LANs which are all Ethernet are connected by bridges, which are described in Chapter 6.

requires an open bus structure, otherwise data packets would circulate endlessly as, unlike token ring, they are not removed by any of the nodes.

However, the network shown in Figure 4.4 does not guard against all failures. For example, there might be a single file server for all four networks, failure of which would disable all applications using the server. The network would still be intact, but it is not much use if its heart has stopped working. Against this kind of failure, some NOSs can provide some protection with the aid of additional hardware, as is explained in the next section.

What is needed for fault tolerance?

In 1976 a US company called Tandem emerged with a new idea, that of a fault-tolerant computer offering protection against failure of key components, such as the processor and disk drive. Such computers were more expensive than others of comparable performance without the fault tolerance, so they were only used for critical applications where it was worth paying to minimize risk of being unable to run key applications. As critical applications move to LANs based on shared file or database servers, there is a corresponding need for fault-tolerant features there also.

Full fault tolerance requires duplication of all key components in the network: such as the disk drives storing data, the processor

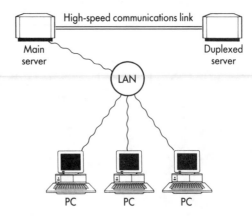

Figure 4.5   Duplicated servers protecting users from server failure and from some disasters. The duplexed server performs every action of the main server, but can be located some distance away – in another building on a large site, for example.

executing applications such as database searches on the server, and of course the communication links themselves. The NOS is responsible for obtaining data from servers for applications. Therefore, fault tolerance based on duplicated servers has to be supported by the NOS. Not all leading NOSs support this. Most NOSs, however, do offer protection against disk drive failure, which is considerably more common than failure of the central processing unit. However, in Novell's fault-tolerant version of its NetWare NOS called SFT (System Fault Tolerant), there will be an option for protection against complete server failure by duplicating the server.

The ability to duplicate the server has a further potential benefit. It is possible to have the mirrored servers some distance apart, so that if one is destroyed by a fire, applications can still run on the other. Given a suitable high-speed communication link between them, duplicated servers can be located several miles apart. Ways in which duplicated servers can be linked are described in more detail in Chapter 10. Figure 4.5 shows a network in which duplicated servers situated in different parts of a building or site provide some protection against disasters external to the network itself, such as a fire or flood. This kind of protection is only possible with a NOS that supports mirrored servers and allows them to be separated by a sufficient distance.

Backing up data

Not all users require, or can afford, duplicated servers. For small networks, the most important aspect of fault tolerance is the ability to

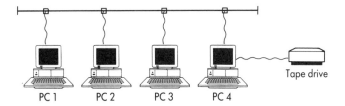

Figure 4.6 Tape drive backing up data on small peer-to- peer LAN. The NOS can support automatic backup of data from each PC to the tape drive attached to PC 4.

4

back up data onto devices such as tape drives. Then, if the primary storage device – usually a disk drive – fails, critical data and applications are not lost. This arrangement also enables a network to manage with a smaller disk drive than would otherwise be the case, because less frequently used files can be archived to lower-cost storage media. Some NOSs provide automatic facilities for backing up data over a LAN at pre-specified times. This may include not just data held on central servers, but also on individual PCs. This means that if any PC on the LAN loses its data as a result of a disk crash, that data can be restored to the condition it was in when the last backup was made. The system used to store the backup data can be a PC on the LAN, or it can be a dedicated storage device such as a tape drive. The advantage of a tape drive is that it is quite inexpensive, which makes it a suitable backup device for small peer-to-peer networks. Figure 4.6 shows a small peer-to-peer Ethernet LAN, with a tape drive to back up data stored in each of the four PCs on the LAN.

NetWare provides a variety of backup facilities, which in Net-Ware 386 (described later in this chapter) have been consolidated into a single menu-driven set utility called NBackup. This allows administrators to back up data from a NetWare 286 or 386 server, or any local disk drive, to a suitable device such as a tape drive. This utility enables backup facilities to operate on networks based on more than one version of NetWare. The utility will not allow data backed up from a device controlled by one version of NetWare to be restored under a different version.

However, except for the smallest networks, the backup facilities provided by the NOS do not help much with overall storage management. They are designed to provide protection against disk drive failure by backing up critical data, but they do not help to clean up the server disk by archiving infrequently used files. On most networks, therefore, some additional backup software is typically used, which may cooperate with the NOS utilities. This software provides additional management information about files stored on the server hard disk. This helps network administrators manage the storage, archival and restoration of data between servers and backup storage devices. Before saying a little more about the role of this software, it is worth clarifying first the hardware options available for backup storage.

What types of storage media can be used for backup

Data can obviously be backed up to a standby disk drive but this is an expensive option, and usually only done for highly critical applications where non-stop operation is required. On most LANs some downtime can be tolerated while data is restored in the event of a failure such as a disk crash. Therefore it makes sense to use a storage medium that provides sufficient capacity but where speed of access is sacrificed for price. The actual option chosen depends largely on the capacity required. There are three main options available.

(1) 1/4-inch tape, providing capacities up to around 500 Mbytes. This is a cost effective option for small to medium sized networks typically with up to about 25 users, although the number depends on the applications. The tapes are typically inserted into a unit that attaches to disk drives via SCSI (small computer systems interface) interfaces. The units are often located inside a PC or server.

(2) DAT (digital audio tape). This provides capacities up to around 4 Gbytes per tape cartridge, although this can be increased to 8 Gbyte with the aid of data compression techniques. Given that DAT systems are also fast and relatively inexpensive, with the ability to access a file on the tape in less than a minute, it is emerging as the preferred method for backing up data on larger networks. Aided by appropriate backup software, DAT systems can be used for unattended operation, allowing backups to be made overnight or at other times when the network is not being use.

(3) Video-8 technology. This is based on the 8-track 8 mm tape cartridges used in video CAMcorders, and provides capacities up to around 5 Gbytes of raw data on a single cartridge, although up to 10 Gbytes with data compression. Like DAT it can be used for unattended backup. It is also

possible to run up to seven devices off a single SCSI controller linked to a disk drive, providing up to around 70 Gbytes of online storage with data compression.

DAT devices were about 50 % cheaper at the time of writing, and also provide faster access to data. Therefore, they appear to afford the best solution for larger networks. However, Video-8 technology does have two tricks up its sleeve. One, existing users that already have libraries of Video-8 cartridges may want to continue with the technology to avoid having to copy files across to new media. Two, Video-8 technology offers significantly higher potential storage capacity on each cartridge. This is because the tapes are bigger. Both Video-8 and DAT use similar techniques for storing data, based on helical scan recording in which data is written across the tape in diagonal stripes, but it just happens that DAT technology has been better exploited at present.

Importance of good backup software

Arguments over which backup device offers the best data retrieval times are rather academic as the key to efficient archival and restoration of data lies with the backup software. It is not much use having a device capable of restoring a file to your server hard disk in 30 seconds if it takes you a day to find that file. The role of backup software should be to help catalogue your data so that it is as easy as possible to find among your backup tapes, and also to streamline the process of archiving data from, and restoring it to, your server hard disk. The backup software should, for example, inform you regularly which files on your server hard disk have not been accessed by any user within a given time period, say three months. These can then be archived to your backup storage because it is likely they will not be needed in a hurry. Your hard disk, which provides almost instantaneous access to data but which is relatively expensive per byte of storage, should only contain files that are accessed frequently.

Network management

The role of management depends on the size of the network. For small networks contained in a single office where all users can see each other, there is no need for sophisticated fault-monitoring and troubleshooting facilities. The main role of management is in monitoring the usage and performance of the network and its elements, notably the server. Traditionally this is the preserve of NOSs such as NetWare, which provides a range of facilities for controlling the server.

However, on larger networks there are other elements to be managed, such as hubs and LAN interconnection devices like routers. The number of functions required also increases with network size. Management of a big network spanning geographically remote sites embraces a number of functions and requires the cooperation of different elements.

NOSs support network management standards

Vendors of the various network components typically provide their own management systems to control their products. The proliferation of different management systems led to growing demand for a standard that allowed them all to interoperate to some extent, enabling the whole network to be managed from a single point. The dominant standard for LANs is the Simple Network Management Protocol (SNMP). As we explain in Chapter 10, where we discuss the subject in detail, NOSs have extended their range of management facilities beyond the server. The major NOS vendors, in particular, are committed to tackling the problems that arise on enterprise-wide networks that were not relevant when NOSs were used solely within single workgroups. An example is support for distributed directories, enabling users to access data on a remote server without knowing its location.

Users of small networks obviously do not need facilities such as support for distributed directories. Some users may not need any management facilities at all. However, even on small networks, basic monitoring of servers will often be useful. We will consider these basic facilities before moving on to more sophisticated management requirements on large networks.

Primary management role of NOS relates to server

For small networks, the primary function of a NOS is to provide access to data held on servers located on a LAN. As we have seen, these servers may be dedicated just to the task of providing data to other computers, or they may also function as desktop PCs in peer-to-peer networks. In either case, the basic role of the NOS in network management is to provide information on usage and performance of the server or servers. For small networks, the main role of NOS management will be monitoring the disk activity of the server. This can provide information about disk errors, which may enable corrective action to be taken before a crash occurs. Also important is to know when the disk is getting full. Some NOSs tell network managers when the disk has reached a certain preset proportion of its capacity, for example 90 %. This gives time for additional disk storage to be laid on before the existing disk fills up completely.

We saw in Chapter 3 that servers can also function as hubs for the cabling through use of add-on cards. We explained how low-cost hubs were becoming standard products based on PC cards, enabling them to slot into standard PCs. To cater for this trend, some NOSs, such as NetWare, now provide hub management facilities as well. This entails monitoring traffic levels along each spoke of the hub and also detecting cabling faults.

Information on disk usage is also required for large networks. But then there are additional requirements. The ability to support a variety of industry standards for communication with different systems and to support distributed applications may be needed. These are discussed in the next section. Also the NOS will probably need to integrate with other large-scale network management systems, such as IBM's Netview and AT&T's Unified Network Management Architecture (UNMA). Novell, for example, has been working with IBM to enable NetWare networks to be managed from the Netview management system.

At the same time, leading NOS vendors are trying to embrace all of a network's management needs. The aim is to provide an umbrella management system for the whole network. To achieve this, NOS vendors support the key network management standards, in particular SNMP (simple network management protocol), which we describe in Chapter 9. They are also working with other vendors to link up their management systems. Novell, for example, cooperated with the leading hub vendor, SynOptics Communications Inc., in this way. This led to SynOptics' hub management system being incorporated into the NetWare Management System.

Another important management facility that NOS vendors need to provide for large networks is a distributed directory service. A large network may interconnect numerous local sites together with a few major sites. Some global networks have over 1000 file or database servers on LANs, and support 20 000 users. In order to provide each user with the ability to access every server on the network, a directory listing their names and network addresses has to be provided. Without that, a server might not know where to send a particular set of data it had been requested to provide.

On a small network based around a single server, a directory is relatively easy to manage. There is just one set of addresses for users on that network, and this can readily be updated from a single management station. The problems begin when there are two servers each having their own directories. Then any updates to one have to be reflected in the other if the overall network based on the two servers is to work. On a large network with multiple servers, the problems are that much greater. The requirement is for a distributed directory service that allows each local site to maintain its own directory, but which synchronizes all directories at regular intervals to maintain consistency across the whole network.

A distributed directory service does not need to be provided by the NOS. It can instead be provided by applications at a higher level. But if the same NOS is used throughout a network, then it can make sense to provide this facility in the NOS. Then all applications can take advantage of a commonly available directory. Indeed NetWare 4.0, announced in March 1993, supports distributed directories across multiple servers.

Support for key industry standards

There are two classes of standard here. One relates to the communication between computers on the network. The other deals with communication between applications that run on the computers. The NOS, controlling the flow of data across a network, needs to support standards at both levels if it is to allow for future change and growth. There are some fundamental standards that are necessary for virtually all NOSs, including the low-cost peer-to-peer ones. And there are others, such as the large-scale network management systems mentioned in the last section, that are relevant only for bigger networks supporting a variety of computer systems.

These two standards groups are both broadly defined within a seven layer interconnection model that forms the basis of interaction between different computers across a network. In Chapter 9 we describe this model, which has been developed by computer and networking systems vendors in a joint effort within international standards forming bodies – such as the International Standards Organization (ISO). Each layer in this model supports a particular aspect of the overall communications and networking process. For example, layer 1 defines physical aspects such as cabling and electrical signalling. The first of our two classes of standard corresponds to the bottom four layers of this communications model, which are concerned with establishing the means of data transport across the network. The top three layers, 5 to 7, are concerned with higher-level interaction between applications software: these correspond to our second group of standards. Here we consider each group briefly in relation to the NOS, with more detail in Chapter 9.

Communications standards

Here the concern is to support communication between computers over your network. The first requirement is to support the basic LAN, usually either Ethernet or token ring. Many NOSs will work over both but a few support just Ethernet.

In addition to the basic LAN communications, the NOS needs to support some data transport protocol so that computers can exchange data files across the LAN without having to understand the detail of the LAN communication mechanism. NetWare has its own transport protocol, IPX, although Novell also supports others so that NetWare LANs can communicate with different networks. On a single LAN serving a workgroup, it does not matter which transport protocol the NOS uses. However, on large networks there are a number of transport protocols that a NOS needs to support to facilitate communication between its domain and others. This includes major proprietary protocols owned by leading computer system vendors, and protocols that enjoy widespread support by different vendors. The latter are sometimes referred to as open systems protocols.

The two most important proprietary ones are IBM's SNA (System Network Architecture) and Digital Equipment's DECnet. The main open protocols are OSI, which offers several data transport options, and TCP/IP. We describe all of these in Chapter 9.

Application standards

The four standards just mentioned (SNA, DECnet, OSI and TCP/IP) all address the application layers of communication as well. Support at this level is necessary to enable PCs to access applications running on remote systems correctly. To do this the NOS has to provide a gateway to convert the high-level communication protocols used by the system being accessed to those used on the LAN. Figure 4.7 shows a NetWare LAN providing access to an IBM mainframe. This requires Novell's gateway software to run in the server, providing PCs with the correct screen emulations and sending the right signals into the IBM SNA network.

However, in this kind of application the PC is little more than a window into the IBM system. There has been growing use of more sophisticated levels of interaction between computers, with the aim of exploiting both the network and the computers attached to it in the

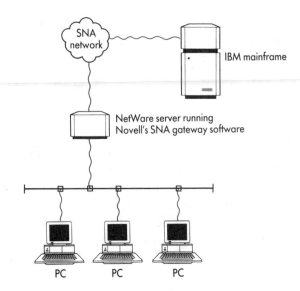

Figure 4.7   NetWare LAN providing access to IBM mainframe for PC users via an IBM SNA network.

most efficient way possible. There are two types of interaction possible between computer applications. These are client/server computing, which is described in Chapter 1, and cooperative processing, which is described in Appendix 3.

Support for interconnection with other LANs

The field of LAN interconnection is discussed more fully in Chapter 6, where we describe the hardware devices needed. Most NOSs will work across networks comprising more than one interconnected LAN. This is needed if a user on one LAN wants to access a server on another. Figure 4.8 shows two remote LANs with servers on each. It is possible for applications to handle the access to different servers without the help of a NOS. But if the NOS supports a distributed directory service, it can save the application from having to determine which server to go to for a particular task such as a database search. Figure 4.8 illustrates how this could happen. Looking at the diagram, suppose PC 1 wants to access a data file contained on server B. The task would first be forwarded to the local server A, which would then pass control over to server B if it did not contain the requested file.

Description of some popular NOSs

We describe two of the major NOSs: Novell NetWare and Microsoft's LAN Manager. We then look at Banyan Vines, the first NOS to be developed for large complex networks. We move on to consider together five NOSs ideally suited for small peer-to-peer LANs: Powerlan, LANtastic, 10Net, NetWare Lite and Microsoft's Windows for Workgroups. We also look at Unix, which can function as both a computer and network operating system. Finally we suggest how NOSs are likely to evolve during the rest of the 1990s.

4

NetWare

For many people NetWare is synonymous with the NOS, having cornered around 60 % of the overall market. Its dominance of the networking section in computer booksellers is even greater. Like all successful information technology products there are as many books about it as there are about John F. Kennedy.

NetWare's success can be put down to three factors. It was the first available for standard IBM-compatible PCs, it performs well and, above all, it has been well marketed. LAN Manager when it emerged in 1987 had some definite advantages such as support for peer-to-peer networking, along with some significant disadvantages

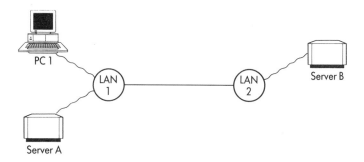

Figure 4.8   Showing how NOS can support interconnecting LANs. The NOS ensures that an application running on PC 1 can access data whether it is held on server A or server B.

on performance. It was unable to make much impression on Novell's well established customer base which in fact continued to grow.

The basic mechanism of NetWare is shown in Figure 4.9. When PCs are stand-alone, that is, not connected to any network, applications issue commands directly to the PC's own operating system. When attached to a LAN, there has to be some way of distinguishing between commands that are for the local operating system and commands for the network. NetWare imposes a software shell between the application and the local operating system, which could be MS-DOS, Windows 3.0 or OS/2. This shell pre-processes a command, and either passes it straight to the local operating system or routes it to the network.

NetWare has now split into three distinct operating systems, with considerable differences. The original NetWare was launched in 1983. Then NetWare 286 arrived in 1985 for PCs based on the Intel 286 processor, introducing a variety of features required for critical applications, including disk mirroring and security features such as lockout features informing supervisors of unauthorized attempts to access servers.

NetWare version 3.11 was then developed to take advantage of the extra power and facilities of PCs based on Intel 386 and 486 processors. NetWare v3.11 increased the number of users that can be supported per server from 100 to 250, with a pledge to go up to 1000 in future. However, the maximum number of users that can be supported in practice will depend on how active they are. The NOS itself is not the only constraint on network size, which also depends on the power of the server and the available transmission capacity of the network.

Novell also redesigned its filing system for NetWare v3.11 to make access of data faster and more suited to client/server applications. Another important addition was the support for extra software

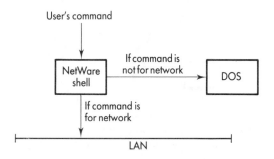

Figure 4.9   Basic mechanism of NetWare in each PC.

modules, called NetWare Loadable Modules (NLMs). These can provide a wide variety of functions for management of the network, communication with other systems outside the network and support for client/server applications.

NetWare had been criticized for failing to support peer-to-peer operation. A dedicated server was mandatory. However, in 1991 Novell remedied this omission with NetWare Lite, designed for small networks. We discuss this in comparison with other peer-to-peer NOSs. At the time of writing, Novell was considering extending peer-to-peer facilities to NetWare v3.11. Then in March 1993 Novell announced NetWare 4.0, introducing support for distributed directories among other improvements. NetWare 4.0 is designed mainly for networks comprising multiple servers.

Unix

Unix is not a NOS, but now most versions of it provide extensive networking support. It is the closest to a universal operating system, being capable of operating on computers of all sizes from PC to mainframe, and also incorporating many NOS functions.

One version of the operating system, BSD Unix, was designed from the outset to operate across distributed systems linked on a network. It incorporated the well-known TCP/IP transport protocols to support communication. These have since become the *de facto* standard for data transport across a wide range of systems, not just computers running Unix.

Other versions of Unix, such as AT&T's System V Release 4, now also support networking protocols. This version of Unix has its own application programming interface (API), called Transport Level Interface, designed to link applications with OSI transport protocols. Many versions of Unix now support Network File System (NFS) as a basis for client/server applications.

The question then arises: if Unix can run on all systems and do most things that a NOS can, why is it not rapidly taking over from all other operating systems? It is growing in popularity, but no more quickly than some NOSs and PC operating systems. There are several reasons why Unix is not a universal panacea for cooperating applications on a network. One is that operating systems do not perform universally well in all situations. In particular Unix was not designed to operate on single-user desktop PCs. Also, it works in the opposite way to most NOSs. On a typical LAN with a NetWare server and PCs running MS-DOS, applications are run by PCs, which control the operation of the server via the NOS. Unix, on the other hand, is a multi-user operating system, designed initially to run on large computers supporting a number of users on dumb terminals rather than intelligent PCs. On a LAN based entirely on Unix, desktop PCs would be under the control of a central machine, which, therefore, in a technical sense is no longer a server but a client.

Figure 4.10 shows a LAN in which PCs, acting as Unix terminals, are subordinate to a central Unix machine. In practice this may not be much different as far as users are concerned to a client/server network controlled by a NOS. Under client/server computing, the desktop PC focuses on tasks that it is good at, such as graphics and word processing. Similarly it is now possible for PCs to access Unix systems to perform tasks such as database searches, using the Unix client/server protocol NFS, and then switch back to their own applications. The more modern PC operating systems, such as OS/2, allow users to access two remote applications on screen simultaneously in windows on the screen, and transfer data between them. Figure 4.11 shows a network where users can access a NetWare server and a Unix system simultaneously.

There are products that enable MS-DOS to access Netware and Unix servers simultaneously. Alternatively, MS-DOS PCs may access the Unix system from a LAN server running a NOS with appropriate gateway server. Figure 4.12 illustrates how this would happen for a NetWare network. When PCs want to access the Unix system to run a program or obtain data, the NetWare server would convert the transport protocol from its own IPX to the Unix TCP/IP and forward the request to the Unix system. On return it would convert the protocol back again, and forward the results to the PC. IPX and TCP/IP are described in Chapter 9.

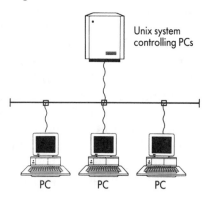

Figure 4.10   Classic Unix configuration in which PCs are subordinate to Unix system.

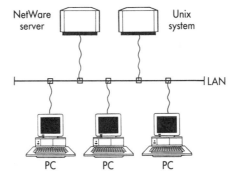

PCs running multitasking operating system
such as OS/2 can access both NetWare server
and Unix system simultaneously on their screens

4

Figure 4.11   A network where users can access a NetWare server and a remote
Unix system simultaneously.

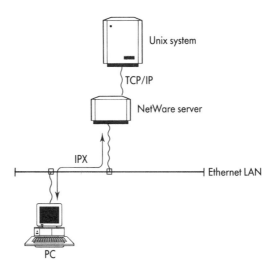

Figure 4.12   How a Unix system can be accessed via a NetWare server.

Unix can support complete end-to-end networking. But more
commonly it cooperates with existing NOSs and desktop operating
systems (although Novell's Univel initiative, described at the end of
this chapter, may increase the use of Unix for desktop applications).
However, one persistent problem is worth noting, which is the lack
of conformance between different versions of Unix. This means that

applications written for one version of Unix may not work on another. It also means that products designed to integrate PC applications with Unix-based servers will not always work. However, there are industry groups endeavouring to unite the different flavours of Unix, so in future it may converge into a single operating system.

Vines (VIrtual NEtworking System) from Banyan Systems

In some ways this NOS was ahead of its time, and although quite successful, never took off like NetWare because it did not address the pressing networking requirements of the mid 1980s. While NetWare was initially designed purely for single LAN workgroups and only later enhanced to support multiple servers across a distributed network, Vines was designed for this from the outset. It incorporated support for several wide area protocols and a global distributed naming system in its initial design, making it ideal for complex large-scale networks. But at that time there were few networks that suited the product, and as a result Vines did not grow as prolifically as NetWare.

LAN Manager from Microsoft

As architect of the world's most successful PC operating system, MS-DOS, Microsoft was determined to triumph again in the NOS area. In some ways the ingredients for a repeat performance were there. As with MS-DOS, Microsoft's NOS – LAN Manager – had been chosen by IBM as the basis for its NOS. IBM called its version LAN Server. Furthermore, LAN Manager was widely considered to be a better designed, technically, superior product than MS-DOS, even allowing for the fact than it was developed almost ten years later. But the difference was it came too late to loosen Novell's grip on the market. MS-DOS had the corporate PC field virtually to itself thanks to IBM's blessing, but this time NetWare was already well entrenched, and continuing to improve, when LAN Manager hit the market. However, the battle may not be entirely over, as we shall discuss in the futures section at the end of this chapter.

LAN Manager came in with two advantages over NetWare. First, it supported peer-to-peer networking, allowing any PC on the network to act as a server. Second, it did not impose a proprietary transport protocol on the network, supporting several popular protocols such as TCP/IP and OSI. Novell now supports other protocols as well, but initially only from the server outwards, still requiring IPX for communication between PCs and the server. Novell maintained this approach because IPX runs more efficiently on PCs than other protocols such as TCP/IP, so there are pros and cons both ways. Now, however, Novell does support TCP/IP as an option on PCs.

In general LAN Manager and NetWare have converged and can be regarded as alternative products, particularly for larger networks where security and resilience are important. LAN Manager was originally designed for PCs running OS/2 but now works with the other major desktop operating systems in the client PC including Microsoft's own Windows NT.

One other advantage that Microsoft claims is that LAN Manager fits particularly well with its Windows 3 PC operating system. This is certainly true, but as Windows 3 is a widely used *de facto* standard operating system like MS-DOS, other NOS vendors ensure that users can exploit the full Windows features. Note that LAN manager is resold under different names, and with additional features, by other vendors such as Digital Equipment and NCR.

Peer-to-peer LANs (LANtastic from Artisoft; PowerLAN from Performance Technology (distributed in the UK by CMS Software); 10Net from Sitka; NetWare Lite from Novell; and Windows for Workgroups from Microsoft

On a peer-to-peer network, PCs can in general be configured for two different modes of operation. They can be clients only, in which case they function just like PCs on a normal LAN without providing any data or services to other users. Alternatively, they can be non-dedicated servers, functioning both as desktop PCs and servers to other users. When configured as non-dedicated servers, some of their main RAM memory needs to be assigned to network operation, and they will probably also need to provide greater hard disk capacities to ensure that there is sufficient storage for all users of the network.

These five products all support peer-to-peer networking and were designed largely or entirely for small LANs from two or three PCs up to around ten PCs, although all will support a greater number than this. In fact these products vary in their expansion capability as well as in their support for the various standards and systems that a network might encounter as it grows.

Partly because Novell already had products for larger networks, NetWare Lite was designed purely for small networks and sits apart from other versions of NetWare. However, it does support up to 24 PCs, although at this level it is more cost effective to purchase full-blown NetWare. NetWare Lite cannot be upgraded to other versions of NetWare.

LANtastic has become particularly popular on small networks because it works very efficiently on low-cost PCs, taking up surprisingly little RAM memory on both the server and workstation, 40 K and 12 K respectively. It also supports voice communication along the LAN via optional voice adaptor cards and telephone-style handsets, although rival vendors dismiss this as a gimmick. Although found chiefly in small LANs, it allows for substantial network growth, supporting up to 300 PCs. It only runs on Ethernet LANs with DOS-based PCs but repays this limitation with excellent performance.

PowerLAN, less well known in the UK than LANtastic, has been successful in the US where it has won various performance accolades in bench tests. It supports both Ethernet and token ring, and can communicate with LANs based on other NOSs, such as LAN Manager and NetWare. PowerLAN supports more of the security and resilience features required for network growth than the other four products in this section, with options for interconnecting different LANs, disk mirroring and a tape backup facility. It allows networks to grow to up to 255 PCs per server, and as already indicated can support multiple servers on different LAN segments. It is, therefore, a more serious contender than the others in this section for large networks. It is not restricted to peer-to-peer operation, also supporting client/server operation.

10Net is pitched fully at the low-end market for small numbers of PCs, although in fact it imposes no limit on the number of users it can support. In practice, however, peer-to-peer operation is really only suitable either for small numbers of users or where network traffic is light. However, Sitka, a subsidiary of Sun Microsystems, does offer a growth path to the company's larger-scale network operating systems.

Windows for Workgroups is really a sequel to Windows 3, incorporating fundamental features of LAN Manager required to support peer-to-peer networking in small LANs. Unlike the other peer-to-peer NOSs in this section, it is a complete distributed operating system combining the NOS and the desktop operating system. No other desktop operating system is needed. It is comparable to Novell's effort of combining DR-DOS and NetWare Lite, but in this instance Microsoft was first with a fully integrated product.

Windows for Workgroups allows users to share the files on their hard disk and also their printer, if they have one attached to their PC. It also comes bundled with a fully fledged electronic mail system in its own right, version 3.0 of Microsoft's MS Mail. This allows users to read, compose, store, forward and manage messages. It also features a 'point and click' address book.

An interesting feature, or a recipe for anarchy depending on your point of view, is a so-called WinMeter allowing users to specify what proportion of their CPU is devoted to their own local applications as opposed to serving other PCs on the network. In this way users can ensure that their PCs are not overburdened by requests from other PCs. However, it does bring the risk of users selfishly preventing others from having reasonable access to files they are entitled to use that happen to be located on that PC. For this reason peer-to-peer networking in general is suitable only for small networks comprising a closely knit workgroup or community of users.

4

The future of network operating systems

Here we must make a nice distinction between network operating systems, or NOSs of the sort we have been discussing, and networked operating systems. The future lies with the latter, which will gradually incorporate the functions of the former. The difference is that a NOS is designed specifically for network operation and typically sits on a LAN server, while a networked operating system embraces both the network and the computers on it. The distinction has already been blurring, as NOSs like NetWare begin to support the same techniques for cooperative processing as computer operating systems. And as we have noted, Unix has most of the ingredients of a networked operating system.

The point is that the NOS was originally designed to extend PCs over a LAN. Now that their applications are being written to support client/server operation, this traditional role of the NOS is fading. The growing requirement, and this applies both to small and large networks, is either for a single distributed operating system that works across the network, or for a standard high-level protocol that supports cooperative processing between applications on different computers, no matter what operating system they are running.

This trend can be seen through the actions of both Novell and Microsoft. In 1991, Novell bought Digital Research, which supplies DR-DOS (a popular version of MS-DOS) to give itself a position in the PC operating system market. A major objective of this merger was to create a single networked operating system by combining the functions of DR-DOS and NetWare into a single product. For the foreseeable future, both will continue to be available as independent products, but as more and more PCs are networked, the combined version should prove increasingly popular.

Microsoft is heading in a similar direction. It has had longer to start tying the two halves together, having always had control of both LAN Manager and MS-DOS. Its sequel to Windows 3, called Windows NT, incorporates NOS functions as well as supporting client/server applications where the server is running another operating system, such as Unix or NetWare. LAN Manager is still required as a separate product to support full server operation in a LAN, as an alternative to NetWare or another NOS.

Novell has responded strongly to the threat posed by Windows NT. In 1992 the company followed up its acquisition of Digital Research with another ace in launching UnixWare, a version of Unix for standard Intel-based PCs. UnixWare was in fact the fruit of a joint venture between Novell and Unix Systems Laboratories, which developed Unix System V.4, one of the major versions of Unix. (Subsequently, early in 1993, Novell moved to acquire USL from the former owner AT & T.) UnixWare is based on this version, and will compete with other versions of Unix for desktop PCs, such as SCO Unix. Exploiting Novell's extensive world-wide distribution channels, it looks set to become a major PC version of Unix. But Novell has a bigger mission, which is to move on from NetWare to the next generation of LAN and desktop operating systems. The initial goal is to make Unix and NetWare more interoperable, so that applications can span both platforms. For LAN servers, Univel is developing a version of Unix that is, in the jargon of the trade, 'NetWare aware'. This means that applications written for this version of Unix can fully exploit services such as backup provided by NetWare, and vice versa. At the same time all the major desktop operating systems such as Windows and DOS will be supported. Univel then gives Novell a position in the fast growing market for Unix, more particularly on servers attached to LANs.

Meanwhile Novell's latest version 4.0 of NetWare competes head on with Microsoft's LAN Manager for Windows NT in the field of networked operating systems capable of supporting distributed computing across a variety of different systems on a network. And for small LANs, its ownership of Digital Research brings the opportunity of building a flexible operating system based on DOS and NetWare to meet the requirements of client/server applications on smaller LANs.

Summary

4

This chapter has established when a NOS is needed, and how products differ. However we have not yet fully emphasized other factors involved in choice of NOS apart from technical merits. In Chapter 7 we point out that quality of product is not the only issue. It is also important to choose products that are well supported and are likely to continue being enhanced.

5

What other devices can I put on my network apart from PCs?

CHAPTER OBJECTIVES

The title of this chapter is largely self explanatory. However, it also covers issues involved in connecting different devices to a LAN. Some parts, such as the discussion about printers, will be relevant to almost all readers, while obviously some of the more specialized devices like bar code scanners may well not be. The following points or questions, some of which overlap with each other, are tackled:

Introduction

5

Just about any computing device that is able to transmit and receive data can be put on a network. This includes computers of all sizes, including Unix workstations, database servers and mainframes. It includes terminals used to access multi-user host systems. It also includes a large range of peripheral devices, including not just printers and disk drives, but also a variety of input devices such as image scanners and bar code readers.

Essentially all computers, and all devices that can be linked to them, can be attached to a network. The motives are various. Expensive resources can be shared. Users can communicate with each other and access information anywhere in an organization from their desks. Applications can cooperate and exploit the computer processing resources in the most efficient way.

In this chapter we describe the issues involved in connecting different devices to the network. In some cases the fact that a product is attached to a network rather than an individual PC will affect the factors that need to be considered when making the purchase. However, the device does not necessarily need to support attachment to a network. A variety of devices, such as printers and terminals, can be attached to a network via servers. The advantage of this is that the server, with a standard PC chassis at the back, can attach to the network via a standard network interface card.

In some cases, especially on larger networks, you may need access to devices or resources that are not located on your own LAN segment. There may be a need, for example, to access data at a remote location. And there may be an expensive high-volume printer at a remote site that you need to access occasionally for large print runs. The issue of sharing resources then extends beyond individual LANs to span the whole enterprise-wide network. Indeed organizations want to interconnect their different local networks so that resources and data can be made available wherever they are needed. We discuss the issues involved in interconnecting LANs in Chapter 6.

One point to note is that the size of the network does not in principle affect the choice of devices you can put on it, given that the fundamental standards such as 10Base-T apply to networks of all sizes. But there are practical considerations. In practice no one is going to attach a mainframe capable of supporting 1000 simultaneous users to a four-node network for example.

What does a device need for attachment to a network?

For direct connection to a network, a device needs to support the relevant LAN protocol, usually either token ring or Ethernet. The normal way to do this is via a LAN adaptor card, commonly called a network interface card or NIC, but it can also be built into the device. Single chip implementations of Ethernet and token ring controllers are now available. These can readily be implemented on the motherboards of PCs, for example. However, the NIC is the predominant method of connecting devices, and as such is worth considering in its own right as something that can be connected to a LAN. Accordingly we devote a section of this chapter to the issue of NICs and the factors you should consider when buying them.

Devices do not have to be directly connected to a network. Instead they can be, and usually are, attached via a server. Figure 5.1 shows a common arrangement in which a printer is attached to a LAN via a standard PC-based file or database server. The advantage of this arrangement is that a standard PC printer can then be used, without any additional networking facilities. This is possible because the file server behaves just like a PC. The only difference is that it will run a network operating system such as LAN Manager. It will usually also be configured differently with a greater amount of

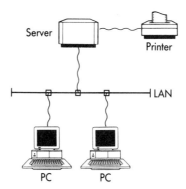

Figure 5.1 Printer attached to a LAN via a server machine that also handles files or a database. Printer is attached to the server via a standard serial or parallel port, just as it would be if attached directly to a PC.

5

disk storage and providing greater protection against faults. In this arrangement the file server rather than the printer takes care of queuing and spooling, so that PC users can submit jobs for printing. We discuss this in more detail in the next section. We are now ready to discuss the devices and surrounding issues in more detail, under eight sections: printers; file/database servers; NICs (network interface cards); input devices such as image scanners; image servers; terminal servers; communication servers; and hubs/wiring concentrators.

Printers

How are printers attached to the LAN?

There are three main options:

(1) The most common method at least on small networks is for the printer to be attached to the LAN via a server. The printer is attached to the server via a standard serial or parallel interface.

(2)   The printer is attached directly to the LAN. For this the printer needs to be designed for network attachment. It needs its own network interface card (NIC) and support for the network operating system (NOS) used on your LAN. It also needs to support spooling, which we describe in the next section.

(3)   The printer can be attached to the LAN via a separate module. The advantage of this is that low-cost printers not designed for network operation can be attached directly to the LAN without tying up a separate server machine. On small networks this can be a cost effective solution. Such modules are specific to particular NOSs, although some support more than one NOS, covering popular ones such as LAN Manager and NetWare.

What is print spooling?

Print spooling (the word spool is an acronym for simultaneous peripheral operation on line) is the fundamental mechanism that allows a printer to be shared across a network. As we have seen this sharing can be accomplished in various ways. The most common is still via a print server that can either be dedicated to printing, or more often, at least on smaller networks, it also acts as a file or database server. Its operation is shown in Figure 5.2. A PC that wants to print something issues a request to the print server via the network. The

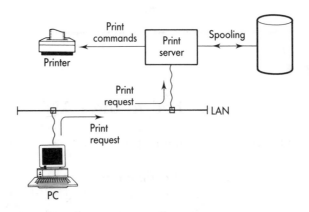

Figure 5.2   Showing the basic operation of printer spooling.

server then 'spools' the print job onto its hard disk, where there may also be other jobs queued up for printing. The server then retrieves print files one at a time from the hard disk into its main RAM memory, according to priority, and prints them.

Spooling solves two problems. First, it enables the server to print files larger than can be accommodated in its main memory. But above all it enables the network to shoulder the burden of managing print queues from each PC. Without spooling, each PC would have to negotiate directly with the printer, and would have to wait for it to be free before transmitting the print file across the network. As the majority of desktop PCs still cannot handle more than one task at a time, this would frustrate users who would have to keep checking whether the printer is free.

5

What are the requirements for networked printing?

On small networks there may be just one printer, and here the aim is to share this among users. The requirement is for queuing and spooling, so that jobs can be submitted and handled independently of each PC. A simple scheme for assigning priority is usually desirable, so that an urgent job can jump the queue and be printed immediately.

On larger networks the NOS needs to offer more sophisticated facilities to enable jobs to be distributed between a number of printers of different types. Figure 5.3 shows a LAN with three printers where printer 1 is designated exclusively for small jobs of high priority, printer 2 for long print runs of low priority, and a third laser printer for specialist jobs that require high-quality graphics. The LAN, usually through its NOS, needs to be able to assign jobs to the correct printer and handle queues for each. It may also need to handle different priorities within each queue, so that, for example, a more urgent long job would come to the front of the queue for printer 2, avoiding what could otherwise be a long wait.

It may also be useful to support multiple print queues on just one printer, as illustrated in Figure 5.4. Here letters and other work are maintained as separate queues. Letters might have automatic priority. The other queue has to wait until there are no letters to send before it can take over the printer. Again it should be possible to have a special urgent category in both queues, which takes precedence over everything else.

In some cases it may be desirable to have one queue shared

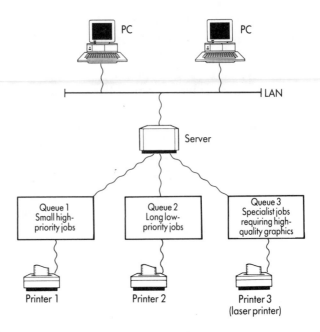

Figure 5.3   How a LAN can distribute different kinds of print jobs among three printers. Within each queue, high-priority jobs can jump to the front. It would also be possible for, say, a high-priority long job to be switched to printers 1 or 3 if another long job was printing on printer 2.

among more than one printer, for example when there are several workgroups supported by a common set of printers on a single net-work. Each workgroup could have its own queue but with the ability to use any available printer. Urgent jobs from any workgroup could then hunt for the first available printer. Non-urgent jobs could utilize all printers when there are no urgent jobs. At the same time jobs requiring a particular printer, for example to produce colour graphics, would obviously have to wait for that particular printer to become free. Figure 5.5 shows such an arrangement, where one queue is distributed among three printers.

In each of these examples, the printer is driven by a LAN server. The operation of the queuing is handled by the NOS running in the server, and therefore presupposes that the NOS provides such facilities. The leading NOSs do. All the facilities mentioned so far are provided by Microsoft's LAN Manager, for example.

It may also be useful to vary the kind of jobs being printed according to time of day. For example, less urgent jobs could be

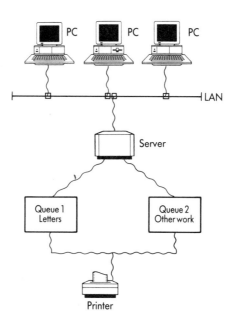

Figure 5.4   Two print queues for one printer.

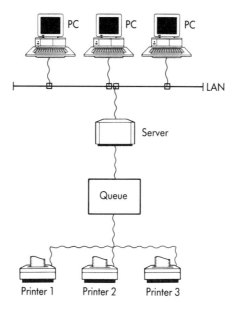

Figure 5.5   One print queue distributed across three printers. The printers could be of different types, with one for high-quality colour printing, one for high-speed urgent jobs and a low-cost one for low-priority jobs.

printed overnight. A typical case might be a network with a single laser printer designated for two quite different kinds of work: printing letters on company headed paper and printing address labels. These two tasks are not interchangeable because they require different paper. The LAN could be programmed to print letters during the day and then switch over to labels by night. Again this facility is supported by some NOSs, such as PowerLAN from Performance Technology (distributed in the UK by CMS Software).

Although such facilities may not be required for small LANs with just one printer, they do at least provide a growth path. In order to sustain network growth, it is not sufficient for the NOS just to support a large number of users on one server. It must also provide the sophisticated LAN control and management facilities that are needed on a large network, and this includes strong print services.

On small peer-to-peer LANs, the immediate need will often be the ability to share a printer without impairing the performance of any server too greatly. This is a point worth considering when purchasing a NOS for peer-to-peer operation. To illustrate the point, let us consider the normal arrangement in a LAN, that is for a printer to be attached to a file server.

On a peer-to-peer LAN this would often be a non-dedicated file server. In Chapter 4 we explained how PCs on a peer-to-peer LAN can be configured purely as clients or as dual client/servers. In the latter mode they need to devote more of their memory to serving the needs of other users on the LAN rather than just their own desktop user. However, if the only requirement is to share a printer with other users, there is no need to configure the PC for server operation. Instead it is only necessary to install some spooling software in the PC, which occupies only a small proportion of its total memory, typically around 4 K. This means that the user of the PC is not significantly affected by the fact that print jobs are routed through the PC.

Access to print queue status information

On networks of all sizes and types it is essential to be able to access and edit print queues to change priorities or erase a job if it is no longer necessary to print. On larger networks it is also necessary to restrict most users from being able to edit print queues for any purpose other than deleting any jobs of their own that they do not want. Without restricting access, anarchy can rule as users vie with each other to bring their jobs to the top of the queue. However, network supervisors need to have full editing right to change the priority of jobs where necessary. In general, access to servers for printing can be controlled in the same way as access to data files. We discuss security and access control further in Chapter 10.

File/database servers

File and database servers may also support other devices such as printers. They may support users' applications as well in non-dedicated mode on a peer-to-peer LAN. However, there are some key issues that are specific to the file or database function, involving provision of shared data resources for a number of users. Among these is the rise of the diskless workstation, that is, a PC without the ability to store data. A diskless workstation costs less because it has no disk drives. It also provides some security advantages (see Chapter 10) because users can neither load data into the system nor remove it via floppy disk drives.

How file and database servers evolved

Data sharing on LANs began with the disk drive only. Users were provided with a larger file store, accessed over the LAN rather than just via their PC system bus. Typically there was no structure to the way data was stored on the LAN. It tended to be used as an overflow for each user's own PC storage.

The next development was the dedicated file server. This was a PC configured exclusively to provide a data storage and management service on behalf of the LAN's users. Now that the data server had a processor, it could support facilities such as record locking required to provide common access to the same data files. Figure 5.6 illustrates how record locking enables data to be shared across a network. Essentially it prevents one user from accessing a particular data record while another is overwriting it. Suppose one user, or more specifically that user's application, issues a command that results in a record on the

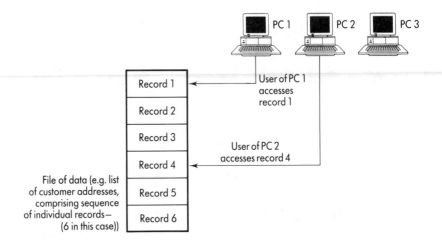

Figure 5.6   How record locking enables more than one user to access a single file without risk of corruption or inconsistent data. While PC 1 accesses record 1 and PC 2 accesses record 4, these two records are temporarily locked. If PC 3 wants to access either of these two, it has to wait until no other PC is accessing it. However, in this case it is free to access records 2, 3, 5 and 6.

file server being updated. Then the file server puts a lock on that record until the update is completed, after which it removes the lock. While the update is taking place the lock prevents any user from accessing the record.

Database servers

You may also have heard of file locking, which is a cruder, less efficient technique more common on older NOS versions. As the name suggests, this involves locking a whole file rather than just the individual record being updated. Under this method, no user would be able to update any record in a customer file, for example, even if another user was just updating one of the individual customer records. Under record locking, only the one record would be unavailable to other users while one user is updating it. Record locking provides faster overall response on the network because, on average, users have to wait less time for records they need to access or update to be available.

However, file servers with record locking still did not make best use either of the network or of the server's processor, as we explained in Chapter 1. Although data could be shared, the task of searching for and identifying individual records was still handled by the desktop PC. Client/server computing was developed so that servers could handle searches and updates on their own. The principles of client/ server operation were described in Chapter 1, where we also described how databases enable more sophisticated and efficient searches for individual records or data items to be accomplished. Here we expand a little further to indicate when a database server becomes desirable, as opposed to a simple file server (note that we are talking about different software, not hardware).

Client/server operation can be used with simple files. For a journalist, such a file could comprise a list of contacts with their addresses and telephone numbers, for example. Under client/server operation, the server could search the file and return a particular contact telephone number upon request from a client desktop PC.

However, more sophisticated searches are possible with a database in combination with client/server operation. A database combines different files each of which describes one particular attribute of a subject list, such as a company's customers. Taking our example above, one table might contain a list of contacts and telephone numbers, while another might list the subject areas relating to each contact. The journalist could instruct the database to obtain the names and telephone numbers of all contacts in a particular subject area who lived in London. Under client/server operation, the database server would first obtain the names of all people in London from the address list. It would then obtain the people in the specified subject area from the subject list, and finally match the two together to provide the list of contacts satisfying both criteria.

This can be accomplished without a database but requires additional programming effort for each application, and also requires a knowledge of where the data is and how it is structured. Databases on the other hand provide a standard access method for specifying searches and updates. This method provides the link with the client/ server protocols. The prevailing standard for accessing databases is SQL (Structured Query Language). The role of SQL in a client/ server network is shown schematically in Figure 5.7. The SQL server software links the LAN operating system or NOS with the database. The NOS processes the client/server instructions coming from the client and translates them into SQL commands that the database can understand and execute.

A database server, therefore, becomes desirable for applications that involve searches based on multiple selection criteria. It enables

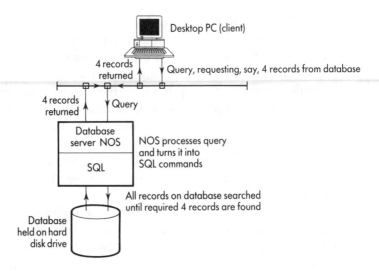

Figure 5.7   The role of SQL (Structured Query Language) on a client/server network.

the search to be completed more quickly. It is also more flexible, in that any combination of search criteria can be used without having to write specific software for it in the server.

Linking file and database servers to the LAN

This is done in the same way as PCs. As far as the LAN is concerned there is no difference between any server and a desktop PC. The differences only arise in higher-level protocols that make use of the LAN service. The relationship between the LAN and higher-level protocols is described in Chapter 10.

In general, machines designed specifically as LAN servers are attached to the LAN's cabling structure via network interface cards (NICs). This is because such machines have PC hardware architectures and can utilize the same NICs as desktop PCs. The role of these NICs and their implications for performance are described in the next section.

On the other hand, large computers that were not designed specifically as LAN servers will probably not attach directly to the LAN. Such computers can be, and increasingly are, programmed to support client/server applications driven from desktop PCs. However, they will typically attach to the LAN via other specialist communications controllers such as front end processors. These controllers may themselves be attached via NICs or plug-in modules. Indeed such controllers are often just LAN servers of another type, supporting the communications requirements of one or more large computers. As such they may be based on PCs linked to the LAN via NICs, just like file servers.

Network interface cards (NICs)

5

Devices called transceivers were required to connect PCs to the early LANs based on coaxial cable. An additional piece of cable was needed to connect each PC to its transceiver.

Now that LANs increasingly run on twisted pair cable, PCs and servers are connected directly to the cable network via network interface cards (NICs). Indeed, any device that connects directly to the network requires an NIC, or a device that performs an equivalent function. Network hubs, for example, may have modules that connect them to the network. These perform the same function as NICs but also handle additional processing needed to support various hub functions such as network management.

In general though, NICs are PC cards that slot into an expansion slot in the back of the PC or server, attaching directly to the motherboard. The NIC in turn is usually attached directly to the network. Figure 5.8 shows how NICs link PCs directly to a 10Base-T Ethernet network running over unshielded twisted pair cable. In the case of a coaxial or fibre optic network, the NIC would not be attached directly to the LAN: instead there would be a separate piece of cable joining the NIC to a connection box on the main LAN cable.

For sending data, the function of the NIC is first to convert data from the form in which it is represented in the PC to the form required for transmission on the LAN. Then it actually transmits the data onto the LAN. When receiving data, the order of events is reversed.

The NIC needs to be compatible with the data packet structure used for the LAN. As Ethernet and token ring require data to be structured in different ways, different NICs are needed.

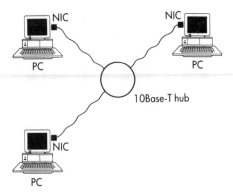

Figure 5.8 How network interface cards (NICs) link PCs to a 10Base-T network. Note: throughout this book, we have omitted to draw in the NICs in diagrams of LANs, for simplicity.

Performance considerations of NICs

The NIC can affect performance in two ways. First, it imposes a slight delay in transmitting data onto the network. Second, by utilizing the CPU of the PC or server, it can slow down the applications using the network. However, the structure of NICs has evolved to tackle both these problems.

First, the delay was reduced by integrating RAM chips into the NIC board as data buffers. This ensures that the NIC can cope with surges of data from either side without requiring a halt in communication. If the NIC receives more data than it can handle on its transmission path between the network and the PC's CPU, it places the overflow in a RAM buffer, while continuing to transmit as fast as it can. Once the rush is over, the NIC reads the overflow back from the RAM and completes the transmission. The principle, which is similar to print buffering, is illustrated in Figure 5.9. The point is that although the NIC is restricting the flow of traffic by virtue of the limited capacity of its transmission path, it cannot be overloaded and maintains the link between the PC and the server throughout a transmission, even when it cannot immediately transfer all the data. This can be particularly important over Ethernet LANs, where as we saw in Chapter 2 overall performance is very dependent on the number of attempts to access the network.

Although the RAM buffer ensures that the NIC utilizes its own transmission channel as efficiently as possible without a break in communications between a PC and the server, the transmission path itself

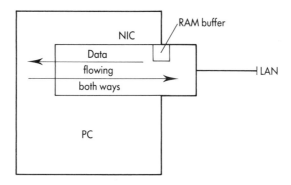

Figure 5.9 Use of buffering on NICs (network interface cards) to cope with varia-tions in traffic or a congested network. The RAM buffer in the NIC stores data tem-porarily if the channel linking the PC to the LAN is overloaded at any time. This could happen if the network is congested, or if the PC is not ready to receive data sent to it by another PC or file server.

can become a significant bottleneck. This largely depends on the width of the bus, which can be 8, 16 or 32 data bits. A data bit is a single binary digit of information. Many early NICs had buses 8 bits wide, which means that 8 bits of information could be transmitted concurrently. Indeed as the NIC cannot transmit data in chunks greater than the PC can handle, they had to be 8 bits wide until the advent of PCs based on the 16-bit 80286 CPU. Now most NICs use 16-bit buses to take advantage of the 16-bit internal buses of modern PCs. In fact the latest PCs based on EISA (extended industry standard architecture) and MCA (microchannel architecture) have the poten-tial to handle 32-bit internal buses, but have been using 16-bit buses. In future PCs may use 32-bit buses, and then NICs may also. In general it is no longer worth considering 8-bit NICs for desktop PCs, as the cost saving is minimal, while throughput onto a LAN from a typical PC is reduced by about 40 %. However, at the time of writing 32-bit NICs cost about four times as much as 16-bit NICs, and were still too expensive for most desktop PCs, except where high perfor-mance is required. They are worth installing in the file server though, as the extra cost when split between each user is relatively small, while the substantial performance gain is enjoyed by everyone.

Another limitation of earlier NICs was their lack of a CPU of their own. This meant they had to utilize the CPU of the PC or server, which reduced the speed at which users' applications were processed. Now most NICs have their own CPU. This means they are computers in their own right, able to perform the data buffering and processing required for accessing a LAN without the assistance of the PC or server CPU.

Input devices

A range of devices for inputting data can be attached to a LAN, either directly or via a server, although usually it must be the latter. The requirements for input devices are rather different than for printers and database servers. It is not so much the network itself that the device needs to access, but the system where the data being input will be stored or processed. This could be the server itself, or it could be a PC on the network designated to handle that particular application. In the case of an image scanner, for example, there may be a PC dedicated to the processing required to organize the image data and catalogue it. The same applies to other specialist input devices, such as bar code and smart card readers. We will consider the main ones in turn.

Smart card readers

Smart cards are typically the size and thickness of credit cards, with a microprocessor chip embedded in the plastic. They have now been used in numerous applications, particularly in France where smart card projects have received extensive investment from government and computer companies. The real potential of smart cards is for multi-service cards, functioning simultaneously as personal identity cards, electronic payment cards, electronic keys for accessing buildings or computer systems, and repositories of medical records. A number of pilot projects in cities or local regions have already shown that smart cards are ideal for such multi-service applications.

Smart cards need some device to read data and also write data to their memory to be of any use. In some cases, for example various security applications, the ability to read is sufficient. In others, as when updating medical records held on the card, the ability to write data is also required. Devices for reading and writing smart cards are typically attached to a computer, which may be connected to a LAN. In this case the role of the LAN is merely in transmitting data to the location where it is required. The amounts of data will not be large, and users cannot access it via the network.

Bar code readers

Bar code readers scan bar codes, which may be stamped on products, labels, or documents such as order forms, into a computer system where they can be stored in digital image form. The principle of operation is similar to that of image scanners which we describe next. The difference is that they are designed to scan just bar codes, which makes them smaller and cheaper. They often need to be portable, so that they can be manoeuvred to the correct position for scanning. However, they may also be embedded in a larger system. Among the best-known examples are the bar code scanning systems used at supermarket checkouts.

Bar code scanners can be attached to a LAN server. In this case they may be used in a production system, where items with bar codes need to be repeatedly scanned and stored. Typically this would be in some data entry application. Bar coded labels are quick and easy to print, and convenient to attach to large objects. In some companies therefore bar coded labels are attached to goods before dispatch. The same labels can also be attached to the accompanying documentation. The labels can be scanned in each case to ensure that goods are being dispatched to the correct address with the right accompanying paperwork. Bar code images generate relatively little digital data, making them much less expensive to archive than full document images. A further advantage of bar code scanning can be that it avoids errors that inevitably result from manual keying of data, which is sometimes the alternative. This applies equally in supermarkets and in other areas where bar coding is sometimes used, such as factories and warehouses.

Image scanners

Document image processing (DIP) is a fast growing field, bringing reductions in cost and improvements in efficiency for organizations that need to store and retrieve paper-based information. DIP involves the electronic storage, manipulation and retrieval of text, graphics and still photographic images. Images of graphical or text information can be generated on a computer but the main advantage of DIP lies in the ability to digitize paper-based documents as they come in. Documents can then be stored and retrieved electronically rather than, as previously, in paper or microfilm form. The benefits are that documents can be retrieved more quickly, storage costs are reduced, workflow is improved because documents are shifted electronically rather than on paper, and less data is lost. Further benefits can follow from use of optical character recognition (OCR) to translate document images into text or numeric data. Then the DIP system can provide input to other conventional computer applications.

Documents can be digitized by conventional fax machines, but this is only useful for low-volume work with no requirement for colour or high resolution. Serious DIP applications require image scanners to digitize images. Scanners come in different sizes to suit varying workflows. For low-volume applications there are simple flat-bed scanners capable of feeding around 100 A4 documents an hour in continuous use. For high-volume applications powerful duplex scanners, which can scan both sides of a page and input over 10 000 A4 pages an hour, are available.

Having digitized the image, scanners compress the resulting data by typically about ten times using techniques such as the CCITT compression for Group 4 fax. On average a compressed A4 page image requires 47 kbytes of storage, although this varies according to the contents of that page.

Given these figures, it is easy to see that a scanner needs to be attached to a fast communications link to deliver documents to an image storage system at the required rate, at least for high-volume work. A byte is a group of eight binary bits used to represent a data character. Therefore on average an A4 document generates 376 kbits of data. So for high-volume work where 10 000 A4 documents are digitized an hour, the required throughput is just over 1 Mbit/s. This means that the scanner either needs to be directly attached to the storage device it is feeding, or must be attached via a LAN. Small scanners may be attached to a LAN via a PC or server but large ones, which contain fast processors themselves to capture and edit images before committing them to final storage on an image server, attach directly.

Image servers

Like image scanners, these are an integral part of a DIP system. Figure 5.10 shows a typical DIP network based on a token ring LAN, supporting image workstations, which may be 386- or 486-based PCs, a scanner, an image server and an IBM host system running standard data processing applications. The image server retrieves existing stored images or creates new ones according to instructions issued either by the PCs or by the scanner. Increasingly often the document image index would be held not on the image server but on the main computer system where it can be related to other applications. In that way the DIP system can be integrated with existing data processing applications.

On the other hand, DIP can also be used on small LANs for straightforward applications such as maintaining an electronic newspaper clippings library. In this case the DIP network might comprise just a few PCs of which one has a low-cost scanner attached, along with an image server leading to optical disk storage. Like other forms of server described in this chapter, the image server usually attaches to the LAN via an NIC.

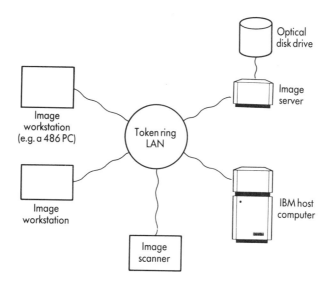

Figure 5.10   A typical document image processing network.

Terminal servers

These are used to attach clusters of dumb terminals to a LAN. They are needed where LANs have replaced other forms of local communication such as traditional multidrop connections. In fact multidrop lines are the immediate ancestors of LANs, having been invented to replace star-shaped host-to-terminal networks in which every terminal had its own wire. A multidrop line is a single piece of wire linking all terminals. Now, as often seems to happen in the computer industry, the cabling story has completed a circle with the move back towards star-shaped LANs in which PCs are directly connected to hubs.

In the 1960s and early 1970s, the computer world comprised large mainframes mostly accessed locally from dumb terminals connected via dedicated wires, as depicted in Figure 5.11(a). These point-to-point lines were then replaced with multidrop lines as shown in Figure 5.11(b). These saved on cable, and also reduced the input/output costs of the host computer because it now needed to support just one cable for all terminals.

This was the precursor of the LAN, with a similar cable arrangement to early Ethernet LANs but only a fraction of the data transmission capacity. A typical multidrop line could support 1200 bit/s, which was adequate for dumb terminals that just need to transmit and receive instructions, but hopeless once users got PCs and wanted to transmit large data files.

LANs were, therefore, installed for PCs, and it made obvious sense to utilize the LAN to connect dumb terminals to mainframes, avoiding the need to retain separate multidrop links. With the falling price of PCs, the terminal population has been declining steadily but there will still be significant numbers around until at least the mid 1990s.

Terminals are attached to the LAN via a server. Another terminal server is required to attach the host to the LAN, as shown in Figure 5.12. At each end the terminal server is responsible for handling conversion between the transmission mode used by the terminals and that for the LAN. The terminal server also has software that makes the network appear to provide dedicated connections between each terminal and the host computer.

This arrangement still has limitations. One is that the host still

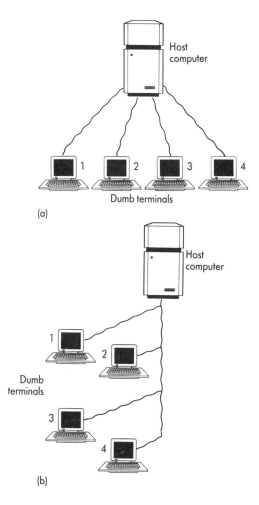

Figure 5.11 How multidrop lines replaced point-to-point lines, paving the way for introduction of Ethernet. (a) Old point-to-point network. (b) Multidrop line connecting same terminals.

needs to support a connection for each terminal, coming out of the terminal server at its end. The need for this can be eliminated by installing software in the host that enables it to support all terminals via a single port, just as it did with multidrop lines. However, the host is still limited to supporting terminal types that it recognizes. As networks grow, there is increasing demand to be able to access hosts over a LAN from a variety of different terminal types. This can be supported across a LAN with virtual terminal protocols. The use of these is illustrated in Figure 5.13.

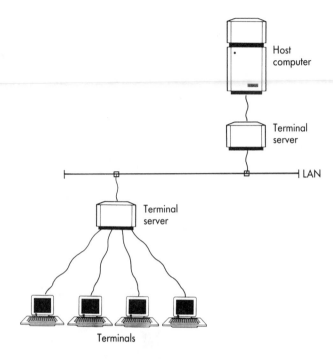

Figure 5.12   Use of a LAN to connect dumb terminals to a host computer, via terminal servers. At each end, the terminal server multiplexes the channels connecting each terminal onto the single LAN channel. This enables the host computer to converse with each terminal as though it were connected to it directly.

The terminal server translates the specific protocols of the terminal into the intermediate virtual terminal format. Then in the host, or in a host end processor, the virtual terminal protocol is translated into the terminal protocol the host expects to receive.

Communications servers: Introduction

A communications server provides users of a LAN with access to applications or data located on another network. These may reside within your organization either on another LAN or on a large host

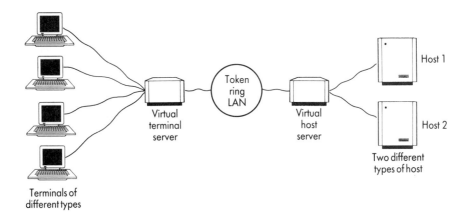

Figure 5.13 Use of virtual terminal network to connect hosts and terminals of different types.

system. Alternatively it could be some external service such as an online database, or a computer within a trading or business partner for exchange of information. An example of the latter is electronic data interchange (EDI), in which business documents are exchanged between trading partners.

Not surprisingly there is a wide variety of products within this category to cater for this range of different types of communication. The common element is that they all enable data to be transmitted and received outside the LAN. In addition the communications server may provide a variety of other facilities such as protocol conversion to access a computer or network based on different protocols. The common ground is that most forms of external communication are particularly well suited to sharing via a LAN. Users rarely all decide to communicate simultaneously, and this means that facilities such as modems can readily be shared between a number of users. Furthermore, a single server machine can often provide a number of communications facilities. For example, it could provide access both to dial-up telephone lines via modems and the ability to send and receive faxes from your PC.

The wide variety of products that provide a communications service on a LAN come in two categories. First, there are products that provide access to a remote service or computer via dial-up facilities. The emphasis with products in this category is in using the LAN to share a facility, such as a modem, that would formerly have been provided for each user individually. Second, there are products for interconnecting different LANs, either by direct local attachment or via an intermediate long-distance link. Bridges, routers and gateways come into this category, where the emphasis is in using the LAN as a building block of a larger network. These products are discussed in Chapter 6. Here we look further at the first category of product, of which there are three main types: modem servers, ISDN servers and fax servers.

Modem servers

In a workgroup or department it is extremely rare for all PCs to be online to a remote dial-up service via a modem all the time. It therefore makes sense to use the LAN to share modems. This saves not just on the cost of the modem but also on the telephone costs if direct lines are used for each modem. Depending on the number of users and the amount of time each one will need to spend linked up to a remote service, more than one modem may be required on the server: it will certainly not need as many modems as there are servers. Two examples will illustrate the sort of calculations that can be made to estimate how many modems are required. Suppose a LAN serves ten users where each one spends on average an hour a day online. In this case two modems are needed to provide each user with about an 85 % chance of finding a line available at any time.

A network with eight PCs where each user on average spends half the time online to a remote service via a dial-up modem connection would require six modems to ensure that there would only be a 1 in 18 chance of not being able to obtain a line at any time. To cope with periods of higher than average demand or to reduce the chance of generally being unable to obtain a line to below 1 in 100, seven modems could be used. In this more extreme example, the savings would be slight, but there are still advantages in using a modem server from the point of view of management and control, as all telephone lines come into a single point. Furthermore, using a modem server enables capacity to be increased smoothly as demand increases. You could start with two modems and add more one by one to maintain an adequate level of availability. It is also possible to have modems of different speeds, reserving the fastest ones for particular applications, or simply allocating them on a first come first served basis.

ISDN server

The principles here are the same as for a modem server, and the points made in that section apply equally here. ISDN is the successor to the standard public telephone network. It provides digital rather than analog connections, and offers greater data transmission capacity per line. Being digital, modems are not needed to modulate digital signals over analog lines. However, this makes little difference as far as users are concerned as special adaptors are still needed to attach PCs to the ISDN network. These adaptors perform a similar function to LAN adaptors, in that they restructure the data into a form in which it can be transmitted, in this case over the public ISDN network.

The main difference with ISDN is its greater capacity and the fact that data, voice, image and motion video can in principle all be transmitted down the same circuit. However, these advantages will not be really significant until broadband ISDN becomes available in the mid or late 1990s. Broadband ISDN will provide dial-up circuits with a capacity of 2 Mbit/s or greater, which will be sufficient for interconnecting LANs. On the other hand, narrowband ISDN provides only 64 kbit/s circuits, which is insufficient for many LAN applications. As we shall see in Chapter 6, there are products that enable LANs to be interconnected over existing public ISDN networks. ISDN is described in more detail in Appendix 1.

Fax server

A fax server enables users attached to a LAN to send faxes using text and graphics generated on their PCs, without having to print out and use a standard fax machine. It also lets them view incoming faxes on their screens and, if required, print them out using either a laser printer or a conventional fax machine. Facilities to do this can be provided in each PC using fax cards, still with the possibility of sharing a printer or fax machine for printing.

A fax card translates data files in the PC into the format required to transmit over a telephone line and be received and printed by a fax machine at the other end of the line. They also contain a modem to handle the transmission at the physical level. In some cases this modem can only be used for faxes but increasingly often they can also be used as conventional modems. In fact there are PC cards now available capable of functioning as either a modem or ISDN adaptor, with the ability to send faxes over both the standard public telephone network and ISDN.

When PCs are attached to a LAN, there are advantages in using a fax server rather than individual fax cards. As with modems, this avoids buying one for each PC and brings all telephone lines to a single point. There is also an important additional advantage for handling incoming faxes. A fax document requires a lot of data to represent it. Users who receive a significant number of incoming faxes would soon find their hard disks filling up completely, unless they erased each one as soon as they had viewed or printed it. A dedicated fax server, on the other hand, can provide a large amount of hard disk storage, with the ability to archive fax images on lower-cost storage media such as tape or optical disk if required.

Hubs/wiring concentrators

In a sense hubs are part of the LAN itself rather than something attached to it. Indeed early, or first generation, hubs were simply multiport repeaters that boosted the signal of a LAN to extend the distance it could cover. Repeaters are described in Chapter 6.

However, there are now more sophisticated hubs that also support, as plug-in modules, a number of devices that attach to a LAN. This includes products for interconnecting LANs, such as bridges, routers and gateways, which we describe in the next chapter. There is a trend towards the hub becoming the focal building block of large national or global networks, with individual LANs condensed into it. Figure 5.14 demonstrates this, comprising local hub-based LANs to which users are attached by unshielded cable of some sort. The LANs in turn are connected by a campus-wide or long-distance backbone network.

There is also the possibility of the hub functioning as a server. In this case other devices such as printers would attach directly to the hub rather than coming into the LAN via a server. Figure 5.15 illustrates this possibility. The first part of the diagram shows a hub with a separate print server attached to it, as well as other PCs. The second part of the diagram shows a hub/server supporting all devices directly.

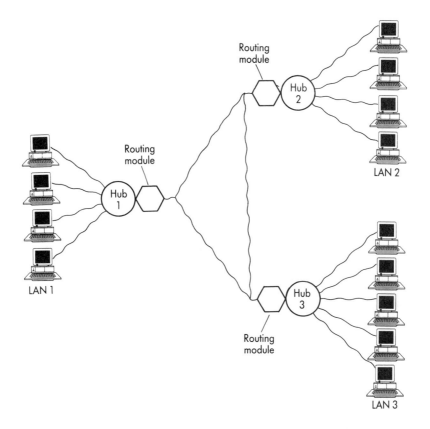

Figure 5.14   Showing wide area network of interconnected LANs attached to local hubs. Each hub has an inbuilt routing module to facilitate the LAN interconnection.

For small networks the more sophisticated hubs are unnecessary and too expensive. In such cases hubs will serve either token ring or Ethernet LANs but not both. The commonest type of Ethernet hub is the 10Base-T hub, while for token ring it is the MAU (media access unit) and CAU (concentrator access unit). Sophisticated hubs for large networks provide both CAU and 10Base-T concentrators in different modules. Hubs are described further in Chapter 3.

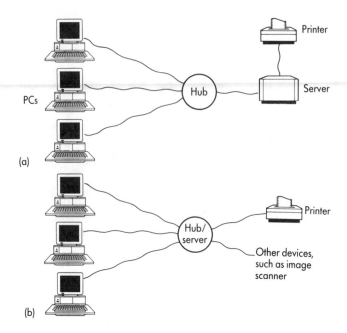

Figure 5.15   Network with hub also functioning as, or containing, the server. (a) Classic hub arrangement, with separate server. (b) Hub/server providing complete focal point of network.

Summary

We have now described the devices that can be attached to a LAN, and how to do it. In the next chapter we examine more closely one particular category: devices for connecting LANs with each other.

6

Can I connect my networks even if they are different?

CHAPTER OBJECTIVES

There are essentially two reasons why devices to interconnect LANs are needed:

(1) To join different LANs into one single network.

(2) To divide an existing LAN into different segments between which traffic flow is restricted to improve performance or security. This second issue is discussed in Chapter 10.

In this chapter we discuss the devices needed to interconnect LANs, referring where relevant to Chapter 10. This chapter is not immediately relevant for small businesses contemplating purchase of their first LAN, but some of the points may be worth bearing in mind if you anticipate your network growing in future. The main points covered in this chapter are:

Introduction

You can connect your networks whether or not they are all the same type. Furthermore, as the networking field matures, the products needed to interconnect different LANs are performing better, costing less and offering greater flexibility. You are increasingly likely to be able to purchase a single range of products to meet all your LAN interconnection requirements with the ability to support future requirements. However, it remains true as a general rule of thumb that connections between networks that are different tend to cost more and perform less well than connections between two identical networks, such as a pair of Ethernet LANs.

In this chapter we first define the various network connection requirements you might have and then discuss the solutions available. The way these solutions work and some of the differences between them are best understood with reference to the seven layer OSI communications model that defines how computers should interoperate across a network. This is described in detail in Chapter 9, to which you may wish to refer if you are unfamiliar with it. However, we describe its basic operation in simple terms in this chapter.

Why not have just one large network?

The first question is perhaps why should there be a need to connect different networks together at all? Why can there not be a single network connecting all computing devices within an organization? Then the only need to interconnect networks would arise when one organization wants to communicate with another.

Certainly organizations are starting to communicate with each other electronically, although this is usually via some third party intermediate network. Applications demanding such connections include electronic data interchange (EDI) for exchange of business documents and electronic payment.

That, however, is not the focus of this chapter. Instead we address the issue posed by the above question of creating a single network within a business or organization. This is not as simple as it sounds because of the way computer communication technology has evolved. LANs have become established as the network for local communication within a building or single site. But LANs are limited on three counts: on the distance they can cover, on the number of computers they can support, and on the amount of data they can transmit. This means that in order to create a larger network serving a whole organization, different LANs need to be connected together. Also, as individual LANs grow, they need to be segmented into components to restrict the amount of traffic and number of devices on each segment. The issue of segmenting LANs for performance reasons is discussed in more detail in Chapter 10, but we touch on it later in this chapter because the devices that divide LANs into different segments are obviously similar to those that unite segments that were previously unconnected into a single coherent network spanning a whole site or enterprise.

The subject of this chapter springs from the physical limitations of LANs, which are the building blocks of large networks. For small businesses this might sound academic because there may appear little likelihood of needing either to connect different LANs together or to divide a single LAN into multiple segments. But there are few businesses that do not hope to grow and they may, in the future, regret having failed to allow for the prospect of an expanding network. It is worth noting that growth may not happen in a predictable way. A business may be taken over by another with a different type of network. A workgroup or local branch of a larger organization may find

6

that it has to access a remote network supporting different protocols.

It is impossible to anticipate all possible avenues of growth or development, especially in relation to computer networking, which is a field where technology and products are changing quickly. However, as we indicated at the beginning of this chapter, there are some signs of stability emerging, bringing the possibility of installing products that provide some hedge against change and growth.

This chapter is really an extension of Chapter 5, with which there is some overlap. There we were looking at the devices you can attach to your LAN. Here we are examining the ways you can expand your network and access computers and services that are NOT directly attached to it. The overlap with Chapter 5 occurs in two senses: first, the devices that you need to interconnect LANs or extend your network obviously need to be attached to your LAN; and second, larger computer systems such as mainframes that you might need to access from your LAN can also be attached directly to it. Alternatively they may be accessed via some intermediate large-scale network, such as an IBM SNA (System Network Architecture) network.

What types of network might you need to connect together?

We summarize five types of network that you may need to access from your local workgroup LAN. Then we describe the various products that provide the required links, pointing out which of the five categories of network connection they provide.

1. LANs of the same type. For example, you may have an Ethernet LAN and want to access one or more other Ethernet LANs. There are two distinct possibilities. One, the LANs may be close together in the same building and connected directly with a single interconnection product that straddles two or more LAN segments. Alternatively, the LAN segments may be a long distance apart, in which case they will be connected by some telecommunications link, which could be either a permanent circuit or a dial-up connection. In this case two products will be needed to perform the connection, one at each end of the telecommunications link attached to each of the LAN segments.

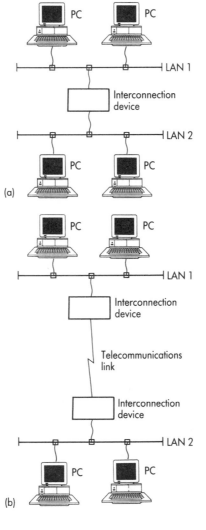

6

Figure 6.1 Showing two LANs joined together. (a) Two LANs directly attached by local connection. (b) Two LANs linked by remote telecommunications.

Figure 6.1 illustrates each of the two possibilities, without at this stage identifying the specific devices needed. Note that a large network may comprise a combination of both locally and remotely attached LAN segments.

2. LANs of different types. For example, you might want to connect a token ring LAN in one office with an Ethernet LAN in another, so that users on each can obtain access to data and applications on

the other. This is a more complex operation than connecting two LANs of the same type and costs slightly more to accomplish, but is increasingly being done. Again, there are two possibilities: the LANs being connected may be either locally or remotely attached.

3. LANs linked to a common backbone network, such as an FDDI ring. We described in Chapter 2 how an FDDI ring is in fact a souped-up token ring LAN. However, its ability to span larger distances and support more devices and traffic makes it a suitable backbone interconnecting different LAN segments. As far as the LANs being connected are concerned, the function of the FDDI network is similar to that of remote connections, except that it provides much greater data transmission capacity.

4. LANs linked to an existing private wide area network (WAN). The WAN may in turn provide access to other LANs, or to a large-scale computer system such as a mainframe. This category, therefore, overlaps with categories 1, 2 and 5. The difference is that in this case the WAN takes over control as soon as data is passed to it. A gateway device is needed to connect the LAN to the WAN as shown in Figure 6.2, where the WAN is based on X.25 protocols. Later in this chapter we shall distinguish between the products required to accomplish this task and those needed in the other categories, with reference to the seven layer OSI interconnection model.

5. LANs providing access to an external computer system. This could be a mainframe or large Unix system, In Chapter 5 we described how terminal servers can be used to connect terminals via a LAN to a host computer. Here we explain how PCs on a LAN can be connected through to a host computer.

Introducing the solutions: What needs to be achieved?

Before introducing the solutions, we need to define more clearly what we are trying to achieve and why organizations need a single coherent network spanning most or all of their computer systems. The basic

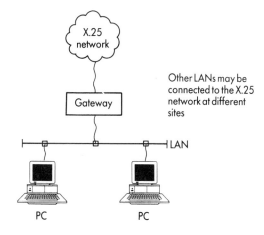

Figure 6.2   LAN connected to a wide area X.25 network.

requirement is to enable users to access all the applications and
sources of data that they need. This does not mean that all employees
need access to every system. Indeed it may be desirable for security
reasons to limit access to various applications and data files. But with
increasing use, for example, of executive information systems to provide senior managers with a snapshot of overall performance within
their company, the need to provide access to information relating to
all activities is growing. Such information is increasingly being computerized, so that to satisfy this requirement for access to all information sources requires a network spanning the whole enterprise.

The provision of widespread access to information requires communication between applications running in different computers. In
Chapter 1 we looked at client/server computing, in which two computers cooperate on a given task. This requires an underlying network
based on commonly agreed communication protocols. The products
we consider in this chapter provide a key part of this underlying communications base across a network comprising more than one LAN
segment, or where a LAN is providing access to an external host
system.

The overall task in which these products play a role generally
involves communication between application software in different
computers. Each application needs to have data presented to it in a
format that it comprehends, and it may need instructions from
another application, again in a form it can understand. For this
overall task to be achieved across a network supporting computers and

software from different vendors, some commonly agreed standards need to be observed. An attempt to develop such standards began in the mid 1970s when the International Standards Organization (ISO) developed its Open Systems Interconnection (OSI) model.

Introducing the OSI model for computer interaction across a network

OSI is described in full in Chapter 9. Essentially it divides the task of communication between two applications across a network such as a LAN into seven distinct layers, where each one relates to a particular task. Not all networks and computers are entirely based on OSI yet, with many still using proprietary protocols for the top four layers at least. However, there has been universal conformance to the layered approach set by ISO, which after all is made up of representatives from leading vendors of computers and networking systems.

The overall aim is to provide a common communications service to applications that is independent both of the computer and operating system they are based on and the network connecting them. By service we mean that data is delivered fully structured in the form the application expects. This could be as files, or individual transaction records, depending on the application.

Fundamentally, as we describe in Chapter 9, the OSI model can be divided into two halves. The top half deals with control of interaction between computers across a network and presentation of the data. The bottom half deals with the network itself, and it is here that LAN interconnection products operate. As we explain in Chapter 9, the bottom half of the OSI model comprises three distinct layers. As we refer to these in the rest of this chapter, readers unfamiliar with the structure of OSI should read the section about it in Chapter 9 before proceeding.

What products are there for interconnecting LANs?

Now we define four types of product for connecting LAN segments together, each of which operates within a different OSI communication layer. Then we discuss which are likely to be appropriate for your network, referring back to the five categories of LAN connectivity requirement that we defined earlier.

The four types of product are repeaters, bridges, routers and gateways. Note that only the last three types of product – bridges, routers and gateways – really address the problems of extending a network. However, the foundations for the more complex internetworking products were laid with the development of repeaters. So for the sake of completeness we begin by describing repeaters, which in any case still play a vital role in LAN hubs. But to begin reading about products that really support network growth, you can skip the repeater section.

Repeaters

Repeaters are the simplest of LAN extension devices, operating purely in the physical layer, which is layer 1 of the OSI model. They play a somewhat different role in Ethernet and token ring LANs, so we discuss each separately before indicating how the function of both has changed in hub-based networks.

6

Ethernet repeaters

Ethernet repeaters extend the length of a LAN by amplifying or regenerating the signal, although their role has changed significantly since LANs were first introduced. Originally Ethernet, when implemented in a physical bus structure using coaxial cable, was limited in length to 500 metres and could support up to 100 nodes, that is, computing devices. However, this length could be extended to 2500 metres, and the number of nodes increased, by use of up to four repeaters at 500-metre intervals.

Token ring repeaters

Token ring, on the other hand, required the signal to be repeated by every node in any case. There was no point using additional repeaters to increase the circumference of the ring because the restriction was not in any case one of total distance. The restriction is in the number of devices that a single token ring LAN can support, which is a maximum of 260 nodes, and the distance between each node, a distance of 100 metres.

Hub repeaters

Now that Ethernet and token ring are often implemented on hub-based networks the role of repeaters has shifted to boosting the signal within the hub. Now instead of the repeater having just two ports for connecting two pieces of cable together, it needs as many ports as there are users attached to the hub. Figure 6.3 illustrates the operation of the Ethernet repeater in its various guises, as explained in the caption. It shows again, as described in Chapter 3, how the use of

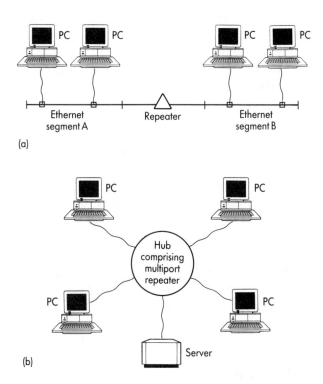

(a)

(b)

Figure 6.3 Various types of LAN repeater. (a) Simple Ethernet repeater. (b) Multiport Ethernet hub repeater for 10Base-T network (described in Chapter 3). When one of the PCs or other devices sends data, the hub repeats it, and broadcasts it simultaneously to all other attached devices.

repeaters enables the different logical structures of Ethernet and token ring to be implemented over the same physical cable network.

An Ethernet repeater regenerates a signal as it arrives from a sending device, and then simultaneously broadcasts it to all other devices attached to that hub. Strictly speaking, an Ethernet hub network comprises multiple Ethernet segments, because each device and its link to the hub is a single segment. However, we have referred to a single hub-based Ethernet LAN as a single segment as it tends to provide the needs of a given workgroup or department.

A token ring repeater, on the other hand, regenerates the signal not in one single action but in a series of hops, which maintains the logical ring structure in which data passes from one device to another in sequence.

Repeaters are useful in enabling a hub to support a large number of devices using token ring or Ethernet protocols. However, they are not helpful for connecting networks together because they provide no ability to filter data, and no support for connection over long-distance links.

6

Bridges

Repeaters operate purely in layer 1, the physical layer, as they do no more than extend the distance of the physical network. Bridges evolved from repeaters by moving up into the next OSI communications layer, the datalink layer, as is depicted schematically in Figure 6.4. Their function is still to connect LAN segments by repeating the signal but the difference is that they can make use of packet addressing information contained in the datalink level to decide on which of two segments to repeat the data. This gives them much greater power. It means they can filter data packets on the basis of the devices they are addressed to. As a result they can restrict the flow of data across the bridges, only allowing across packets destined for the other side. Data packets addressed to a device on the same segment as the device that transmitted them are filtered, by repeating the signals for that packet only on that segment. Figure 6.5 illustrates the principle. A packet transmitted by device A to device B on segment 1 will be filtered, with the packet being repeated only on segment 1. A packet transmitted

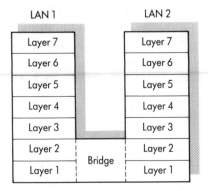

Figure 6.4 Showing how bridges connect LANs at the datalink level, which is layer 2 of the seven layer OSI interconnection model.

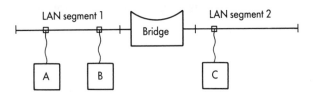

Figure 6.5 Illustrating how bridges handle data packets. The bridge filters packets transmitted from A to B, to stop them crossing unnecessarily to segment 2. But the bridge forwards packets transmitted from A to C, because they need to cross between the two segments. The same applies to packets transmitted from B to C, or from C to either A or B.

by device A on segment 1 to device C on segment 2 will be forwarded, with the signal being repeated only on segment 2.

With this principle of operation, bridges can connect two LAN segments in an efficient way, containing local data traffic within each segment, and forwarding only data that needs to be forwarded. This has two important consequences. First, it means that bridges can be used to divide a LAN that has become too large into different segments. Each segment then becomes in effect a separate LAN. A LAN divided into two segments can, therefore, support twice as many computing devices as the original LAN and it can also carry substantially more traffic. The use of bridges to segment LANs in this way to allow a LAN to grow without losing performance is discussed further in Chapter 10.

The other consequence of being able to filter traffic is that the bridge can connect two remote LANs. In this case two bridges are needed, because the two segments are now separated by a telecommunications link, as shown in Figure 6.6.

Networks comprising more than two LAN segments can be constructed using bridges. However, two different techniques evolved to handle bridging on larger networks. One, and only one, of those methods, called Spanning Tree bridging, is used for Ethernet networks. Spanning Tree is also used for some token ring networks, but IBM developed another method called source routing bridging. The name is confusing because routing has for long been considered an alternative to bridging. We shall clear up the confusion when we introduce routing in the next section. First we discuss the whole field of Ethernet bridging, which also applies to some token ring networks. Then we describe source routing bridging, used by IBM for token ring networks. We proceed to describe a standard, called Source Routing Transparent that unites the two forms of bridging. We finish by describing translation bridging and how to bridge LANs together via an FDDI backbone.

6

Ethernet bridging

Early bridges had a weakness in lacking support for alternative routing, as they simply provided a point-to-point link between two LAN segments, as in Figure 6.6. This meant that the network was severed in the event of a single link failure.

When bridges were used to build larger networks and to carry data traffic in more critical applications, this inability to provide resilience by supporting alternative routes around the network became a serious limitation. In the case of networks comprising multiple Ethernet segments, it appeared at first sight impossible to support

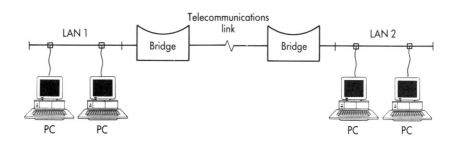

Figure 6.6 Two LAN segments connected remotely by two bridges.

alternative routing, because Ethernet required an open bus network topology. For there to be alternative routes between any pair of nodes on a network, there has to be at least one closed loop.

To solve the problem a technique called the Spanning Tree algorithm was developed. The basis of this algorithm is that you only need to open an alternative route when the primary one fails. Therefore, it is possible to obey the Ethernet insistence on an open bus structure by keeping one link on standby, and only invoking it if another link fails. The principle is illustrated in Figure 6.7, where two LAN segments are interconnected via bridges by two separate links. The link between segment 1 and segment 2 across link A is normally closed, so that an open bus is maintained. But if, say, link B fails, the Spanning Tree algorithm automatically opens link A, so that as the diagram shows, there is always a link between any two nodes, except in the unlikely event of a second link failing. Note that although Figure 6.7 shows two separate bridges on each segment, many bridges provide more than one port. Thus in many cases a single bridge will attach to both the primary and secondary links at each end.

Spanning Tree became an IEEE standard for operation of Ethernet LANs – see the glossary for a detailed list of LAN standards. But although it solved the redundant link problem, Spanning Tree

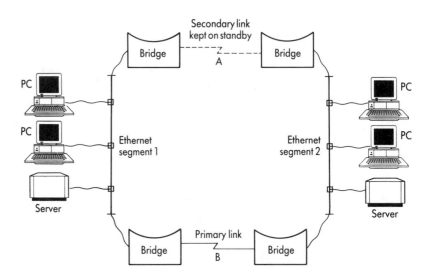

Figure 6.7   Shows two Ethernet LANs interconnected by two separate telecommunications links, where one is designated the primary link (B). The Spanning Tree algorithm ensures that the secondary link (A) is kept on standby unless and until the primary one fails.

failed to do anything for another growing problem, that of increasing data traffic being transmitted across bridges between LAN segments. There was the option of installing a faster link between LAN segments but given the cost of wide area circuits, it seemed wasteful to have a perfectly good link standing idle.

No standard has been developed to remedy this, but several vendors of Ethernet LAN bridges developed their own proprietary solutions, an example being the adaptive routing algorithm from Retix Systems. The principle of all these proprietary techniques is similar: it is to split traffic equally between two routes where there is a choice, while maintaining the appearance of a closed bus to the network as a whole.

The principle is illustrated in Figure 6.8, which shows the same network as Figure 6.7, except that now one of these new routing techniques is used. Traffic between segments 1 and 2 is now shared between the link A and link B. As before if one link fails, the Spanning Tree algorithm is used to open the other link. But now during normal operation the two bridges on segment 2 supporting link A and link B are both programmed to filter out packets that they originally forwarded as they return round the network. Otherwise data transmitted across link 1 would return via link 2, and continue to circulate endlessly. However, the bridges on segment 2 avoid repeating data back onto the links 1 and 2.

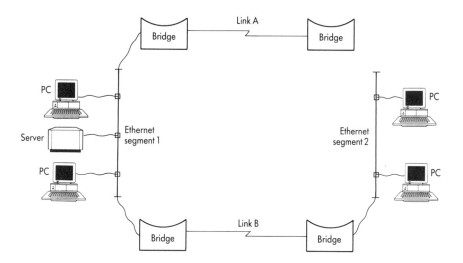

Figure 6.8   Showing how proprietary techniques allow inter-LAN traffic to share both links of a Spanning Tree network. Both links are in active use, but the bridges prevent packets completing a whole circuit of the network.

Even with this kind of technique bridges are not generally used for large networks comprising many interconnected LAN segments, where routers are generally more suitable. We shall discuss the pros and cons of bridging and routing later in the chapter.

Source routing bridging

Source routing bridging, used on IBM token ring networks, operates differently from Spanning Tree bridging, although the underlying principle is the same, to interconnect two LAN segments. Alternatively, and this amounts to the same thing as far as locally connected segments are concerned, the function is to divide a ring that has outgrown its size into two segments. The latter function is discussed further in Chapter 10.

In the case of a simple bridge linking two segments, there is no real difference between these two types of bridging. In both cases the bridge determines whether to filter or forward a packet by reading the address header in the packet.

The difference arises on more complex networks when there is a choice of routes between LAN segments. As we have seen, Ethernet uses a Spanning Tree method in which bridges determine the route a packet will take. If the normal link is open, the bridge on that link will forward a packet addressed to a destination on the other side. If the link fails, the bridge will filter the packet, which will instead be forwarded by the bridge on the spare link.

IBM developed a different procedure called source routing. With this procedure, the source, that is a device such as a PC sending data packets onto the network, ordains what route each data packet will take. The source inserts precise details of the route into each packet. Each bridge on the way reads this routing information and either filters or forwards accordingly. The operation of source routing is illustrated in Figure 6.9, where the packet starting from ring A has two choices of route to reach ring E. It can go via ring B or via ring C and ring D. The source routing method would determine at the outset, when the network is first configured, which of these two routes is best. From then on packets continue to take that route until the network is changed in some way, for example when a new PC is added to one of the rings, or if a link fails.

Source routing has two advantages over Spanning Tree. One, it

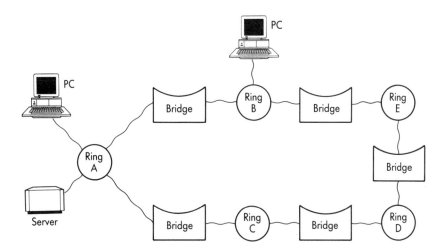

Figure 6.9 Operation of source routing bridging on token ring networks connected locally. Packets from Ring A to Ring E can travel via Ring B, or via Rings C and D. But the source routing method ensures that they always go via one route or the other, until a link fails or some other change occurs.

6

can fully utilize all routes, although Spanning Tree networks can also do this with the help of proprietary techniques developed by some vendors, as described in the last section. Second, source routing does not require any additional processing in the bridges, which still simply filter or forward. The disadvantage is that it does require additional processing in the source, which has to recalculate all potential routes each time the network is reconfigured.

Routes are static, in the sense that a packet will always take the same route between any two nodes until the network needs to be reconfigured when a link fails, or some change is made such as the addition of a new PC to one of the rings. But at the outset, and whenever a change is made such as the addition of a new node, each source has to recalculate every route, making decisions according to factors such as shortest distance and sharing the load equally.

In the case of the network shown in Figure 6.9, the source at ring A would send out exploratory packets across each route to every potential destination. Each exploratory packet records the route it takes and then returns to the source, which assesses each route and sets its routing table accordingly. After that all packets follow the predetermined routes, until the network changes and the whole process has to be gone through again. The need to go through this process whenever the network is reconfigured, which could be when a link fails, causes a slight hiccup in performance each time it happens.

Another point to note about token ring bridging is that, for timing reasons, no packet is allowed to cross more than seven bridges. This imposes a practical upper limit on the size of a bridged token ring network, although given that each ring can support 260 nodes, the network can in fact be very large.

Source Routing Transparent (SRT)

As already noted, not all token ring networks use source routing bridging. Some use Spanning Tree bridging, which is sometimes called transparent bridging because the packets do not carry any information describing their route. They simply carry a destination address and let the bridges on the way decide which route to take.

The situation arose that some larger organizations had implemented token ring networks of both types and wanted to connect them together. The SRT standard was developed to allow bridges to interconnect both types of token ring LAN in the same overall network. It can also be used in combination with translation bridging to connect Ethernet and token ring LANs where source routing is used.

The operation is simple. If a packet reaching an SRT bridge contains source routing information, the bridge obeys that information just like a source routing bridge. If it does not contain any source routing information, the bridge assumes that the packet came from a Spanning Tree network, and behaves just like a Spanning Tree bridge. In this case the bridge either filters or forwards the packet according to the address of the packet and whether the link is open.

Translation bridging

Many organizations have both token ring and Ethernet LANs and want to interconnect them. The usual way of doing this is via routers, which make use of OSI layer 3 and avoid the need to translate between Ethernet and token ring protocols at the datalink level. We describe routers in the next section.

There has been some demand for bridges that connect Ethernet and token ring LANs without needing the additional complexity of implementing a network layer 3 protocol to provide routing information across a network. Such demand has come largely from organizations with a lot of token ring LANs supporting IBM systems, and perhaps just the occasional Ethernet network to link into their network. Unfortunately using bridges to connect Ethernet and token ring LANs also brings additional processing complexity, because of the need to convert protocols at the datalink level. This tends to defeat the object of bridging, which is to have relatively simple devices that provide high performance at a reasonably low cost.

Translation bridging is needed to bridge Ethernet and token ring LANs without using a network layer. The technique involves translating between the Ethernet and token ring packaging of data. In addition, where source routing is used for token ring bridging, the bridge needs to support the SRT standard, to be compatible both with the source routing network on one side and the Spanning Tree on the other.

Translation bridging has not become a major force in the market because it suffers from the disadvantages of bridging, which are described later in this section, without offering the advantages of simplicity and a high performance/price ratio. However, translation bridges are available, the most notable supplier being IBM.

FDDI bridging

We saw in Chapter 3 how FDDI backbone networks are being used to interconnect local LAN segments, linking computing facilities around a university campus, for example. Bridges can be used to connect either Ethernet LANs to each other or token ring LANs to each other across the FDDI backbone. However, such a bridge cannot connect LANs of different types across an FDDI backbone. To connect an Ethernet LAN to a token ring LAN via an FDDI backbone would require a router.

FDDI bridging requires an additional technique called encapsulation. Normal bridges operate by directly connecting two segments, or via a transparent point-to-point connection that faithfully conveys the signals between the two LANs. But FDDI is a LAN in its own right with its own data packet structure. Bridges that operate via FDDI therefore have to make the packets they are transmitting appear as FDDI packets while they are on the FDDI ring. Figure 6.10 shows how this works for two Ethernet LANs interconnected by an FDDI backbone ring via Ethernet-over-FDDI bridges. Bridge 1 on

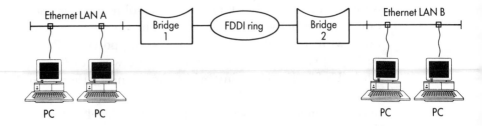

Figure 6.10 Shows how Ethernet LANs can be connected via bridges across an FDDI network.

LAN A accepts all data packets addressed to devices on LAN B. It wraps them for transmission across the FDDI network with appropriate protocols including the FDDI header. It then places the packet onto the FDDI ring, where it is transmitted to bridge 2, which intercepts the packet as it is addressed to a device on LAN B. Bridge 2 then strips off the FDDI protocols and places the packet onto LAN B, where it is broadcast, and received by the appropriate device.

Token ring-over-FDDI bridges operate in a similar way. The process of wrapping the Ethernet or token ring packets in FDDI protocols is known as encapsulation.

Limitation of bridging

For networks that are small in terms of the number of different segments that need to be connected, and where all the LAN segments are of the same generic type (all Ethernet or token ring), bridging will often be the best solution. By small we mean comprising typically six or fewer remote segments. There are some much larger networks comprising many segments where bridging is used, particularly at sites using predominantly IBM computers. Generally, however, the larger the network, the less suitable bridges become.

The principal limitation of Ethernet bridges is inability to provide more than two alternative routes between any two nodes of the network. Token ring networks with source routing can support more than two alternative routes, but even then the network becomes hard to manage if it is very large.

Picture a big Ethernet network comprising perhaps 100 remote branches each with an Ethernet segment. With bridging, each branch would be connected to two others in point-to-point mode. For every branch there would be one other that could only be reached by hopping across 50 other Ethernet segments. Even with the help of the Spanning Tree algorithm, such a network is exposed to failure of individual links, and the need to hop through so many intermediate segments will diminish performance.

Bridges only satisfy the first of our five interconnection categories completely. Translation bridging satisfies category 2, connecting LANs of different types, but is rarely used. Encapsulation bridges for FDDI partially fulfil category 3 of interconnecting LANs via a backbone. But they do not support communication between LANs of different types, or with devices attached directly to the backbone network.

But Ethernet switching can provide local bridging without some of the performance limitations

6

For networks on a single site, a technique called Ethernet switching has emerged as a cost effective alternative to local bridging for Ethernet LANs. This allows a single Ethernet network to be subdivided into a number of segments with high-speed switching between them. Ethernet switching is discussed in more detail in Chapter 10 in the section on segmentation of LANs under the overall heading of performance.

Routers

Routing adds a new layer of sophistication to LAN interconnection. The essential difference is that routers enable more complex mesh networks to be supported, in which there are multiple links between any pair of segments. They are also able to balance the load of traffic across the routes by making dynamic decisions about which path to take, provided a suitable routing technique is used.

Furthermore, routers can make routing decisions based not just on the network layer address, but also on the type of data packets.

This enables them to distinguish between different protocols and make routing decisions accordingly. Similarly they can also filter according to packet type. This enables them, for example, to block data of a particular type for security reasons, preventing certain users from accessing prohibited parts of the network.

Routers operate in layer 3 of the OSI protocol stack, the next one above the datalink layer in which LANs are driven. Layer 3 or the network layer provides the ability to specify a route across a network spanning a number of individual links. For example, it could describe the route from the PC on the Ethernet LAN to the server on the token ring LAN in Figure 6.11(a), via the link connecting the two LANs together locally. The operation of routing in this example is shown schematically in Figure 6.11(b). Each node on the overall network has a unique network address. As data enters the Ethernet LAN from the PC, the network address is contained in each data packet, and this is used to generate the Ethernet LAN address of the router in the datalink layer.

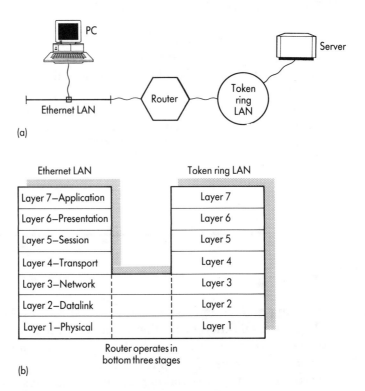

Figure 6.11 Showing how a router can interconnect an Ethernet LAN with a token ring LAN. (a) Physical structure of network. (b) How router operates within seven layer structure of OSI model.

The router intercepts packets that are addressed to it from the Ethernet LAN, and strips off the part of the packet specific to Ethernet such as the Ethernet address header. The router then reads the network address in each data packet and uses this to restructure the packet into token ring format with the correct datalink address. The token ring LAN then delivers the data to the server. In this way the router connects the Ethernet and token ring LAN without requiring direct translation between the Ethernet and token ring packet formats. In this case there is just one direct route between the two LANs, but as we shall explain, routers can, unlike bridges, choose between different routes.

At this point we can finally explain the distinction between IBM's source routing, which is a form of bridging, and true routing. Source routing is static in the sense that once the routes have been determined for a given network configuration, they are fixed until a further change is made to the network. True routing, on the other hand, allows routes to be determined dynamically, which means that they are calculated as data is being transmitted. The calculation is based not just on which route is the shortest, but also on which is currently being least used, and perhaps which costs the least. However, as we shall see, there are several routing methods, and some are more sophisticated than others.

6

Routers, then, offer three advantages.

(1) They can filter and route according to packet type.
(2) They support multiple links between LAN segments, which provides additional protection against link failure.
(3) Routes can be calculated on the fly to take account of prevailing data traffic conditions on the network.

Taken together, the second and third of these two advantages yield a fourth benefit, at least on large networks. The fact that multiple routes are supported with the ability to choose between them dynamically means there is a better chance of finding a route when the network is heavily loaded.

Figure 6.12 shows how this could happen. There are three routes between the PC on LAN A and the server on LAN D. The router on LAN A has three choices, and would base its decision on prevailing conditions. Obviously if route 1, the direct route between the two LANs, failed, the router would choose one of the others. Less obviously, if one of the other routes, although less direct, offered greater bandwidth, it might be preferred for transmitting large files.

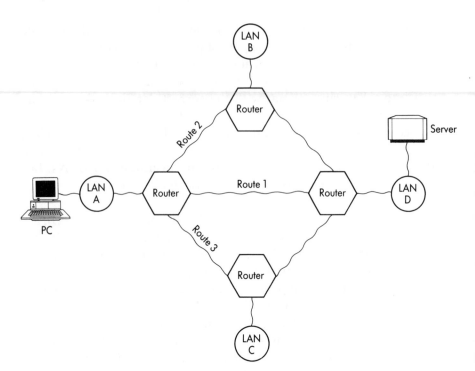

Figure 6.12 Showing router network offering choices of route between the PC on LAN A and the server on LAN D. In this case all LANs are token ring, but they could be Ethernet, or a mixture of the two. Note that in practice a router network would support many more PCs and devices than are shown in this diagram.

However, a note of caution is worth sounding. Routers from different vendors do not necessarily understand the same routing protocols. Although many will interoperate in the sense that they can be used on the same network, they may provide only a low level of routing function.

Routing methods

The issue of which routing protocol to use is especially important on large complex networks where there is a variety of different types of link, or where routers from different vendors are interoperating. Most vendors have used a proprietary routing protocol for networks built exclusively from their products. But there is increasingly demand on large networks for routers from different vendors to interoperate. There are three main independent routing methods that allow this to be done – these methods are independent not just of the make of router but also of the communications protocols being routed.

In ascending order of complexity they are PPP (point-to-point protocol), RIP (routing information protocol) and OSPF (open shortest path first). PPP merely allows routers to interoperate, without providing any support for choice of routes. It tends to be used for routing between two networks where dissimilar protocols are being used in the layers above the network layer where the router operates.

The PPP protocol enables the two routers to inform each other about the basic structure of the data packets they are sending so that they can interpret them correctly. Information exchanged would include the size of the packets being transmitted and details of any data compression technique used. RIP goes further by allowing a choice of routes, but it always makes the same choice – the shortest route. For this reason RIP, although an improvement on PPP, is still flawed as a routing protocol, because it takes no account of prevailing conditions on the network, or of costing issues. It is still really a static protocol, in that faced with a choice of routes, it will always take the same one. Another fault with RIP is that signals need to be transmitted at regular intervals between routers just to check they are still working. This continual polling occupies bandwidth on the links that could otherwise be used for transmitting data required for users' applications.

These weaknesses are remedied in OSPF, which is the most suitable routing protocol for large networks. With OSPF, devices do not need to maintain a constant dialogue just to reassure themselves that all is well even when there is no data to send. Instead they only transmit information when something has happened on the network. For example, a link might have failed, in which case all routers need to know to avoid trying to send data across that link.

But most important, OSPF can calculate not just the shortest route between two network nodes that is available at a given time, but also the one that costs least. The basis for the costing calculation can be specified by the users of that network, who can obtain a balance between cost and performance. In fact OSPF allows routes to be calculated according to a combination of four key factors: delay, determined largely by the number of hops; data throughput, measured in terms of link capacity; reliability; and cost.

On top of this it allows the network to specify routes that particular types of data should take. This enables data from a critical application to be given preferential treatment by being assigned the fastest route. OSPF can also distribute data automatically across available routes, while obeying instructions based on the factors already described, to balance the load across available routes.

A growing number of routers now support OSPF, although there can be problems using OSPF to communicate between routers from different vendors. However, vendors have started to cooperate in testing the interoperability of their respective routers. The number of different products that can communicate using OSPF has been increasing accordingly.

Local, remote and FDDI routing

Essentially routers can be used in the same situations as bridges. However, a major difference already noted is that routers can readily interconnect token ring and Ethernet LANs. Suppose, for example, a building contains a large Ethernet LAN that needs to be divided into smaller segments to maintain overall performance. Suppose there is also a token ring segment that needs to be brought into the big network picture. The router can fulfil an identical function to the bridge in segmenting the Ethernet LAN into two parts, but at the same time it can link up with the token ring LAN as well. Figure 6.13 shows the arrangement.

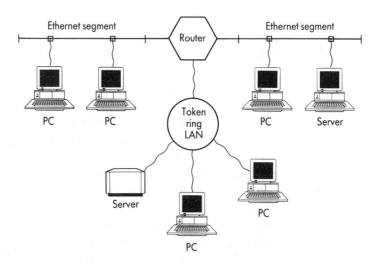

Figure 6.13 Use of a router to split an Ethernet LAN into two segments, and at the same time link up with a token ring LAN, where all are in the same building.

Routers can also be used to connect LANs over long-distance links, as well as via an FDDI backbone network. In the case of FDDI there is no actual routing to be done, because FDDI is just another type of LAN in which data packet addresses are specified in layer 2.

But over FDDI, routers have the advantage of being able to interconnect Ethernet and token ring LANs across the FDDI backbone. Indeed a general advantage of routers is that they are not restricted to a particular LAN type. A router can interconnect FDDI, token ring and Ethernet LANs, supporting both local and remote connections. A bridge, on the other hand, is specific to the pair of LANs it interconnects. For example Ethernet-to-FDDI bridges can only connect Ethernet LANs via an FDDI backbone network, as explained in the bridge section.

Multiprotocol routers

As routers make use of information in OSI layer 3, the network layer, to determine routes, they need to support a specific network protocol. Examples are the Internet Protocol (IP), which is part of the popular TCP/IP protocol stack, and Novell's IPX used to route between PCs and servers on NetWare networks. Initially routers tended to be specific to one particular network protocol, and were useless when presented with data packets using another network layer protocol. This was a significant disadvantage compared with bridges, which were independent of the network layer protocol. Consider, for example, the two LANs in Figure 6.14, both of which have a NetWare server accessed via IPX protocols and a Unix server accessed via TCP/IP protocols. Both networks therefore support two network layer protocols: IPX and IP. The two networks could be interconnected with either a bridge or router.

A bridge would automatically allow both IPX and IP data packets to be transmitted between the two LANs, because it is oblivious to information in the network layer. On the other hand, neither an IP nor an IPX router would work, because neither would be able to handle both IP and IPX packets.

To overcome this handicap, multiprotocol routers were developed. Most routers are now multiprotocol, being capable of supporting all the popular network protocols. They can read the network addresses of data packets formatted in any of the network protocols that they support. Note, however, that a multiprotocol router cannot route data between two LANs that support different network layer

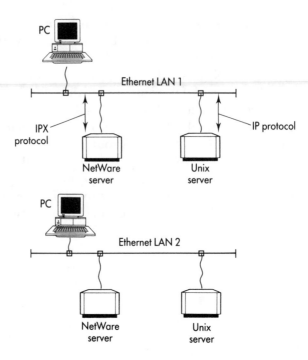

Figure 6.14 Two LANs (Ethernet in this case, but could be token ring, or one of each) supporting a NetWare server and a Unix server. These two LANs could be interconnected with a bridge, but if a router is used it must support both IPX and IP protocols.

protocols. This is because routers do not translate between different protocols. There is no router equivalent of the translation bridge we described earlier. The point of a multiprotocol router is that it can connect LANs running more than one network layer protocol, but only where the same protocols are supported on both the LANs being connected. To connect two LANs running different network layer protocols, a gateway is needed. Gateways are described in the next section.

However, routers can be used to interconnect a group of LANs over an existing wide area network. This is the equivalent of the Ethernet-over-FDDI bridge which we described earlier, except that this time the encapsulation takes place in the network layer rather than the datalink layer. We look at routing encapsulation later in this section.

So multiprotocol routers, like bridges, can interconnect LANs on which a variety of network layer protocols are running. But unlike bridges, the routers can act on information in the network layer to determine the best route.

This advantage is shown in Figure 6.15, which is in two parts, each showing the same network of four Ethernet LAN segments but with one interconnected by routers, the other by bridges. With routers, each of the LAN segments can be connected directly to all three of the others. This means that data never has to travel more than one hop, and the network can guarantee to provide a service to all users even if two individual links fail. With bridges, the best that can be done is to connect the four segments in a loop.

On a network with more than four remote LAN segments, however, the use of a full mesh network, in which each segment is connected to every other, could result in unacceptably high tele-communication costs. Suppose, for example, an organization with six

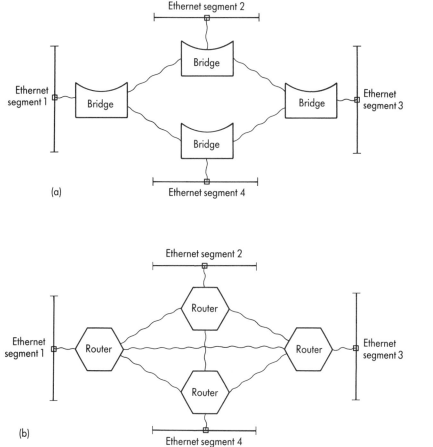

Figure 6.15 Showing four Ethernet LAN segments interconnected (a) with bridges; (b) with routers, where each LAN can be directly connected to every other in a mesh network.

locations had a LAN segment in each one. For there to be a mesh
network with each location connected directly to every other would
require a total of 15 long-distance links, which might be quite out of
proportion to the amount of data traffic.

In practice most organizations have some locations with greater
data transmission requirements than others. A typical solution would
be to have a core network linking major sites, with smaller branches
connected to the core by point-to-point links. Figure 6.16 shows such
an arrangement, comprising a core mesh network linking three major
sites, and seven satellite branches linked in via point-to-point connections. The satellite links could be via routers or bridges, but the core
network would be built with routers.

Encapsulation routing

Routers, like bridges, can encapsulate packets to support connection
of LAN segments over another network. The difference is that bridges
encapsulate at the datalink level, or OSI layer 2, to facilitate interconnection of Ethernet or token ring LANs over another kind of LAN,
usually FDDI. Routers encapsulate in OSI layer 3, that is the network
layer, to enable data packets built using one layer 3 protocol to be
routed over a network based on another. Routing encapsulation is
used mainly in two situations:

(1)   To connect LANs via an X.25 packet switched wide area
       network. A number of organizations established X.25 net-
       works before they needed to interconnect LANs. By encap-
       sulating the LAN packets, which typically use IPX or IP
       routing, over X.25, the packets can be transmitted. In this
       case the X.25 network handles the routing of data between
       LANs. The router merely packages the data up so that the
       X.25 network can handle it, and then unpacks it again at
       the other end. Figure 6.17 shows LANs interconnected by
       an X.25 network.

(2)   To enable IBM SNA network data to be routed over a
       backbone network comprising routers. In a sense this a
       reverse of the X.25 situation. This time a more recently
       installed router network is used to transport traffic from a
       longer-established wide area network. The router backbone
       would typically be connecting several large sites, like the
       network illustrated in Figure 6.16.

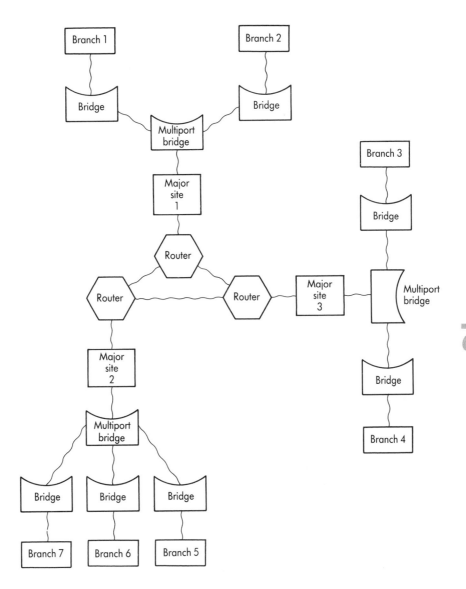

Figure 6.16   Showing a large network based on a core of three major sites and seven smaller satellite sites. Here the satellite sites are connected via bridges and point-to-point links, while the three major sites are linked with powerful routers. But often routers would be used throughout. Note: the bridges at each of the major sites are multiport bridges, supporting more than one link. In effect they function as more than one single bridge.

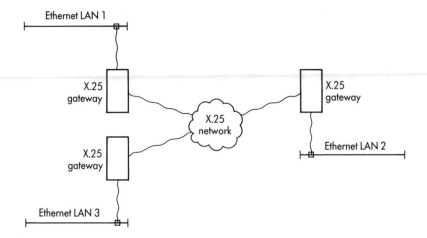

Figure 6.17   Showing an X.25 network interconnecting three Ethernet LANs via X.25 gateways.

Brouters

These are devices that combine the advantages of routers and bridges. Protocols that can be routed are routed, but those that cannot be routed are bridged. The point is that there are a few protocol stacks that do not contain a network layer, an example being Digital Equipment's Local Area Transport (LAT) protocol. Brouters function as multiprotocol routers, supporting different network layer protocols, but also have the ability to bridge LAT, as well as IBM's source routing protocol that we described earlier.

Disadvantages of routers

We have discussed the advantages of routers, in particular their ability to determine routes dynamically taking account of costing factors and prevailing data traffic conditions. We have also mentioned one disadvantage, their dependence on the existence of a network layer protocol. However, we also pointed out how multiprotocol brouters largely eradicate this problem. This leaves two other traditional router snags to deal with: cost and performance.

Early routers cost substantially more than bridges, and were also slower at transmitting data between the LANs they supported. Both these problems followed from the fact that routing is more complex than bridging. Bridges only act on layer 2 addresses. Routers need to base their decisions on both layer 2 and layer 3 addresses, and also need to perform complex routing calculations. However the increasing power and falling price of microprocessors have eroded this argument in favour of bridges.

This has led to the situation where both routing and bridging functions are being implemented in the same products. And as we noted in Chapter 3, routing and bridging are now being implemented as modules in hubs.

What do routers and bridges look like?

In fact bridges and routers can now be obtained in three forms. They can be cards for existing PCs, which then may either operate in dedicated mode or may also perform some other role such as file serving. They can also be hardware devices designed specially for the task. Or they can be modules that are specific to a type of hub.

6

What interconnection requirements do routers fulfil?

Routers fulfil the requirements of the first three of our interconnection categories, and partially fulfil the fourth. They are undoubtedly preferable for almost any large network. The uncertainty arises on small networks comprising just a few segments, where the issues of performance and cost need to be balanced against the need to cater for future change. We shall discuss this further in Chapter 8.

Routers do not fully handle the fourth category, involving connection of LANs to an existing wide area network. We saw earlier in the section how routers can connect LANs over an X.25 wide area network and also allow IBM SNA traffic to be carried over a router backbone. But they cannot connect LANs into an SNA network in the same way as over an X.25 network. This is because SNA is more than just a network layer 3 protocol. It also handles interactions at higher communication layers. Therefore to connect a LAN to an SNA network, a gateway is needed to provide protocol conversion between whatever high-level protocols are used on the LAN and the SNA protocols.

Gateways

These are the most sophisticated devices for interconnecting LANs, requiring even more processing power than routers. Gateways not only perform a routing function across a network but also translate between two different protocol sets. For example, a NetWare LAN would need a gateway to access an IBM SNA network. This is because all of the data's packaging layers are different on the two networks. Therefore for a DOS-based application on a PC using IPX routing protocols to communicate with an IBM mainframe on the SNA network, the protocols need to be translated from layer 3 right up the stack to layer 7. A router on the other hand is transparent to all protocols from layer 4 upwards, just as a bridge is from layer 3 upwards.

The subject of gateways goes rather beyond the LAN, which is why we do not describe them in as much detail as bridges and routers. However, the principle is easily illustrated with reference to letters sent through the post. For a letter to be routed from sender to destination, it is only necessary that the address can be understood by everyone who has to handle the letter on its journey. A common naming system based on a single alphabet is quite sufficient, which is why a letter posted in the US can be delivered easily in Italy.

But if the letter is to be perfectly understood by an Italian who does not read English, the contents also need to be translated. A gateway performs such a translation service for computers. There are two alternatives. One is for one of the computers to learn the language of the other, by implementing its complete protocol stack covering all seven layers, or at any rate the crucial upper five layers as the lower two layers can be taken care of by other devices on the network such as routers.

This is known as emulation, the computer equivalent of the Italian being able to read English. The other alternative is for both computers to speak an agreed common language, the equivalent of the human Esperanto language. The computing equivalent of Esperanto is OSI. Cynics would say, with some justification, that OSI is no more widely accepted than Esperanto. In practice a number of computer vendors have adopted an alternative set of protocols, such as TCP/IP, which we have already mentioned. Computers, like people, are reluctant to abandon a language they speak for a new supposedly independent language. In practice, therefore, many more computers use TCP/IP protocols than OSI. In any case the two are slowly converging towards a common standard protocol set.

A final point to note about gateways is that the function can be provided in the same computing frame, for example a PC, as routing or bridging. For example, Novell's NetWare/SAA services, which is gateway software for connecting NetWare networks to IBM SAA (System Application Architecture) networks, can run in the same server as the company's routing software. There is a trend, at least on larger networks, towards all LAN interconnection functions being provided within a single server or a smart hub, which then becomes a network building block.

Gateways in principle can handle any of our five communication categories. Unless protocol conversion is required, however, there is no point in paying for the additional functions of a gateway. In practice therefore they are used only for categories 4 and 5, where protocol conversion is often required.

A typical situation where a gateway might be used is shown in Figure 6.18. PCs on a NetWare LAN access an IBM mainframe via

6

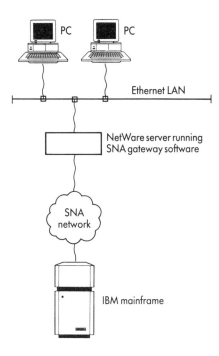

Figure 6.18 Use of a gateway to access an IBM mainframe from a LAN. Here the NetWare server functions as a gateway to access the mainframe using IBM's SNA protocols.

an SNA gateway. The gateway translates protocols from the LAN into a form the mainframe expects.

Summary

Having now described the issues of LAN interconnection, all the major components of a LAN have been covered, except one, network management. On larger networks, management is closely linked to LAN interconnection devices, as will become clear in Chapter 10.

7

How do I choose my own LAN?

CHAPTER CONTENTS

CHAPTER OBJECTIVES

The elements of a LAN have now been covered, except for network management, which to some extent is independent of the underlying LAN platform. In this chapter we look beyond the technology at perhaps the most important choice, that of supplier. Basic questions or issues tackled are:

Introduction

Choosing suppliers can be both the most important and most difficult decision you have to make regarding your LAN. There are many to choose from at different levels, ranging from straightforward commodity vendors to total solution providers. The latter can hand hold you through the whole selection and installation process, and even get your applications running as well. On the other hand commodity suppliers, while providing no added value service, will offer keener prices. Various different options in between these two extremes are also available.

The best choice depends on the level of expertise within your business, and on the size and complexity of the network you are installing. The key point to bear in mind is that LANs are more complex to install and manage than single PCs, and that going for the cheapest option will not save money in the long term. Somewhere along the line you will have to pay for the expertise necessary to implement a LAN. This expertise may be obtained in one of four ways:

(1)   In the cost of the equipment, by not using a commodity supplier. In this case the supplier will install the network at no further cost.

(2)   By employing a consultant if you buy the equipment at minimum cost from a commodity supplier.

(3)   By employing staff with the relevant skills.

(4)   By educating yourself or one or more colleagues.

This chapter will examine these options. The various categories of vendor and supply channel will be defined, outlining the various options available. Then we shall turn to the subject from the point of view of the customer, describing in turn how each type of supplier relates to a variety of network situations. By looking for the section most relevant to your needs, you should be able to identify the types of vendor and supply processes most pertinent to your organization.

We distinguish first between network size, identifying three categories: small networks of 1 to 10 users; middle sized networks from 11 to 49 users; and what for our purposes we call large LANs supporting upwards of 50 users. There are large sites with segmented LANs supporting far larger numbers of users than this, in some cases over 1000, but this book is primarily aimed at users of smaller networks.

Another important distinction is whether the LAN being commissioned will need to link up with other networks. Different factors may need to be considered when purchasing, say, a small network for a single business such as an architectural practice than when considering the same network for a workgroup within a large organization. We look at the various interconnection possibilities within each of the three sections for the different sizes of network.

Then at the end of the chapter we look at the important related subject of training. It is not much use having a sophisticated NOS and LAN management system if no one in your business is able to exploit them properly. There is now a wide variety of training courses available, covering the NOS, database management systems, network management, LAN interconnection and other related topics.

7

Categories of supplier

The same LAN components can be obtained from many suppliers of several different types. Table 7.1 summarizes the options, which range from large well-known suppliers of IT systems such as IBM and AT&T to small local dealers that sell LAN components or complete LANs from a variety of manufacturers. There are also suppliers that specialize in parts of the network such as cabling systems or network management systems. For larger or more complex networks it can be advantageous to involve more than one specialist supplier each of whom is strong in a particular area.

Alternatively a single total solution provider may subcontract various parts of the overall network to such specialist providers on your behalf. This is particularly likely to happen with cabling, which requires specialist expertise quite distinct from higher-level protocol and application issues.

Also, some suppliers that specialize in one field may be capable

Table 7.1   Range of possible suppliers, summarizing possible advantages and snags.

Supplier type	Possible advantages	Potential disadvantages
Dealer	Close proximity	Lack of expertise, especially in more complex networks
	Competitive prices	Not completely impartial advice – will only provide products it deals in
	Some choice between different products	
Consultancy	Expertise – should have already dealt with similar situations	Expensive
	Impartiality. Should be independent of networking vendor	No guarantee that consultants will have expertise in all relevant areas, e.g. cabling
		May not be financially secure. A number of networking consultancies went bust during the recession of the early 1990s
Cabling company	Expertise in cabling	Means having to deal with other suppliers for other components of network
	Cabling may be cheaper than from non-specialist suppliers	If cabling company does offer other components of network may lack relevant skills
Network management specialist company	Expertise in network management which is crucial in larger networks	May not give impartial advice, particularly with respect to the management system itself
	Will choose or recommend components that can be embraced by a single management system	May be expensive
Application software company	Could be best bet for a total solution ensuring that network chosen is suitable for applications you want to run	May not have sufficient grasp of networking field to recommend appropriate components
		Again, may be expensive

of installing other components as well, saving you the aggravation of dealing with more than one vendor. In fact there are a growing number of 'one stop LAN shops' that can sell you complete LANs including PCs, servers, network operating system and installed application software. These are aimed at businesses that know what they want, and just want to obtain the whole solution as cheaply as possible. However, such an approach is only recommended for relatively small networks. Some suppliers will install the network and ensure that all applications are working properly. Others sell by mail order, leaving buyers to set the network up. Obviously the latter option is the cheapest. As a rough guide, a complete 'shrink-wrapped' mail order LAN for four users would cost about $16 000, or £12 000, for a basic application. Costs increase if sophisticated applications are required, or if help is needed with installation, followed by ongoing support.

Using consultants

Apart from suppliers of actual network components, there are consultancies that can help you find the right source of supply, and can also supervise the installation process and ensure that all the pieces work together at the end. Their price might seem high, but for larger networks at least it may be a price worth paying, provided you have chosen good consultants. Like other elements of the supply chain, consultants can be judged by talking to other customers of theirs. If any supplier cannot or will not provide references, it may mean that they cannot keep their customers happy for long.

There are several points worth considering, though, before hiring consultants. Given the high price they charge, it is important to ensure that their role is clearly defined and focused. Some consultants are only too happy being busy doing nothing useful while gobbling up fees. The following checklist can be applied:

1. Define clearly what you want the consultants to achieve and the scope of their work. This can range from merely helping select other suppliers to managing the whole acquisition and installation process on your behalf. At this stage timescales for the project should also be clarified.

2. Having established a framework for the project, the little matter of cost needs to be discussed. The way in which costs are determined

is particularly important for consultancy, because some methods of payment can lead to unexpectedly high bills. Payment can be a fixed fee for the project; or costs plus, in which case there is a set fee with bonuses for work that was not described in the initial contract; or it can be on a time basis with additional payment for materials and expenses.

All have their merits and minuses. Fixed fee has the advantage that costs are largely predetermined, but can mean paying more than the project merits, although this can be mitigated by seeking quotes from several different consultancies. Time and materials contracts are of course open ended, and need to be tightly linked to carefully worded contracts that relate fees to targets. Contracts should be carefully scrutinized by a solicitor or lawyer with expertise in the general field of consultancy contracts.

3. Ensure that there is a proper reporting structure. The consultant or consultants should have someone in your company to report to, rather than being vaguely answerable to more than one director or manager. Even when the consultants are taking full charge of an installation, there should be close liaison with someone in your company to ensure that timescales and milestones are met.

4. Standards and documentation. It is important that consultants adhere to well defined procedures and technical standards, and that the project is well documented, so that you are not left stranded if for some reason they pull out of the project. Specify key components such as the NOS, LAN type, communication protocols and database. Consultants may give useful advice about these – indeed this may be partly what you hire them for. But the ultimate decision is yours and needs to be spelt out clearly in contracts.

5. Guarantee and acceptance of job. Many businesses have failed in the past to ensure first that there is a clear definition of what constitutes a completed project, and then that consultants provide an adequate guarantee worth the paper it is written on. The answer is to be specific both about what constitutes a completed project, and about acceptable levels of faults or problems with the resulting network. At this stage it is well worth specifying any maintenance and ongoing support agreements, and their costs.

In some cases consultants will be called in just to help evaluate proposals and perhaps oversee other suppliers. In this case some or all of the above principles will apply to each party concerned. For example, ongoing support and maintenance may be provided by the installer of the network, but it is still important to define clearly what consultants are expected to achieve for a given fee.

Distribution channels

From the customers' point of view, the distinction is not so much between suppliers, but between channels through which the product may be obtained. Large suppliers of computers and networking systems have a number of channels through which they send products to market. Digital Equipment (DEC) is a fairly typical example. Like other large manufacturers, it first of all distinguishes between direct and indirect channels. Direct means selling straight to customers, while indirect means distributing through dealers or value added resellers that incorporate Digital Equipment products into complete LAN-based solutions.

Digital Equipment had two main direct channels operating in the UK during 1992, and the picture was similar in the US. One was a direct merchandising arm, operating by mail order, allowing customers to specify purchases over the telephone and pay by credit card if they wished. Then it had a direct-end user sales force, split into three units each offering different levels of service.

One such unit offered a complete network service, from initial design through installation of equipment and cabling, culminating in testing of the network itself and if required of applications that ran on it. At the other extreme was a high-volume sales team handling lower-value items such as terminal servers.

The company also had two types of indirect channel. One was the value added wholesaler, acting as an intermediary between DEC and smaller local resellers or dealers that may not have particular expertise in the company's networking systems. In these cases the wholesaler may use Digital Equipment systems as part of total networks including equipment or software from other vendors. The wholesaler then distributes such network solutions through local resellers or dealers.

The other type of indirect channel in DEC's case is the value added reseller, which unlike the value added wholesaler sells directly to customers. The value added reseller is more likely to incorporate Digital Equipment systems in complete solutions which because of their complexity would need to be sold direct to customers rather than via another tier of distribution.

7

Other major IT vendors operate similar channels of distribution in both Europe and the US. However, in the UK the world's largest computer company, IBM, has opened a new channel by using self-employed salespeople to sell complete networks to small businesses. The idea is that such people should have greater incentive to sell systems that individually are very small for a company of IBM's size, but which collectively add up to a lot of business. For users, the salient question that has yet to be settled is how well systems and networks purchased this way will be supported compared with those obtained through more traditional channels.

Some medium sized manufacturers of networking systems have decided they cannot afford direct sales forces, and therefore sell only through indirect channels. Taking a fairly typical example again, Proteon, which manufactures products such as routers for LAN interconnection, has a few key first-line distributors some of whom rebadge the products with their own logo. These distributors in turn may have both direct and indirect channels of sale by which they reach the market. Although they distribute Proteon's products, these distributors may also manufacture other products of their own. In fact it is quite common for manufacturers of LAN systems to distribute products from other vendors as well as their own to fill gaps in their catalogue, so that they can offer complete networking solutions.

Authorized dealers and value added resellers

Vendors of network operating systems (NOS) also sell through dealers and value added resellers. Such dealers will sell copies of the NOS by itself, but some specialize in complete solutions, including PCs, for customers that do not have these already. They may, for example, be dealers for Novell NetWare and at the same time for PC manufacturers such as IBM, Dell and Compaq, as well as for LAN components like NICs (network interface cards).

From the viewpoint of manufacturers of LAN components, such dealers lie at the end of their distribution channel. The dealers themselves represent a number of different component suppliers, and in most cases see their role as being suppliers of complete IT solutions. But the extent of their coverage varies.

Identifying the right supplier is difficult

Some dealers cover the whole LAN including PCs, but do not get involved in application software. Therefore a customer wanting to computerize its business at a stroke would need to find alternative suppliers of database software, if they need a database, and for applications such as accounting that would run across the LAN. However, some dealers, as we noted earlier, offer complete computing applications, of which the LAN is the underlying platform.

Given the complexity involved in setting up a network complete with applications from scratch, it may be tempting to go for a single supplier that promises to shoulder the whole job. Unfortunately not all suppliers that profess to have all the relevant skills actually possess them. Again, it comes down to a judgement of the competence of the supplier. However, judging a supplier can be difficult for a firm that has no great experience in dealing with IT matters. One way out is to appoint consultants with well-established practices in IT to take over the project and be responsible for choosing suppliers. The cost of doing this needs to be balanced against the reduced risks and savings made through having the project controlled by people who, hopefully, know what they are doing.

7

Dealers authorized by NOS vendors are worth considering

For the NOS in particular, dealers authorized by the vendor are worth considering. Both Novell and Microsoft have élite dealers, sometimes described as systems houses, that undergo extra training and vetting. They are supposed to provide greater expertise than average high-street dealers. These systems houses will also be expert in other aspects of LAN installation and support.

The NOS vendors themselves will be able to supply you with a list of authorized dealers in your area, and may be able to indicate which are most appropriate for your requirements. Although these élite dealers will not always be superior, they should be given preferential consideration, particularly for larger networks.

In general you should scrutinize dealers closely, and quiz them about their level of expertise. Ask to speak to qualified staff about your requirements, and base your judgement on how satisfied you are with the response. Unfortunately dealers can obtain certification without extensive qualifications from NOS vendors, after undergoing a fairly rudimentary training course. So it is worth approaching dealers with an open but sceptical mind.

In general it is worth paying for a reasonable level of support, unless there is someone in your business already fairly expert at LAN installation and ongoing management.

LANs are more complicated than stand-alone PCs: more can go wrong, and the value of good support from vendors is correspondingly greater. It may be possible to obtain substantial discounts on the NOS, for example, but support will probably be poorer as a result.

Solution should be driven by business requirements

In some cases it may not be obvious what type of network is best suited to the requirements you have. Some companies may not even be sure if they need a network at all. Others may not be able to judge clearly between several alternative solutions. For example, it may not be apparent whether to go for token ring, Ethernet, or even some other LAN topology such as Arcnet. It may not be clear which NOS suits your needs best. Or there may be uncertainty whether to go for a peer-to-peer configuration, or one based on dedicated server operation, or a combination of both.

However, you should at least have a clear idea about the business objectives your network is expected to meet. A clear set of business objectives can be turned into a broad outline of the type of network and applications you need. This outline should consider the basic applications needed and the number of users the network will have to support. It should also consider requirements to access information throughout your organization, which may be a trivial matter for a small firm, but will require considerable thought for a workgroup within a large company. The plan should also take account of anticipated changes in requirements in the foreseeable future. Some of the basic questions that such an outline plan should answer are listed in Table 7.2.

Such an outline can be presented to potential suppliers, who can then come up with a detailed proposal of a network designed to meet these requirements. These proposals may differ. For example, some suppliers may propose a peer-to-peer network, while others put forward a more centralized server-based LAN. Others again may even propose a solution based on a minicomputer linked to dumb terminals rather than PCs.

The suppliers can then be judged on the strength of these proposals alongside whatever references they have provided. Perhaps

Table 7.2   Some basic issues that should be addressed in an outline plan for a LAN.

1 Total number of users, both now and in the future.

2 What applications are needed to implement now, and in the foreseeable future. These may include word processing, accounting, financial planning, electronic mail and other office applications. There may also be a need for remote communications to access public online services or other systems within your organization.

3 How the applications relate to users. In particular users can be split into different workgroups, each of which requires only some of the applications. Establish whether the workgroups need to communicate with each other via electronic mail.

4 Having established a basic logical structure of the network based on workgroups and applications, this needs to be turned into a physical diagram related to where the users are actually located in the building. From this a rough idea of cabling requirements can be obtained.

5 Users will differ in the load they and their applications make on the network. Some profile of each user's activity will help establish how much capacity needs to be provided. In most cases this will affect not the physical network itself, but the PCs and any servers attached to the network. For example, with PCs attached to a network the main factors influencing performance are the processor and the main memory. Disk performance on the other hand is more important on the server. However, on a peer-to-peer LAN, where as explained in Chapter 4 desktop PCs may also be non-dedicated servers, disk performance is likely to be important on all PCs. But it will be especially important on machines that are designated as non-dedicated servers and, therefore, shared by other users.

7

some of the suppliers have met similar business requirements at other sites, in which case you may be able to judge how well the reality matched the promises.

Evaluating proposals

It is not much use seeking competitive proposals from suppliers or consultants unless you have some idea how to differentiate between them. That is why it may be worth hiring a consultant experienced in the field to assess other proposals. On a large project it may even be worth having one consultant assessing other consultants, provided you can be sure they are not from related companies.

But the first step is to establish a clear request for proposals (RFP) that sets out succinctly what the project involves. For relatively small-scale networks of the sort primarily addressed by this book, it is not necessary to invest substantial time developing a massive RFP. An example of a typical RFP is given in the concluding chapter which considers a fictitious case study summarizing the key points of this book.

When evaluating proposals, the first step is to eliminate proposals that obviously come from vendors unable to supply the products you want. For example, if you specified a token ring-based solution and the proposal cites Ethernet, the vendor either has not read your RFP or else cannot meet your requirements. In either case the vendor should be discarded.

Importance of adhering to standards

Other technical points include adherence to standards. Solutions that include proprietary components should not necessarily be ruled out, depending on what they are and on whether you plan to expand your network in the near future. But virtually all networks will change at some point, and if they are based on proprietary standards for management or communication, it will be harder to expand or change without scrapping existing components. In general, therefore, suppliers that propose proprietary products should at least have a firm commitment to migrate to accepted standards in future. This should be written into the contract.

Price is not the only factor

Pricing is naturally important, although cost should be balanced against the nature of the proposal. The first step is to ensure that the proposal has been costed accurately and that prices reflect the actual task in hand. For example, a proposal might sound cheap because cabling installation costs, which usually account for a substantial proportion of an overall LAN installation, have been omitted.

When considering proposals, relative costs and technical merits are not the only points to bear in mind. Equally important is the nature of the supplier and its reputation. For a substantial project, suppliers that have limited resources or appear to be financially insecure may not be suitable, even if their proposals look sound and cost less than rival ones. We expand on the question of vetting suppliers later in the chapter.

Another point to consider is that big suppliers may not be best for relatively small projects. It is best to have a match between supplier and project, where each is important to the other.

Two examples of selection process

In the first case (company A), a network is required in a large warehouse enabling staff to access screens to find where particular stock items are located. In this case a LAN may not be the ideal solution for several reasons. One, there is no requirement to share data between users. More importantly all users have identical requirements, to access the same application, and there is no need to access external systems. Furthermore, the distances involved may be too great for LANs based on low-cost cabling, unless repeaters are used to boost the signal, adding to the cost of the network. In this case there is no real advantage in having a LAN at all.

An alternative solution is to use products that turn a relatively low-cost PC into a multi-user system serving either other PCs or more likely dumb terminals. If the requirement is just to look up stock items, there is no need for the power of a PC for users, and lower-cost dumb terminals can be used instead. There are several companies offering products that can support applications such as this in which standard PCs drive a number of dumb terminals, without requiring a LAN. Alternatively a traditional minicomputer could be used, but a standard PC may well be able to fulfil the same function more cheaply.

Standard cabling structures can still be used, with the possibility of connecting with LANs elsewhere within the organization. Figure 7.1 shows a network in which a standard PC is linked to several distant controllers that could be up to perhaps 1000 metres away. These controllers could be located at suitable points in the warehouse, and around each of these are small clusters of dumb terminals. Several suppliers offer solutions of this type, which may be worth considering as alternatives to LANs. However, it is important to ensure that such solutions do not restrict future options, and do not lock you in to a particular supplier.

Indeed a LAN could be used for such an application, and may be preferred if the system needs to link with other LANs within the

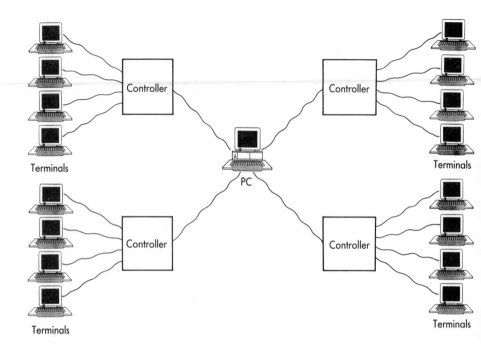

Figure 7.1   An alternative to a LAN, in which a standard PC runs applications accessed by dumb terminals. This is more like a traditional host computer set-up. The links from the PC to the controllers could run across a large site such as a warehouse, at distances up to 1000 metres typically. Alternatively they could in some cases be extended via telecommunications links. The terminals would, however, have to be within 100 metres at most of the controllers.

same building. The fact is that LANs have become a standard building block of large networks, so they may be installed even when they do not appear to be the best solution to current requirements.

In the second case, a publishing company (B) wants a computer system for its editorial department producing a weekly magazine, with the ability to link with other systems in the building. The aim is to enable reporters and feature writers to produce copy on screen, and pass it across to sub-editors (called copy editors in the US) for editing. At the same time other editors will sometimes want to access work in progress.

This is a classic workgroup situation, in which files, in this case editorial copy, are passed between users. Furthermore, different users have different needs. Reporters need a powerful word processing system. Copy editors may need this too, but also require a system for inputting the instructions to printers or typesetters. Other editors may want to annotate copy with their comments, without necessarily changing the content. Therefore, not all users want to run the same software, which makes the application less suited to a centralized multi-user system such as the one recommended for company A.

On the other hand, a single dedicated server holding files of finished articles may well be required, along with the ability to exchange files between users. Several possible configurations might be recommended, but there is a strong case for a LAN. It does not really matter whether it is Ethernet or token ring. However, if other departments in the building have, say, token ring LANs with corporate applications based on an IBM mainframe, it may well be wise, although not essential, to seek a token ring solution. But more important is that the LAN chosen, and the NOS driving it, should support interconnection with other LANs via bridges or routers, given the need to communicate with other departments.

These points should be considered before seeking proposals from potential suppliers. Then the solutions on offer can be judged on their relative merits, in the knowledge that they should at least fulfil the fundamental requirements.

7

Supplier considerations

Small networks of 1-10 users

In other chapters we have discussed the pros and cons of the key LAN types, NOSs and cabling structures. These need all to be considered together when choosing a LAN. When choosing small networks, you are more likely to have a clear idea of the type of network you want, as the options are fewer. The following key questions should be posed.

(1) What applications will I be running, and how many users will need access to each one? How much data will each application require? How much network traffic will each generate?

(2) How many users does the LAN need to support altogether? Will they all be located in the same room, or will they be scattered around a building or site?

(3)   What other networks do I need to connect my LAN to, if any? If I do not need to connect to any others now, am I likely to need to do so in the near future?

(4)   What other future changes are likely? Is my LAN going to support a growing number of users over time, or is it likely to remain fairly static? Will it have to support new applications that increase the traffic load on the network? What types of computer will need to be connected?

The answers to these questions will narrow the range of potentially suitable products. Suppose, for example, that although the network currently only needs to support six users, it is likely to expand quickly to bring on another 18 users within the year. This means that if, for example, you choose a hub-based solution, as discussed in Chapter 3, the hub must be capable of supporting up to at least 24 users, preferably more. Also, with over 12 users it will be desirable that the hub supports network management, even though this may not be necessary for six users.

Equally important is that the NOS can support the extra users. Some NOSs, such as NetWare Lite, are designed purely for small workgroups and are meant to be replaced as the number of users approaches 20. Many of the NOSs such as LANtastic aimed particularly at small networks can handle larger numbers of users. But in many cases performance degrades significantly when the number of users exceeds 20. However, there are some NOSs that support small numbers of users and that also perform well for quite large networks of 100 or 200 users.

Most NOSs have been evaluated in benchmark tests by various computer or networking magazines. When assessing the options, it may be worth asking to see reviews as well as seeking reference sites where networks of similar size have been installed.

In some cases the ability to expand significantly will not be a factor. Then choice of NOS can be made on other criteria, such as price and performance for small numbers of users. This may leave two or three candidates. You can then seek quotes from dealers of these particular NOSs. These dealers may also be able to provide the rest of your network. Alternatively, you may wish to have a cabling system installed by a specialist company, or you may wish to go to a larger supplier that can offer a choice between a variety of NOSs.

Having installed a LAN, there can be problems in getting applications to work on the network. Although a growing number of applications are 'network aware' in the sense that they can function correctly when accessing data from a server across a LAN, many are still not. It may be that you have existing applications running on single PCs which you want to transfer to your LAN after it is installed. This should work, but cannot be guaranteed. So if, for example, you have elected to have cabling installed by a specialist supplier with no expertise in software and then bought the remaining components as commodity items, you may be in trouble.

For this reason there are a growing number of LAN specialists setting up in business to provide consultancy for smaller networks. It may be wise to hire such a consultant to oversee your installation. This would not preclude the involvement of specialist suppliers, but means there is someone responsible for ensuring that all the components, including applications, work together. For the smallest networks, on the other hand, the involvement of an independent consultant is neither necessary nor cost justifiable. The simplest LANs, for example, involve just two users, such as an executive and secretary, where the latter's machine runs as a non-dedicated server. In such cases there is probably no need for a specialist cabling supplier, as the LAN can by set up just be connecting the two PCs together with a standard piece of coaxial cable. Then if the LAN needs to grow, a more organized cabling system may be considered later.

7

Medium sized LANs 11-49 users

As the number of users rises above ten, performance considerations are likely to become increasingly important. You are not likely to consider some of the bottom-end NOSs at this level, especially as the price of the NOS is usually very small compared to that of the whole network. And depending on the applications, there may be reasons for preferring a particular LAN type, as discussed in Chapter 2.

Another point to consider, more probably for larger LANs in this category, is segmenting the LAN to reduce overall traffic levels and thereby increase performance. The role of local bridges and routers in segmenting LANs for performance reasons is discussed in Chapter 10.

Another key factor is the physical size of the LAN. As discussed in Chapter 10, LANs based on unshielded twisted pair are limited in range. For example, with 10Base-T the maximum distance between the hub and each device is 100 metres, which is sufficient to span most floors and many buildings, but not if the LAN extends across a larger site. A 10Base-T solution can still be used where some devices are more than 100 metres away from the hub, but requires some back-bone network or cabling to extend the range.

As discussed in Chapter 3, coaxial or fibre optic cable can be used to extend the range of a 10Base-T network. There can either be a separate backbone network, based for example on FDDI, or if the requirement is just to extend the LAN to a handful of more distant devices, a single piece of cable can be used.

Potential suppliers can be judged on the way they approach such problems. Different solutions may be proposed and can be judged against the criteria you have now. It may be that you are prepared, and can afford, to pay more than the minimum required to solve your immediate problem. The more expensive solutions are not always the best, but on the other hand the cheapest may cost you dear over a longer period. If the solution you have adopted cannot accommodate future expansion, you may have to write off your investment and start again.

However, it is worth noting that in the case of software such as the NOS, it is not always wrong to ditch current products and start again, provided the supplier offers a smooth and economical upgrade path. Sometimes, as with Novell products, it is possible to have your existing product coexist with the more powerful one you are migrating to. This means you can gradually phase out the old product and fur-thermore, if the supplier allows you to trade in the old one and obtain a generous discount off the new one, then the fact that you have to move to a different system may not matter too much.

The situation is different with hardware. Hubs, for example, can often be expanded by cascading them together, as shown in Figure 7.2. But there is usually a limit to the maximum number of devices that can be supported in this way. To exceed this limit, you have to move to a new hub and write off the cost of the old one. In this case any trade-in is not likely to be so generous.

Beware of charlatans

The middle sized network sector is particularly exposed to vendors making promises they cannot meet. No vendor likes to turn down business, and some are tempted to install networks larger than they can cope with, when they are only really capable of dealing with small LANs. With larger LANs there are new issues such as performance and network management that require considerable expertise. If you are unsure that a prospective vendor has the right qualities, you can say "Where's the beef?", and ask them to furnish examples of

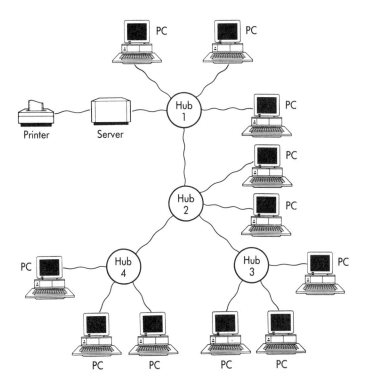

Figure 7.2 How hubs can be expanded by cascading them together. In this particular example, a hub with four ports has been attached to other hubs of the same type to support 11 PCs plus a server.

7

similar sized networks they have previously installed before making a decision.

Of course, there has to be a first time for every vendor. But such a vendor should be open about its lack of experience and perhaps offer a reduced price, rather like suppliers have beta test sites that cut the teeth of a new product in return for significant discounts and perhaps free technical support.

Alternatively, if you have already decided on key products, such as the NOS, you can seek advice from the ultimate suppliers. For example, if you elect to go with NetWare, you can ask Novell to recommend a suitable NetWare dealer or reseller in your area. That also gives you some extra leverage if things go wrong and the dealer fails to come up to scratch as you can always raise the matter with Novell.

In fact NetWare is available not just through Novell's own

distribution channels but through those of other large IT vendors as well. IBM and NCR, for example, sell and support NetWare through their channels.

Large networks

A network can be large by geographical spread, or by the number of users it supports. It can comprise many small geographically remote LANs, or a single large network on one site or within a single building, or it can be a combination of both. Our interest here concerns single purchases of a network supporting 50 or more devices. The LAN may stand on its own or be an extension of an existing network that already supports a substantial number of users.

As with medium sized networks, performance, reliability and network management are important issues, only more so. And a growing concern with larger networks is security, to prevent data being corrupted either deliberately or accidentally, and to minimize the risk of unauthorized access to systems.

Table 7.3 summarizes the key issues that need to be considered when buying a larger network. The ability to support protocols already used elsewhere in the organization is likely to be a requirement, as is the need to be compatible with other systems and LANs.

Even more care needs to be paid to the cabling system that underlies the network, as mistakes are harder and more costly to rectify on a large network. Also, it may be more difficult to predict how much capacity will be needed over the next few years. Issues involved in ensuring that networks are as proof as possible against the future are discussed in the next chapter. The point here is that you need suppliers who understand the issues and can recommend appropriate solutions. It may be desirable with a large network to have a specialist company install the cabling, to ensure that the network is as flexible as possible. It may well be that a whole floor or even building needs to be cabled, making it imperative that the network can accommodate relocations of individual staff or even whole workgroups, and also that it can support emerging LAN technologies.

One of the most popular structured cabling systems is AT&T's Systimax (previously known as Premises Distribution System), which we discussed in Chapter 3. This is based on unshielded twisted pair cable and provides a sound base for expansion. If you decide to go for PDS, it is important to choose a cable installer approved by AT&T. For very large networks, it may be worth involving AT&T

Table 7.3 Summarizing key issues that need to be considered when buying a large network.

---

1 Cabling system needs extra careful consideration, to ensure that it provides sufficient physical coverage to reach all users and that it is manageable.

2 Care must be taken to ensure that the network is compatible with other systems already established in the organization, and that it supports the relevant protocols.

3 The network may be accessed by users elsewhere in the organization other than those for which it is originally intended. In any case loading on the network is almost sure to increase. Capacity needs to be planned carefully to ensure that the network can cope with future expansion, but without unnecessary over-investment.

4 Security is more important than on smaller networks. If external access is going to be allowed via public dial-up networks, extra protection, such as dial-back security, may be desirable. Just as important as such absolute protection is multi-level security to discriminate between legitimate users. Some information may be sensitive for access only by selected senior managers. Security is discussed in Chapter 10.

5 Extra care needs to be taken in choosing suppliers on a large network. The consequences of choosing a supplier that goes out of business, or a product that restricts future choice or change, is more serious.

---

itself to ensure that all components of the cabling system conform with Systimax standards.

Having established a sound cabling infrastructure, it is important to ensure that all the higher-level components work together and also integrate smoothly with other elements of any existing network. There are suppliers, often called systems integrators, that specialize in building complete IT solutions of which the whole network is just a part. The major computer vendors such as IBM, Digital Equipment, Hewlett Packard and AT&T all have systems integration units that can put together complete solutions, and also if required take care of cabling. However, they will naturally be biased towards their own products. They are therefore only worth considering if you have decided that some of their products are suitable for your network. There are also some relatively independent systems integrators that offer mostly networking products from other manufacturers.

Trends in network supply

During the early 1990s the network has increasingly been regarded as part of the overall IT solution. The term network computing has become popular to describe applications in which different computers cooperate in an overall task. In Chapter 1 we described client/server computing while in Appendix 3 we shall look at cooperative processing. These both involve participation of two or more computers in a single overall application.

This trend has had a major impact on the way IT systems are supplied and supported. There has been a spate of mergers and cooperative agreements between vendors that previously supplied just computers and those that specialized in networks.

For example, IBM now sells NetWare as part of its complete network computing solutions. Many PC manufacturers now sell their systems automatically configured to operate over a network. With the advent of single-chip LAN controllers, for example, it is becoming possible to produce PCs that will automatically attach to a LAN. Furthermore, a growing number of application software products such as spreadsheets and word processors are now 'network aware', so that they will operate in client/server networks without requiring additional software.

The consequence is that total networking solutions can be obtained from a wide variety of sources. It is important to choose a supplier that you consider is strong in the required areas. For example, a PC supplier may not have the expertise to help you manage your network or cope with the issues involved in establishing a complex mesh of interconnected LANs.

Another development linking computers with the network between them is the convergence between the NOS and computer operating systems, as we discussed in Chapter 4. Operating systems such as Windows NT and OS/2 now contain many of the ingredients of a NOS. This makes it possible to buy single operating systems that embrace both the computer and the network. Also, network management is becoming more closely integrated with computer system management. The only separate networking issue that needs to be considered when looking for a LAN supplier then becomes the cabling system, which remains an area of expertise quite distinct from computers and applications software.

Other considerations

Stability of suppliers

It is common practice when placing a contract to ascertain that potential suppliers are financially stable as well as technically sound. Even for smaller networks, the results of a supplier going bust can be serious, as it may leave the user without any support. Sometimes the supplier will be bought by another company that will take over maintenance contracts, but a number of firms in the cabling and LAN business vanish almost without trace.

Several prominent and well-respected networking consulting firms in the US and UK closed down during the early 1990s, leaving some customers with unfinished projects. The costs in terms of disruption and delay to implementation of networks can be serious.

Naturally suppliers will not tell you if they are in serious financial trouble but there are ways now of narrowing the angle. The most recent financial results can be obtained, and there are various databases containing details of credit worthiness and recent performance. Such databases can be accessed via standard public electronic mail networks.

Adherence to open standards

On large networks especially, it is important that your suppliers are committed to existing and emerging open standards. Without such commitment you cannot be confident that your network will be capable of embracing new products and emerging technologies in the future. Note that a bland statement of commitment to standards is not enough. Suppliers should actively participate in conformance tests to demonstrate that their products can actually interoperate with others using open standards. The importance of strong conformance to open standards can be stressed in tender documents for networking projects, as a first line of defence against unfit suppliers.

In Chapter 9 we discuss which standards are relevant for your network.

Ability to support optical fibre networks (not relevant for most smaller networks)

As discussed in Chapter 3, FDDI networks based on fibre optic are increasingly prevalent for backbone networks, and in a few cases to support local LAN traffic right to desktops. Installation of fibre optic networks requires particular care at terminating points, and at junctions where cables are joined together. Furthermore, the network can degrade over time as cables move slightly out of alignment, bringing the risk of data loss or corruption. This means that suppliers should be sought that not only have sufficient expertise to install the network correctly, but that will also make regular maintenance visits.

Optical fibre is an option provided with the main established cabling systems, such as Systimax and the IBM cabling system. Authorized suppliers of such systems should be able to install a fibre network and make regular maintenance visits every six months or so.

Training

The most complex component of smaller networks is the NOS. This after all controls the server, which is the heart of the network, and provides facilities for key functions like backup and control of access to data. From relatively humble beginnings, the NOS has evolved into a sophisticated software product which requires considerable expertise to exploit fully.

For users of smaller LANs with less than 25 nodes the NOS is therefore the most important component of the network in which to receive training. In fact some training courses based on the leading NOSs will also embrace other aspects of LANs such as network management. For larger networks there are in any case numerous higher-level courses that focus on LAN interconnection via bridges and routers, interfacing LANs with mainframes, enterprise-wide network design and other topics well beyond the needs of most smaller businesses.

Who provides training courses?

The two leading NOS vendors, Microsoft and Novell, both authorize education centres that provide a range of courses related to their respective systems. In Novell's case some of these are distributors, of which there are three or four in the UK. In addition there are several specialist training companies approved by Novell, which provide courses in NetWare in addition to other aspects of networking and computing. These specialist training companies also have to be approved by Novell, but may equally be approved by other vendors to give courses relating to their products. Novell itself gives courses to the trainers at its own education centre, but does not directly train end customers.

Microsoft has a similar approach to training. Courses are taught by Microsoft-approved training centres at selected locations around the country.

Other NOS vendors have less organized course structures, in some cases providing training through dealers and distributors. In most cases the NOS vendors should be able to point you towards suitable courses in your area.

What sort of courses are available?

Courses on Microsoft's LAN Manager can be categorized in ascending order of difficulty. The most basic covers planning, configuration and administration of a LAN, embracing routine tasks such as backup and network monitoring. Next up the scale comes a course in installation and more detailed management for those who have already sat the first course or gained appropriate experience. Then there are some more advanced courses covering connectivity and integration into wide area networks, and more sophisticated tuning of a network to optimize performance.

For NetWare there is a wider range of courses available, because Novell has been at the game longer than Microsoft and has a much larger customer base. Courses range from a basic one day introduction to networking and NetWare, to more advanced but still general courses lasting several days on NetWare management service and support. Then there are more specialized courses not relevant to all users in areas such as NetWare TCP/IP, which deals with maintaining NetWare networks running TCP/IP protocols.

Who should receive training?

Training courses are expensive, measured not just in the upfront cost but also the staff time lost. It is, therefore, important that training should be focused where it is needed. Then the investment in time and money will be more than recouped through greater staff productivity and avoidance of mistakes that are themselves costly to rectify.

Generally, businesses installing a LAN for the first time should put at least two people through a basic course covering the NOS and fundamentals of LAN operation. These two can then teach others how to perform straightforward LAN operations and users should be able to take off from there, with the aid of manuals where necessary.

In many cases, however, it is a good idea to have someone with a higher level of technical expertise to act as a fount of knowledge and assistance embracing all aspects of the particular LAN installation. Free telephone support may be available from a supplier, but this may only cover part of the whole picture. Generally the larger and more complex the network, the less you can rely totally on an external supplier to provide universal support and help.

An exception is where a large network has been handed over to an external supplier under an outsourcing contract. In this case that supplier has total responsibility for providing a full networking service. But otherwise it is important that someone within your organization has sufficient all round knowledge to determine broadly the nature of any problem and know which supplier to call to fix it.

For a typical LAN with 12 users, it may be sufficient to have someone trained to intermediate level on the NOS, sitting a course lasting perhaps three days. For larger networks it will be a matter of deciding which courses are relevant. Where there are several remote LANs interconnected by routers, for example, it may make sense to send your leading network administrator or engineer on a course covering LAN internetworking.

Other sources of information: User groups and bulletin boards

Apart from training, ongoing information about the LAN can be obtained from two main sources: user groups and bulletin boards.

User groups are a valuable source of solutions to practical problems and tips that you may not obtain from a formal training course. Also, as new revisions of key software, in particular the NOS, are released, new problems and issues arise. Within a user group there will often be someone who has already experienced and solved a problem that has just struck you.

User groups evolve around particular vendors of hardware or software, or around a specific well-established product like Microsoft Windows. There may be several relevant user groups, possibly one for your NOS, one for your PC, and others for applications software such as word processing and spreadsheets.

It may not be necessary to join all of them: the NOS group will cover most aspects of LAN operation, for example. Vendors or dealers should be able to put you in touch with relevant user groups.

Electronic bulletin boards that can be dialled up from a PC are another useful source of information, particularly about widely used products such as NetWare. Like user groups, they can provide information about fixes to bugs in a new release of software and tips that may help you exploit some of the less well-known features of a product.

Bulletin boards also provide a wide variety of other information, including details of courses, products for sale, and relevant news items in a particular field. Bulletin boards are available on well-known public electronic mail or information networks such as Compuserve, CIX and BT Dialcom's services (Telecom Gold in the UK). These include bulletin boards that deal specifically with popular LAN and PC products. For example, on both CIX and Compuserve there is a NetWare bulletin board, on which Novell itself displays information about new products or solutions to particular problems. Subscribers can also display information freely, with the only cost being the online charge of the particular service.

Novell has also launched a dedicated information service called NetWare Express, which has various bulletin board features. This is available worldwide on GE Information Services' BusinessTalk System 2000 electronic mail and bulletin board service. It provides access to sales and marketing data pertaining to NetWare, complementing already existing bulletin board services offering mainly technical information. It can be used to order some lower-cost NetWare products and utilities.

A possible criticism of bulletin boards is that they appeal most to enthusists, with the material often haphazard and poorly laid out. But for people familar with using them, they provide a congenial way of keeping abreast in general with the given specialist field.

7

Summary

We have now covered the non-technical issues in choosing suppliers. The next chapter draws this together with the all-important question of how your network is likely to evolve in future. Clearly suppliers that are here today but gone tomorrow are not going to help your network the day after that.

8

How do I design my
network so that it will last
and can be easily
extended?

CHAPTER CONTENTS

CHAPTER OBJECTIVES

This chapter returns to topics discussed in earlier chapters,
looking at how they interrelate from the point of view of
expandability. The role of the following factors is considered:

Finally we consider from the point of view of expandability
whether the traditional mini might not after all be superior.

Introduction

The general answer is to choose LAN components, particularly cabling and the network operating system (NOS), that provide plenty of flexibility and scope for growth. The requirement may not be just to support growing numbers of users, but also to cope with increasing network traffic, new applications and different protocols. It may also be necessary to connect with other LANs and remote computer systems via telecommunications links. Another vital ingredient of networks that are built to last and be expanded is that their components conform as far as possible to universal standards. The role of standards is discussed in Chapter 9, but is also touched on where relevant in the rest of this chapter. At the end of the chapter we discuss the principal alternative to LANs, minicomputers, from the standpoint of expandability.

NOS is crucial

The role of the NOS in expandability is crucial. The NOS is the least expensive part of the network, yet the wrong one can severely hamper future growth. Therefore it is important to select one with a good record for provision of upgrades and compatibility with previous versions. The NOS vendor should also have a proven record for development and evolution of products. This tends to limit the choice to just a handful of leading vendors.

The questions of durability and extendability are closely related in that a network that cannot support growth and has to be replaced obviously has a limited life span. If a network has not been designed to support increasing traffic, both performance and reliability will begin to degrade with time. The other aspect of durability is related to the quality of the components, the way the network has been built, and how well it is maintained. The importance of finding suppliers that will provide adequate ongoing support and backup is discussed in Chapter 7. Then the role of good management in ensuring that the network continues to provide high levels of service to its users is dealt with in Chapter 10.

In this chapter we discuss the issue of future proofing for each of the relevant LAN components. For this purpose we recognize four elements: cabling, including hubs; LAN servers, which can be either dedicated or non-dedicated or a combination of both; the NOS; and finally the LAN type. The ability to access other networks is also important; this is covered in the discussion of these four elements. Another important aspect of LAN growth is segmentation of the network to minimize overall traffic levels. The actual process of segmentation is really an ongoing management function, and is therefore discussed in Chapter 10. However, it is important to ensure that the cabling system, hub and NOS will support the division of LANs into segments, and so we touch on that aspect in the relevant parts of this chapter.

Cabling and hubs

Even for small networks the cost of installation is usually significantly greater than that of the cable itself. Similarly the cost of altering a cable network to cater for change, especially if this needs to be done repeatedly over time, may exceed the entire cost of the cabling hardware. It is therefore worth taking some trouble and spending some money on ensuring that the network originally installed will cater for as many users as can be physically accommodated in that particular office space.

From the user's perspective the principle is similar to the electricity supply, in that it should be possible to plug a PC or other computing device directly into the network from any desk position. However, unlike the electricity supply, it is not usually possible to attach more than one device to a single outlet. Hence, it is important not only that outlets are reachable via a short lead from all potential desk positions, but also that there are at least as many outlets as there are users.

Table 8.1 summarizes the features that need to be considered when installing a cable network. Another consideration is the type of cable itself, where the general principle is to choose as good a grade as you can afford: the higher the grade, the greater its potential capacity. We noted in Chapter 3 that advances in transmission

Table 8.1   Features to consider when installing a cable network.

1 Cable type should be capable of supporting the type of LAN you want over the required distances. For small workgroups or businesses unshielded twisted pair copper is usually recommended. But if you anticipate a need to support higher data rates to the desk, for example 100 Mbit/s, shielded twisted pair should be considered. And for distances greater than around 100 metres, coaxial cable, or fibre optic will be required. The latter is becoming a standard for backbone networks interconnecting different LANs across a large building or campus.

2 The cable network should not restrict relocations of staff within the office or building. In some cases an office will be flood wired, so that access points to the cable network are as frequent as power sockets. At any rate care needs to be taken to match the cabling to anticipated location of network users.

3 Except for very small networks, the cabling should be structured, which makes it easier to manage and maintain. Large networks should be based on a recognized cabling scheme such as Systimax (previously known as Premises Distribution System (PDS)). This ensures that standard cabling products and procedures can be used.

4 When the network spans more than one floor, the cable network should be split into separate vertical and horizontal components. In some cases different cable will be used for each of these. For example, optical fibre may be used for the vertical, and unshielded twisted pair copper for the horizontal. Care should be taken in location of both vertical and horizontal cabling. For example, vertical risers should if possible be distributed across different parts of the building to reduce risk of the network being severed by a localized accident.

5 The structure of the horizontal cabling should be related to the proposed computer and network equipment. For example, you may decide to install composite server/hubs (described in Chapter 3). In this case the cabling will need to be star shaped, radiating out from some central point. It may be desirable to have enclosed closets to house the server/hub, with cabling fanning out from the closet to sockets on the floor.

technology are increasing the amount of data that can be sent along cable of various types, but the ratio between the actual capacities of different types of cable tends to remain constant.

Table 8.2 shows the prevailing capacities of the major cable types in 1992. Note that transmission rates always decrease with distance. This means that there is a limit to the distance over which any cable type can sustain a given transmission speed. For example, 10Base-T networks based on unshielded twisted pair (utp) cable operate at 10 Mbit/s, but only at distances up to 100 metres. Fibre on the other hand will support 100 Mbit/s for much greater distances. Furthermore, fibre has the potential to transmit at even greater distances and speeds in future.

For this reason some sites that have the luxury of comfortable

Table 8.2 Capacities of main types of cable used in LANs.

Cable type	Distance	Transmission speed
Unshielded twisted pair (standard data grade)	100 m	10 Mbit/s
Unshielded twisted pair (high grade)	100 m	16 Mbit/s
Shielded twisted pair	100 m	100 Mbit/s
Optical fibre	100 km	100 Mbit/s

1. Distance and transmission capacity have a reverse relationship: the greater the distance, the slower the transmission speed. You will notice for example that while the speed we have quoted for optical fibre is the same as for unshielded twisted pair, the distance is 1000 times as great.
2. The examples we have given are somewhat arbitrary and are not absolute. Technical improvements in the equipment used to transmit data across the media means that speeds are constantly improving. So although for example we have cited 16 Mbit/s as the limit for high grade unshielded twisted pair over 100 metres, it will soon be possible to reach 100 Mbit/s in favourable environmental conditions.

budgets and long distance networking vision have installed fibre networks right to the desk even when they do not yet require the capacity. In the short term this involves unnecessary expense. But over time it is likely to save money provided it is fairly certain that fibre optic cable will be needed at some time in the future. For most smaller businesses this is unlikely, given the increasing capacities of copper networks, and in any case most will not be able to afford it. However, as costs of attaching to fibre continue to fall, it will become viable for more companies.

A cheaper option than fibre is shielded twisted pair (stp). As discussed in Chapter 3, both stp and utp can now extend FDDI networks to the desktop at 100 Mbit/s for short distances. However, stp has so far proved more reliable, having less problem with electromagnetic interference. Therefore the extra expense may be worthwhile for networks that are likely to transmit substantial amounts of data in future. This includes networks supporting applications in computer-aided design and modelling, and in multimedia where audio and video signals also need to be transported. However, where the requirement for as far into the future as it is possible to see is only for standard business and office applications such as word processing and accounting, utp will almost certainly be quite adequate for final distribution to desktops, always going for as high a grade as the budget will allow.

However, where the network has to span different floors, or various offices in a building, some backbone cabling will be required, because individual cable segments may exceed 100 metres in length. As discussed in Chapter 3, this can either be coaxial cable or fibre optic, with the latter increasingly being preferred, especially in locations such as lift shafts where there is considerable electromagnetic interference. Where it is just a matter of connecting two or three floors, individual LANs on each floor can often be interconnected with a single piece of backbone cable. Typically each LAN is connected to the backbone via routers or bridges that are either integral to or connected to cabling hubs on each floor. A typical arrangement is shown in Figure 8.1. Such an arrangement will provide plenty of room for traffic growth provided the overall physical shape of the network does not change much.

Additional cabling consideration for large networks

On larger distributed sites, however, there is an additional consideration. When several local LANs are being interconnected over a large site such as a university campus, the backbone also has to be well structured. The prevailing standard for backbone networks is FDDI.

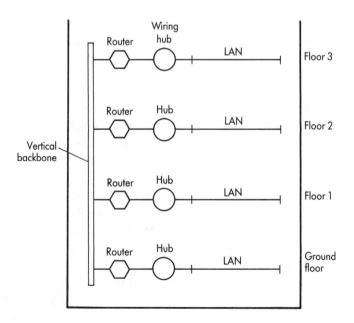

Figure 8.1 LANs on different floors of a building interconnected by vertical backbone cable.

In some cases a site may not need, or have the budget, for, a complete FDDI network. But given the growing consensus behind FDDI as the protocol for high-speed LANs, it may be worth installing your network now in such a way that a migration to FDDI in future will be as straightforward as possible. To achieve this, cable has to be installed in the FDDI structure even though it will not yet support FDDI protocols. Essentially this means laying a double ring of fibre, although as we pointed out in Chapter 3 this does not necessarily imply that the network looks physically like a ring. The expense of installing two rings rather than one will not be significant compared with the labour costs of installing the cable in the first place. More to the point, such costs are insignificant compared with future costs that may be incurred if the initial cabling network requires alteration. The golden rule with cabling is to look as many years ahead as you can afford. Even if FDDI does not really take off, or if it is quickly superseded by new technologies, it is still worth adopting FDDI-like cabling structures.

Hub considerations

As we saw in Chapter 3, cabling hubs are becoming increasingly popular. Even for small LANs there are plenty to choose from. One reason for their proliferation is that hubs make it easier to design and manage cable networks. Ideally a cable network will satisfy your requirements for the foreseeable future, as we explained in the last section.

But it is not always possible to anticipate the future completely, and sometimes a cabling system will need to be expanded or altered. In this the role of the hub is crucial. Most hubs have a maximum number of devices that they can support.

What are the main hub options?

It is worth noting at this stage that the hub market roughly splits into three parts. First, there are relatively low-cost hubs for Ethernet and token ring LANs, typically without any management facilities. Then there are larger more expandable hubs with management facilities, but still dedicated to a particular LAN type such as Ethernet. Third, there are sophisticated hubs that support both Ethernet and token ring, with the ability to interconnect the two via bridging or routing modules, as discussed in Chapter 6. For the majority of readers, the lower-cost hubs designed specifically for either Ethernet or token ring, but not both, are likely to be most relevant. However, later in the chapter we indicate where more sophisticated hubs should be considered. For Ethernet, the most widespread type of low-cost hubs are the 10Base-T concentrators, for 10Base-T networks running over unshielded twisted pair cable. For token ring, low-cost hubs are either MAUs (media access units), or CAUs (concentrator access units). These are all described in Chapter 3.

It is important to choose a hub that can be expanded to support the number of devices you will need in your workgroup, department or building. This calculation is not always easy, and depends on the way your overall network is structured. For example, if you have a building comprising a number of floors, you could well have a separate hub on each floor with each hub linked via some backbone network. On a large site, there may then be a larger backbone concentrating hub acting as the local point of the whole network. Figure 8.2 shows such an arrangement. In this case the backbone hub may provide remote routing or bridging to connect the whole site-wide network to other networks via telecommunications links. Figure 8.3 illustrates schematically how such backbone hubs operate.

Different considerations apply to these backbone hubs with respect to future expansion than to smaller scale hubs for each floor.

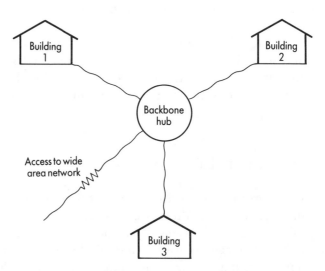

Figure 8.2 Showing backbone hub on a large site, with more than one building. Each building in turn may have smaller hubs for local LANs.

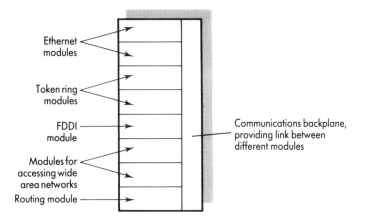

Figure 8.3 Function of backbone hub or Rub. Notes: (1) The Rub may provide bridging or routing functions as part of its internal structure, or these may be supported by additional modules. The Rub in the diagram is of the latter type, with an additional routing module. (2) The structure of different Rubs varies considerably, and the diagram is only intended to serve as a basic guide to the functions provided.

With the latter, choice depends on the size and structure of your network. To discuss some key issues that need to be examined, we will consider three categories of network. First we will look at small LANs that do not need to connect to any other network and will not need to for as far ahead as we can see. Second is individual LANs, typically on a single floor of a building, that may need to connect to other LANs either within the same site, or remote sites, or both.

Third is complete site-wide networks that embrace a number of individual interconnected LANs, such as you find on university campuses or large manufacturing complexes. In fact the hub market has split into three sectors along these lines, with each sector addressing one of the three types of network we have just defined.

Hub considerations for small stand-alone networks of 12 users or less

Early hubs were mostly designed to support either token ring or Ethernet LANs, but not both. Subsequently a number of vendors developed small hubs without any management facilities to keep costs as low as possible. These hubs are aimed specifically at small networks supporting at most 12 users, and in some cases just eight. With this size of network there is no point in paying for sophisticated management facilities. A number of dealers offer such low-cost hubs, from manufacturers such as Hewlett Packard and 3 Com, bundled as part of complete low-cost LAN packages that also incorporate a low-end NOS such as NetWare Lite. Such hubs usually support Ethernet only.

Such solutions are ideal for a small business, providing a tidy solution with limited expansion capability. Generally the hub cannot be expanded beyond 8 or 12 users, so the choice depends on how many users you anticipate your network will need to support over the next few years. It is possible to string such hubs together to support more users. However, with larger networks the lack of management facilities can be a serious handicap with hubs strung together in cascades. If you anticipate expanding beyond 12 users, it is worth investing in a larger, modular, manageable hub, as we describe in the next section.

It is possible to use such manageable hubs for small networks, but they are more expensive. However, another option for smaller networks that does provide some scope for expansion is the card-based hub that slots into a server, as described in Chapter 3. This is an elegant solution for networks that have a central server, which then becomes the focal point for everything: cabling, the NOS, database and any shared applications.

The disadvantage is that you need a NOS, such as NetWare, that supports a card-based hub. On the other hand you have a choice of vendors supplying hub cards. Novell in 1991 published a software specification called Hub Management Interface (HMI), allowing hardware vendors to design cards for the server.

However, card-based solutions are not suitable for larger networks with over 50 users, and are really aimed at LANs with 20 users or less. Given that servers have other functions to support as well, potential for growth is less than with dedicated hubs. Also, as noted in Chapter 3, card-based hubs are not designed for use with structured cabling systems, without which a larger network is harder to manage.

Hub considerations for larger networks on single floors

With larger networks the future becomes less predictable. At this level you want a modular, manageable hub that meets current needs and that appears to have as good a chance as possible of migrating in tune with your network through the addition of new modules. Ideally the hub vendors' development plans should correspond with your own.

On larger networks it may be worth considering so-called smart hubs that support both Ethernet and token ring LANs, with the ability to interconnect the two. For example, you may just need to support Ethernet now, but do not want to rule out a move to token ring in future, or even running separate Ethernet and token ring networks off the same hub. You may find a modular hub that meets all your current requirements, but does not yet have a module for token ring. However if, as usually will be the case, the vendor is developing a token ring module, and can convince you that it will be available well before you will need it, then it is probably worth going for.

One point to note is that modules are proprietary to the hub. The situation is not like PCs and servers, which have standard internal structures into which you can attach cards for a wide range of added functions from many different vendors. With hubs, the internal structure, or backplane, is proprietary to the hub manufacturer. Many hub makers have cooperated with other firms that have relevant expertise to develop modules for routing, bridging and management. A well-known example has been hub maker Synoptics' agreement with router maker Cisco Systems. But this still means users can only buy modules from a single group of vendors. It may be worth sacrificing the freedom and potential cost savings of 'cherry-picking' your LAN components from a wide variety of vendors in order to attain the advantage of a single integrated hub-based network. But if the hub vendor runs into trouble, so might your network, if support for the hub and associated modules deteriorates or disappears. This is unlikely, admittedly, with the largest vendors, but is a point to bear in mind.

Another point to consider is that some vendors have been contemplating the development of a common hub backplane architecture. This would allow makers of routers and other LAN interconnection or management products to develop modules that would attach to a variety of hubs, leading to economies of scale and falling prices, just as happened with PCs and servers. At the time of writing there had been no concrete agreement between major hub vendors to develop a standard for hub backplanes. It looks likely that a standard backplane will emerge in a new generation of hub products between 1993 and 1996. These will be based on a new internal switching mechanism called asynchronous transfer mode (ATM), which we discuss in the next section as it is particularly relevant for large backbone hubs.

However, there may be a standard in the immediate future for smaller hubs serving single LANs of 60 users or less, taking a logical step forward from the card-based server mentioned in the last section. The idea is to build a complete dedicated hub using standard PC architecture. This would support a greater number of users than a normal server, because it does nothing else. It would have a larger number of slots for cards than usual, each one taking a hub card that may serve in the region of 8 to 12 users. Using a standard PC architecture, there would be nothing to stop any vendor developing cards. Indeed there is no reason why such a product should not also support cards for routing and bridging as well. Again, this is a development to watch out for over the next few years.

Backbone hub considerations

In 1991 the first large-scale backbone hubs emerged. These varied in detail, but the essential idea was to provide a single hub as a focal point for a large network on a single site or campus. Internally such hubs may provide shrunk-down FDDI networks to support high-speed bridging and routing between modules attached to them. Figure 8.3 illustrates the function of such a backbone hub, sometimes called a routing hub, or Rub. Essentially the hub provides the equivalent of a backbone network shrunk down into a single box. Individual local hubs on different floors of a building may be connected to the backbone hub, which in turn provides a path between them.

Such an arrangement provides scope for growth in numbers of users and changes in the network configuration, because additional modules can be plugged into the backbone hub. Such modules can support additional users or LANs, and can provide extra functions. For example, you may start just with bridging modules, and then move over to routing as the network grows in size. The distinction between bridging and routing is discussed in Chapter 6.

A possible caveat to all this is that the internal structure of large-scale backbone hubs is likely to change substantially in the mid 1990s. The reason for this is that having invested in such a large hub, there is naturally demand to use it not just for LAN data but for all forms of electronic information, including voice, video and image where relevant.

On telecommunications networks, asynchronous transfer mode (ATM) is emerging as the switching technology of the future. LANs do not use switching in which data may take one of several paths depending on network conditions. Instead LANs provide a single path linking all devices, and require no switching decisions to be made.

Data enters the LAN, and stays on it until it is stripped off by a device to which it is addressed. Having emerged from the LAN world, hubs have adopted the LAN mechanisms. However, given the different physical structure of modern hub-based networks, and the emerging need to link up with ATM-based telecommunications networks, vendors have started to re-engineer large-scale hubs. The next generation of hubs will use ATM switching internally, so that they can connect readily to future telecommunications networks and support voice and video as well. Given that backbone hubs are a substantial investment, some larger sites may consider waiting for the next generation of ATM switches, and make do for now with smaller less expensive hubs within each floor linked by a standard backbone network. This is especially true for sites wanting to use the same hub to switch voice and other forms of data onto a wide area telecommunications network.

LAN servers

The choice of server depends not just on the size of your network but also on the way it is organized. A network does not need to have a dedicated server at all, as we saw in Chapter 4 in the discussion of network operating systems that support peer-to-peer operation. In such networks there is no single central machine that is shared by all users but not under the direct control of any one user. However, as soon as a network grows to more than ten users, it is usually preferable to have a dedicated server that does not have to run applications such as word processing and spreadsheets for users. With larger networks, peer-to-peer LANs with non-dedicated servers become increasingly hard to manage.

Apart from the fact that it does not allow users to access it directly, there is no difference between a dedicated server and any other type of computer. With the trend towards client/server applications, which we described in Chapter 1, a number of larger computers such as IBM mainframes are beginning to function as servers, providing desktop PC applications with access to central data. They may do this alongside their traditional role as multi-user systems accessed by dumb terminals. For most smaller networks, however, servers are usually powerful PCs dedicated to their task.

Servers perform a number of roles that we have described at various stages of the book, the primary ones being database management, printing and communications. Applications running in desktop PCs then make use of the database and printing facilities on the server. It is therefore important to consider not just the expected growth, if any, in number of users, but also the impact of new applications that might make heavier use of the server. As with other computers, the server has two essential elements that limit performance, these being the disk drive and the main processing unit. There are various related factors, such as the disk drive controller and the speed at which data is switched internally within the server. But it really comes down to the ability of the server to be expanded with new components that increase its speed and data storage capacity.

With many database-intensive applications, the server's disk drive, on which all data is stored and accessed, is first to feel the strain. Disk drives are improving all the time, and it is usually possible to upgrade your server with a drive that has both higher capacity and faster data access. However, the processor may then become the bottleneck, given that client/server applications transfer to the server all the calculations required to select specific data items from the database. Some servers allow processing boards to be replaced, so that the machine can be speeded up substantially without the greater expense of replacing it outright.

However, all may not be lost if you cannot expand your server. It may be that the server currently runs everything, including printing as well as database management and perhaps some shared applications. Instead of replacing the server completely, it should be possible to install a second server to take over the printing functions, for example. This may well restore performance to acceptable levels. A typical configuration, in which printing and file or database functions are provided with separate servers, is shown in Figure 8.4. In fact as a percentage of total LAN cost, the expense of having an extra server dedicated just to database management is relatively low, except on the smallest networks.

The same argument applies to other functions that a server performs. For example, a server may provide some routing functions as well as database management. With increased inter-LAN traffic, the load placed on this server for routing calculations may start to degrade its overall performance. With time such a server might be unacceptably slow both for routing and accessing the database. Again the answer would be to install a new server dedicated just to routing.

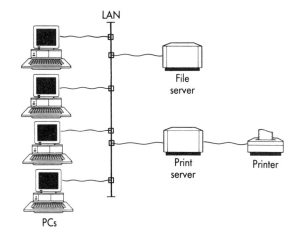

Figure 8.4   Showing network with separate file and print servers.

The network operating system (NOS)

With the NOS there are several factors that need to be considered over and above basic support for any expected growth in number of users. Table 8.3 summarizes these factors, most of which grow in significance with size of the network.

8

NOS and support

Probably the most important aspect of the NOS to consider is its 'hinterland', that is, the range of support and services available not just from the NOS vendor itself but also from other parties. It is no use having a technically excellent NOS capable in theory of supporting all your future needs if the vendor goes out of business leaving the product effectively in limbo. There are eight factors to consider under the general heading of support:

(1)   Availability of third party products that enhance the value of the NOS.

(2) Availability of training (discussed in Chapter 7).

(3) Range of publications such as user guides (NetWare wins hands down on this count).

(4) Existence of user groups and bulletin boards that provide useful information (again see Chapter 7).

(5) A healthy supply of qualified people with experience in the NOS.

(6) Stability of the product and expectation of future innovation to enhance the NOS.

(7) Extent and quality of dealer network and of first-line distributors for that product.

(8) Technical support such as online help and site maintenance available from source of supply (this overlaps with number 7 as dealers will often supply and support the product).

On all these counts NetWare and LAN Manager score highest, as they have extensive dealer networks, and substantial investment in research and development from Novell and Microsoft respectively. Furthermore, the huge user base ensures that these NOSs attract a healthy range of products from third parties, especially in NetWare's case. However, some of the other leading NOSs are now relatively stable and have established sufficient market presence to attract third party products, Vines and LANtastic being the best two examples. However, there is a risk in opting for some of the other smaller NOSs that the product may not stay in the front line and will fall behind technically.

Table 8.3 Factors to consider when choosing a NOS that will last and grow with your network.

1 NOS support

2 NOS performance

3 NOS and network management

4 NOS and ability to access other networks

5 NOS and new applications

NOS performance

Performance of course is important for networks of all sizes. The point here is that some of the peer-to-peer NOSs described in Chapter 4 were designed primarily for small networks. So although some of them may claim to provide a growth path up to several hundred users, performance typically degrades progressively when the number exceeds 20. However there are exceptions. One is the NOS known as PowerLAN, which supports both peer-to-peer and dedicated server operation. So with this product a LAN can start off operating in peer-to-peer mode and then move to dedicated server operation as the LAN grows. The point is that managing a peer-to-peer LAN with more than about 20 nodes becomes difficult.

However, performance does not depend on the NOS alone. It is also contingent upon the desktop PCs, as well as the capacity and configuration of the network itself. With increasingly sophisticated graphical user interfaces (GUIs), demand for main memory, central processing power and disk capacity on PCs is rising all the time. In many cases, it is the desktop PC rather than other components of the network that has the greatest impact on performance as perceived by users. It is now possible to buy PCs that can be upgraded by adding more powerful processors as well as adding memory and installing faster higher-capacity disk drives.

Then there is the network itself. As the number of users and amount of traffic increases, the network may need to be rearranged and upgraded to ensure that users do not experience deteriorating response time with networked applications. However, in order to know that changes may need to be made, information is required on traffic levels and network utilization. This is a function of network management, which we discuss in detail in Chapter 10. However, we touch on some of the network management issues relating to the NOS now.

NOS and network management

Several of the factors summarized in Table 8.3 come under the heading of network management. The ability to reconfigure a network, for example to bring on additional devices, is one. Another is the ability to monitor faults, to enable corrective or preventative action to be taken as quickly as possible. The ability to monitor usage of the network is also important, for accounting and security purposes. It may, for example, be desirable on a large network to apportion usage costs to individual departments. It may also help with planning future capacity to know which users, which workgroups and which applications are generating most traffic across the network. This can only be done if each user is effectively metered. This also enables network administrators to track any unauthorized use of the network for security purposes. Security is discussed in more detail in Chapter 10. The point here is that both security and management features, especially the former, are increasingly being provided by the NOS.

Novell and Microsoft have both invested heavily in giving NetWare and LAN Manager the sort of security and management facilities found on large centralized operating systems for mainframe computers. But in the case of NetWare, the full range of security and management facilities are only available in the top-end versions of the product, NetWare 3.11 and NetWare 4.0. Therefore, organizations expecting to require comprehensive management and security features across a large network, especially one comprising multiple interconnecting LANs, would be best off going for NetWare 3.11 or NetWare 4.0 straightaway. In fact these are now generally recommended except for small networks with limited expectations of growth. This is partly because NetWare 286 is likely to be phased out, and to enjoy ongoing support, users would need to upgrade anyway.

However, Novell does offer an upgrade route of sorts between its products, in that they are all able to coexist on the same network, running on a common server. Novell then offers trade-in discounts to encourage its customers to upgrade when they reach the point at which such a move is desirable.

LAN Manager on the other hand is a single product, with no need to upgrade as your network grows. Versions of LAN Manager differ according to the underlying operating system they require on the server. Whereas NetWare requires no specific underlying operating system, LAN Manager in various flavours works on top of a variety of operating systems, including OS/2 and Unix.

NOS and ability to access other networks

The products required to access other LANs and systems are described in Chapter 6. If you need to access other networks now or envisage having to do so in future, it is worth checking either that this is supported by the NOS or that there are suitable third party products available for that NOS. With NetWare 3.11, for example, there are various third party products available as NetWare Loadable Modules (NLMs).

Most NOSs do support basic LAN interconnections via bridges or routers. But they vary in their provision for access to remote applications and host computers. For example, if you want to access an IBM SAA (Systems Application Architecture) network you need some sort of SAA gateway facility. If your LAN is going to become part of a larger network it may make sense to be able to manage the LAN from a central point within that network. For example, an SAA network may be managed by IBM's NetView network management system. It would then be a good idea for your NOS to support NetView. LAN Manager, for example, allows a NetView management station to take control of the LAN. The kind of management information exchanged by such links is discussed in Chapter 10. When choosing the NOS, it is worth ensuring that relevant links to external management systems and networks are provided.

NOS and new applications

This relates to the final item in Table 8.3. As discussed in Chapters 1 and 4 there is increasing cooperation between computers across a network to achieve an overall aim. In client/server computing for example, a server machine may retrieve information from a database on behalf of a wide variety of client applications running typically on desktop PCs.

There is a variety of techniques used to support the communication processes that facilitate interaction between applications on different computers. These need to be supported by the operating systems of the computers involved. For client/server computing on a LAN, this usually means the NOS. However, in some cases PCs are connected via a LAN to a large computer such as a mainframe which has its own operating system. In that case there may be no need for a NOS but the operating systems must be able to communicate across the network.

LAN type

We put this section last because it is usually least important as far as future expansion is concerned. As we discussed in Chapter 2, Ethernet and token ring have various pros and cons, but for most applications either will suffice. However, there are a few pointers, summarized in Table 8.4. Growth in user numbers is not usually the main factor. More important are the anticipated traffic patterns and the nature of any other network you may need to connect to. Suppose, for example, a new LAN is being installed for a remote branch of a large firm that has already installed many token ring LANs in other locations. Even if there is no immediate requirement to access these other LANs, it would make sense to install a token ring, if other factors are equal. It would then be easier to interconnect with the other LANs at a later time. However, if other factors were not equal, and there was some reason for installing an Ethernet at the new site, there would usually be no strong reason for not doing so. It is becoming easier to interconnect Ethernet and token ring LANs, although at slightly greater expense.

The other factor to consider is traffic profile. In Chapter 2 it was explained how Ethernet is best for networks with large numbers of users but where frequency of access to the network is relatively low. This means Ethernet is the best choice if you anticipate your network developing this way. On the other hand, where heavy use of a network is anticipated, token ring may be preferred because its performance is more predictable under such circumstances. By comparing your plan with the pros and cons of each LAN type in Chapter 2, you should be able to judge which would be the best choice. This does depend of course on being able to judge how your network will develop. Given an uncertain future, token ring may be preferred, again because its performance degrades more smoothly under increased loading, giving more time to make changes that improve performance.

Table 8.4 Factors to consider in choosing LAN type.

1 Anticipated data traffic profile. How this relates to Ethernet and token ring is explained in Chapter 2.

2 Other networks that need to be connected to.

3 Cost. Ethernet still tends to be cheaper than token ring.

Are LANs better able to support changing requirements than minicomputers?

One of the major advantages of LANs compared with traditional minicomputers is in their greater flexibility and support for change. For this reason companies such as Digital Equipment and Data General that grew up in the 1970s as suppliers of minicomputers have moved into the LAN server market. In some cases traditional minis are being deployed as LAN servers running a NOS such as NetWare. However, such servers tend to be more expensive, and certainly perform worse in this situation than powerful PCs based on microprocessors from Intel or Advanced Micro Devices.

In their traditional form, however, minicomputers are multi-user machines accessed by relatively dumb terminals. It is true that this pattern is changing, and it is now possible to buy central machines, typically running the Unix operating system, that combine some of the advantages of minicomputers and LAN servers. However, for small businesses there is still in many cases a distinct choice between two principal alternatives: a server-based LAN or a minicomputer with dumb terminals.

Minicomputers may be expandable with options of increasing memory, disk capacity and the number of users supported. But expansion tends to come in quantum leaps, requiring sudden and costly upgrades when a site reaches the limit for number of users and performance. LANs allow more organic growth, provided the LAN components have been chosen carefully.

Another important point to consider with regard to change is the range of choice available in both hardware and software. Minicomputers used to be completely proprietary, so that having installed one, you were virtually stuck with it for the rest of its life, because no other make could run the same applications. This has changed now that most minis use the Unix operating system. Unfortunately incompatibilities between different versions of Unix mean that applications are not yet completely portable between all Unix machines. The situation is improving with greater convergence toward Unix System V.4, but it is still not quite the single universal operating system that its protagonists claim it soon will be.

With PC LANs on the other hand there are well-established universal standards in Windows, MS-DOS, NetWare and so on. Users of LANs can choose PCs and servers from a wide variety of manufacturers safe in the knowledge that they will run existing applications. And the range of choice in applications themselves is greater on PC LANs, so there is more prospect of finding off-the-shelf software packages that meet your needs.

Applications for minicomputers used to have one advantage in that they were designed for multi-user operation. The first generation of PC LAN applications were on the other hand essentially single-user PC applications tweaked for use over a network. However, with a growing base of client/server applications designed to split the processing load between desktop computers and servers, this argument in favour of minis is waning.

One situation where minis may be favoured is for businesses that want to run just a single application such as accounting or sales order processing shared between a number of users. However, the number of businesses that want computers for just one application is declining.

Another situation where minis score is where users need to share data and/or applications over a site that extends beyond the distances that can be covered by a LAN. A traditional minicomputer solution linked to dumb terminals requires only a fraction of the data bandwidth of a LAN and works quite satisfactorily over dial-up telephone lines.

It is worth stressing, however, that in general the traditional argument between minis and PC LANs is waning as the two sets of solutions begin to converge, and it is quite likely that before the end of the decade, the distinction between PC LAN servers and minis will have ended.

We can now summarize the pros and cons of minis as follows.

Advantages

(1) Can be more cost effective where a number of users need to share just one application.
(2) Tend to be best for supporting widely dispersed users, as opposed to workgroups contained in a single office or building.

Disadvantages

(1) Less flexible, requiring expansion in quantum leaps.
(2) Fewer hardware options.
(3) Does not have the vast choice of software applications that PC LANs have.

(4) Provide less freedom for end users to install their own personal applications.

(5) Organization may already have PCs installed that can more readily become part of a LAN without much additional expense.

In summary, then, PC LANs provide a much more flexible environment, enabling an organization to decide how much control is exercised over end users, keeping future options much more open.

Summary

We have hopefully established that LANs tend to provide more flexible, expandable solutions than traditional minis, except in certain specialized cases. However there is no reason why minis and LANs cannot coexist, and they often do.

8

9

What is an open system and is it important to me and my network?

CHAPTER CONTENTS

CHAPTER OBJECTIVES

This chapter is more by way of a reference, to back up points made in other chapters. For example, in Chapter 6, LAN interconnection is described with reference to the OSI model, which is described in detail in this chapter. Readers unfamiliar with OSI are advised to acquire at least a fleeting familiarity with it.

Basic points and issues covered in this chapter are:

Standards are important

An open system for computer networking is one that conforms to agreed international standards for communication or interoperability. It certainly is important for your network even if you do not know it, because the basic LAN types, Ethernet and token ring, are themselves international standards. Beyond that, it is only through conformance by vendors to universal standards that you can connect your network up to others and access remote applications. Standards are also required to support the emerging paradigms for distributed computing where applications on different systems cooperate across a network.

The benefits of open systems in general are summarized in Table 9.1. All the advantages spring from the fact that universal communication standards make it possible to have a common network shared by all users, applications and computers. Apart from greater freedom of choice in hardware and software, this brings cost savings through avoiding the need for separate networks to support different applications. Above all it provides a path to the future, because you can be sure

9

Table 9.1   Benefits of open systems summarized.

1 They provide a basis for a common network supporting all users, providing widespread access to key systems, applications, and information.

2 Freedom of choice in systems and software – you are less likely to be tied into particular vendors.

3 They provide a framework for future applications in which there is greater cooperation between different computers.

that new products and emerging technologies will conform to or be based on open standards. This is provided of course you choose the right standards.

But there are pitfalls

We will see later in the chapter how some OSI standards have failed to gain widespread acceptance, being unable to budge earlier *de facto* standards. Even where standards have gained wide acceptance, there may be a sacrifice to be made in adopting them. Products conforming to open standards may be more expensive than equivalent ones based on proprietary protocols. They may also perform less well in situations where there is a proprietary alternative.

However, the point of open standards is that they facilitate communication between systems that do not support the same proprietary methods. Increasingly the aim with open systems is to achieve full interoperability between different systems on a network, so that low-level differences between software or hardware do not prevent applications cooperating on a network. The objective is communication and integration, not necessarily homogenization. Seen in this context, open systems and proprietary systems are not complete opposites. An example is Novell's IPX protocol stack (described later in this chapter), which although undoubtedly proprietary is now widely supported and ideally suited for many LANs. There is no reason to spurn it just because it is labelled proprietary. The need is for standards, whether proprietary, *de facto* or *de jure*, that work and are widely supported. Those are the criteria by which we have selected the standards described later in this chapter.

Who sets standards?

In this chapter we describe the relevant standards and how they relate to your LAN. This includes so-called *de jure* standards that have been set by committees comprising a cross-section of the IT (information technology) industry. It also includes proprietary *de facto* standards which are established by the market power of a particular vendor and then gain wider support. An example of the latter is Novell's IPX routing protocol. Sometimes such standards later become adopted by international committees as *de jure* standards. An example is the token ring LAN standard, originally introduced by IBM and later adopted first by the US Institute of Electrical and Electronic Engineers (IEEE) and subsequently by the International Standards Organization (ISO). The role of these various committees will be described at the end of this chapter.

We begin by describing the seven layer OSI (Open System Interconnection) model developed originally by ISO in the 1970s. This model provides the foundation not just for ISO's own OSI standards, but also most proprietary sets of networking protocols. The TCP/IP protocols, for example, which are widely used instead of OSI in computer networks, are based on a similar seven layer model. IBM's SNA (System Network Architecture) is also based on a similar model, with some minor differences. A working knowledge of the OSI model is therefore a prerequisite for understanding how computers and their applications interoperate across a network.

Introducing the seven layers of OSI

For applications to cooperate across a network, there needs to be a hierarchy of ingredients ranging from a physical communications link at the bottom to some agreed structure for the information being transmitted at the top. As computer networks began to evolve during the late 1960s, it soon became clear that anarchy would prevail unless some effort was made to establish a common framework for the various tasks involved in communication.

9

The first such framework was IBM's SNA network architecture, introduced in 1974. The basic form of SNA served as the basis for the OSI protocols that emerged gradually during the 1980s and early 1990s. The difference was that while SNA was purely for networks comprising systems either manufactured by IBM or compatible with IBM standards, OSI was designed for open networks comprising computers from a wide variety of vendors.

This inevitably meant that OSI standards took longer to evolve, as they were set by committees representing all the major vendors. In the lower two layers of communication, which deal with LANs, OSI standards are now well established, not just in multivendor networks, but also in SNA networks. But at the higher levels, where greater complexity is involved, OSI standards have been slower to mature and to be implemented in products. In some cases the standards have been so slow to arrive that other *de facto* standards have already won widespread support. A good example is the TCP/IP protocol stack, which is widely used on LANs and is described later in the chapter. In some cases the equivalent OSI protocols are then modified so that networks based on the established *de facto* standards can migrate smoothly towards them. At the same time the *de facto* standards sometimes move gradually towards the equivalent OSI ones, so that the two sets gradually converge.

This is happening in the case of network management, where the SNMP protocols developed originally for TCP/IP networks are moving closer to the CMIP protocols. This is discussed further in Chapter 10 which looks in detail at network management.

Basic structure of OSI model

The motive for having seven layers rather than one is that it breaks the overall task of building a network down into manageable components. The network as a whole is then easier to install, maintain and enhance. For example, a change may just affect one or two layers of the OSI model. To implement the change then only requires amendments to the layers that are affected rather than the whole network.

Each layer performs a specific set of tasks required for computers to interoperate across a network, and communicates only with the layers immediately above and below. Each layer, except the top one, provides a service to the layer immediately above. And each except the bottom layer requires the service of the one immediately below. The whole networking process then comprises a set of seven interrelated groups of tasks.

The overall model is summarized in Figure 9.1. The seven layers fall into two groups, the upper application layers and the lower internetworking layers. The upper three layers ensure that two computer systems understand each other, so that they can work together. They deal with the structure and presentation of data, and coordination between the systems that are interworking. But they do not worry about how the data gets from one system to another, this being the function of the lowest three layers. The bottom three layers then handle the transmission of data packets across the network, and do not worry what the contents of the packets are.

This in fact only makes six layers. We have left out the one in the

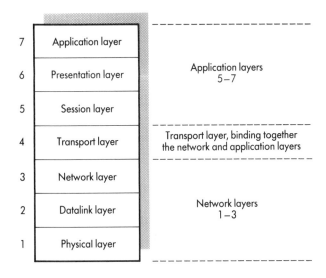

Figure 9.1   Structure of seven layer OSI model.

middle, the transport layer, which binds together the upper and layer layers, ensuring that it is actually possible to transmit data over the network. There might be an error or the network might be overloaded, in which case layer 3, the highest of the lower layers, informs layer 4, the transport layer, that it is not possible to transmit data at that time. The transport layer in turn informs layer 5, which may lead to a session being suspended with users perhaps receiving an error message such as network temporarily unavailable.

It is possible to implement OSI without all seven layers. In this case the function of a missing layer is fulfilled by joining together the layers above and below it. For example, it is possible to manage without a transport layer, in which case layer 3 communicates directly with layer 5 to handle transmission of data across the network.

The upper layers

Layer 7, the application layer, delivers the complete OSI service to user applications so that they can interoperate. One example is support for file transfer, which is required by many applications and provided by the OSI FTAM standard (file transfer access method). Another example is OSI-TP, required to coordinate the sequence of events for transaction processing systems that are distributed across different processors on an OSI network.

Among the best known layer 7 standards is X.400 for message transfer between office and electronic mail systems, although the ISO name for this is actually Motis (message oriented text interchange system). X.400 was developed by the CCITT, but is now aligned with Motis. The overlapping role of standards bodies like ISO and CCITT is described at the end of the chapter.

Layer 6, the presentation layer, ensures that data is delivered in an agreed format to the application layer. Any conversion required between different data representations would take place in this layer. An example would be conversion between two different character codes, such as ASCII to EBCDIC. ASCII characters are represented by different combinations of binary bits from EBCDIC characters, and the translation between the two codes would take place in the presentation layer.

Layer 5, the session layer, controls the dialogue between two applications on different computers. For example, when a PC user is accessing an IBM mainframe via a LAN, a session will be set up and controlled within layer 5. This would ensure that applications are kept informed of any problems, and would define what kind of session it would be.

For example, it might involve just onscreen interaction, or file transfer, or both simultaneously. The actual process of transmitting data from the PC via the LAN to the mainframe and back again is handled by the bottom four layers, which therefore provide a transport service to the session layer.

Layer 4, the transport layer, is responsible for providing a path between applications and ensuring that data is delivered correctly along that path. Layer 4 normally performs error recovery, although some of this may be done in layer 3.

Layer 3, the internetworking layer, is responsible for finding a route across the network, and in some cases for error recovery. The exact facilities provided in layer 3 depend on the type of network provided. A simple network comprising a few LANs linked by bridges would not need a layer 3 at all, because there is no routing to be done and error recovery is handled in other layers.

On a more complex wide area network, however, layer 3 performs a vital role, in providing resilient routing capable of avoiding single points of failure, and in guaranteeing error free delivery of data.

Layer 2, the datalink layer, is responsible for ensuring that data is faithfully transmitted across the physical medium itself between devices attached to it. Such devices may be PCs attached to a LAN or routers on a wide area network, the function being to ensure that data is not corrupted during its transmission between any two such devices across the physical link between them.

This link may be fixed such as a fibre optic or copper cable, or it may be a wireless link.

This layer corrects errors that occur on the medium, but cannot cater for problems arising in higher protocol layers. LANs such as Ethernet and token ring operate in this layer.

For LANs, layer 2 is divided into two sublayers. The lower of these two sublayers is the media access control layer (MAC), which deals with access to the actual physical medium. The upper sublayer is the logical link control (LLC), which controls the flow of data between devices on the LAN and ensures that data is reassembled correctly when it leaves the physical medium. All ISO LANs, including both token ring and Ethernet, are based on a common LLC sublayer. They differ only in the MAC layer, which defines how they access the physical medium – CSMA/CD being the access method for Ethernet, and token passing for token ring.

Layer 1, the physical layer, specifies the medium itself and the physical method used to access it. It is not concerned with how data gets across the link. Therefore this layer may define first the cable itself, and then characteristics of the signal, such as the maximum length allowed without repeaters. The medium might be unshielded twisted pair (utp) copper cable, for example, in which case layer 1 describes the electrical characteristics of the signal and at what distances it should be regenerated. Layer 1 also defines the sockets for attaching devices to the medium. An example of a layer 1 standard is the 10Base-T standard for running Ethernet LANs traffic over utp cable.

9

Relationship between layers 3 and 2 on LANs?

The interaction between layers 3 and 2 can be understood more easily with reference to LANs. Layer 2 (in conjunction with physical layer 1) is concerned with enabling data to be transmitted in individual packets between two devices. The way this is done for both token ring and Ethernet is described in Chapter 2. The job of layer 3 is then to construct a coherent end-to-end network connection that can deliver data between two devices for as long as they need to. So while at layer 2 a pair of devices communicate intermittently packet by packet, layer 3 constructs a continuous link from these intermittent streams of packets.

What OSI standards are relevant to LANs?

We have already discussed the primary layer 2 LAN standards, Ethernet and token ring. For communication between LANs over a wide area, layer 3 standards have traditionally been used, to support routing over a mesh of different paths. For some years the most popular OSI wide area standard has been X.25. The problem with X.25 protocols is that they are very slow compared with LANs, and so impose a bottleneck on any network with significant inter-LAN traffic. The role of a typical X.25 network used to interconnect LANs and other systems is shown in Figure 9.2.

More recently networks of LANs have increasingly been interconnected using routers that communicate over telecommunications links using TCP/IP protocols. These protocols allow the LANs to make use of higher-speed point-to-point telecommunications circuits operating at speeds up to 2 Mbit/s. The TCP/IP protocols are not OSI standards. But they have become much more widely used than any equivalent OSI protocols and are likely to converge with OSI over the next few years. We describe the TCP/IP standards a little later in the chapter.

Frame relay

This is especially relevant for LANs because it is ideally suited to transmitting LAN traffic over a wide area network. It is really a sequel to X.25. Like X.25, Frame relay provides an interface to a switched wide area network handling data in packets. But it is more efficient than X.25 and supports much higher speeds, particularly for interconnecting LANs. It provides a basic communications service in layer 2 of the protocol stack, beneath network layer protocols such as the IP part of TCP/IP. Many routers can access a frame relay network, enabling LANs to be interconnected at high speeds over a separate wide area network. In this case the Frame relay network provides what appears to each router as a point-to-point connection, although in fact there is a switched network in between the routers.

This principle, which also applies to X.25, is illustrated in Figure 9.3. Figure 9.3(a) shows a network of three routers interconnected by direct point-to-point circuits leased from a telecommunications operator. Figure 9.3(b) shows the same network interconnected via

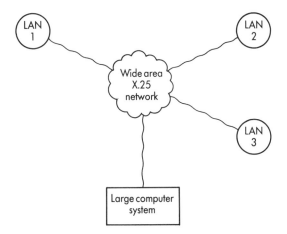

Figure 9.2 Role of X.25 network for interconnecting LANs.

a public frame relay network. One advantage of the frame relay network is that, being based on a large public network infrastructure, it should provide greater protection against failure of any single circuit. It could also save money, because it avoids the need to pay for permanent dedicated links between each pair of routers. As far as the routers are concerned, the frame relay network simply provides direct point-to-point connections, so that the two networks shown in Figure 9.3 are functionally equivalent.

9

ATM (asynchronous transfer mode)

This will not be relevant for small networks in the immediate future, but as so many vendors are talking about it, and as it is seen as a possible universal networking technique in the future, it is worth mentioning. The aim is to create a universal transmission method for voice, video and indeed any form of electronic information that can be digitized, including LAN data. Eventually some vendors and standards makers expect it to replace current LAN technologies such as Ethernet and token ring, erasing the barriers between LANs and WANs (wide area networks) and dispensing with the need for bridges and routers. But more immediately it will become a high-speed switching technology for WANs and also within top-end smart hubs. The

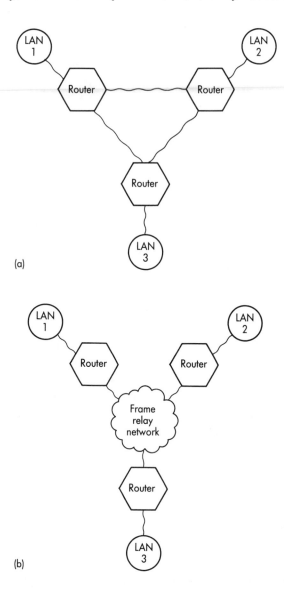

(a)

(b)

Figure 9.3 How frame relay network provides the equivalent point-to-point connections between LANs. In this case the LANs depicted are token ring. (a) Three routers interconnected by point-to-point links. (b) Same LANs, but this time the three routers are connected to a public frame relay network, which provides the same functionality.

ATM standard, developed by the American National Standards Institute, will support a range of transmission speeds between 100 Mbit/s and 2 Gbit/s.

ISDN (integrated services digital network)

ISDN is the emerging digital successor to the standard public telephone network. Its communications structure is based closely on the bottom three layers of the OSI model, which are all it needs to establish a connection between two points across a public switched network. More detail on ISDN can be found in Appendix 1.

Higher-layer OSI standards

Any LAN that conforms to the OSI standards, including Ethernet and token ring LANs with the exception of some older versions, should support any higher-layer OSI application standards. However, not all combinations of the higher layers automatically work together, as we shall explain at the end of this OSI section.

As already mentioned, the transport layer standards bind together the higher applications layers and the lower network layers. However, many implementations of higher-layer standards automatically include a transport layer. Therefore, in order to implement a complete set of OSI protocols on your network, it is often not necessary to understand the subtle differences between the various transport layer protocols. Hence, we confine our attention to the various higher layer options.

There are separate higher-layer standards for different types of applications. We identify six main standards groups:

(1) The X.400 standards for message handling. There is also an important related standard called X.500 which defines the structure of a distributed directory capable of locating users and systems across a multivendor network.

(2) The FTAM (file transfer and access management) standards for transmission of files between computers across a network.

(3) The office document architecture (ODA), which facilitates transfer of formatted documents between different computers across an open system network.

(4) The virtual terminal (VT) standard, which ensures that the screen handling and keyboard operations of PCs and terminals operating across an open network are compatible.

(5) The OSI-TP (transaction processing) standard, which allows transaction based applications to be distributed across an open network. Transaction based applications generally involve large numbers of identical short tasks that involve frequent access to and updating of databases. Common examples include booking systems for airline tickets or hotel accommodation, and order processing systems.

(6) The CMIS/CMIP (common management information service/common management information protocol) standards for network management. The aim here is to enable a network comprising components from a variety of vendors to be managed from a single system. This is discussed more fully in Chapter 10.

There is some overlap between these six groups. This is particularly so with the first three, which all address exchange of data files between applications. The first, message handling, specifies how to exchange basic unformatted messages between systems. Its main function is electronic mail (email) and office systems, and is designed to make the transmission of frequent relatively short messages as efficient and fast as possible. Before the advent of X.400 it was generally only possible to exchange messages within proprietary office or email systems from a single vendor.

An important extension to message handling are standards that support electronic data interchange (EDI), which facilitates exchange of detailed business messages such as invoices between companies. The principal open system EDI standard is called EDIFACT. This uses X.400 as its framework for inter-company message communication, with the addition of standards that define how items such as invoices and purchase orders should be formatted. They can then be processed by any company's computer systems.

FTAM on the other hand is not concerned with individual messages, but larger bodies of information that may not relate to a specific task. It could in theory be used to provide a messaging service, but is better suited to handling larger data transfers between systems and also provides facilities for accessing and managing databases or file stores.

ODA is related to FTAM and X.400 in that it also supports transfer of data between systems or applications. But it differs by allowing the high-level structure of data to be maintained. So, for example, documents exchanged between office systems supporting ODA would retain their format as well as their basic content. It also supports interchange of graphics and images between systems, and in future will extend this to allow documents annotated with voice comments to be transmitted.

Importance of functional profiles

As hinted earlier in this section, not all OSI standards are compatible with each other, strange as this seems. The explanation is that the whole set of standards often referred to as OSI is in fact a diverse group of protocols designed to meet a wide range of requirements. The discrepancies mostly occur within the higher layers, for as we have noted standard LANs should support any OSI application. The problem is mainly that not all transport layer protocols will support all higher-layer protocols. However it is possible to select subsets from the overall OSI group of standards that are totally compatible. Such subsets are called functional profiles. They define a profile of OSI standards that function correctly together. The principle of functional profiles is illustrated in Figure 9.4. As can be seen, such profiles define a vertical slice through each layer of the model. As we pointed out in Chapter 7, OSI functional profiles can be used when specifying the supply of components for networks. This reduces the chance that new components will fail to interoperate correctly with existing ones.

There are some well-known functional profiles defined by large computer user groups that are able to exert pressure on vendors to conform. The best known is Gosip (government open systems interconnection profile) defined by both the UK and US governments (although UK Gosip and US Gosip are not in fact the same).

TCP/IP

The TCP/IP standards are sometimes confused with OSI ones. Their structure is very similar, as can be seen from Figure 9.5 which compares the two models. In fact in the bottom two layers they are

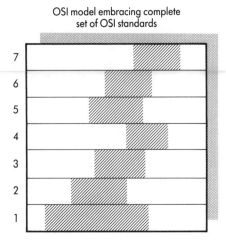

Figure 9.4 Illustrating the principle of OSI functional profiles. A set of functional profiles defines specific standards within each OSI layer for use in a particular organization or group of organizations, or for a specific type of application. In the diagram, the whole block depicts the complete OSI model, while the shaded areas represent subsets of each layer corresponding to a set of functional standards.

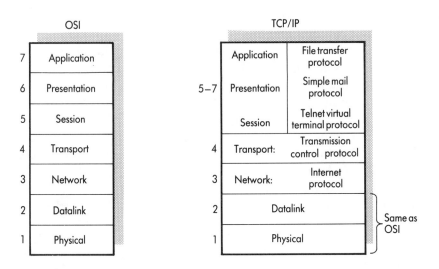

Figure 9.5 Comparing structure of TCP/IP with OSI. Note that TCP/IP higher-layer protocols embrace all three upper layers. Note also that in practice many TCP/IP networks do not use the upper three TCP/IP layer protocols – OSI ones such as X.400 are more popular.

identical, as TCP/IP uses the OSI standards such as Ethernet and token ring LANs. The two differ from layer 3 upwards, but there are also signs of convergence in the top three layers where OSI standards are starting to predominate. TCP/IP is completely different from OSI in layers 3 and 4 which define how to establish end-to-end connections between systems attached to different LANs. It is in these middle layers, for transporting data across a network, where TCP/IP protocols are widely used. The higher-layer TCP/IP standards are sometimes used, but on many networks, TCP/IP standards are found only in layers 3 and 4. The upper layers may comprise OSI standards or proprietary ones. So when people talk about TCP/IP, they often mean just the third and fourth layers of that protocol set. Here TCP/IP has become so firmly established that it is quite likely to become part of the OSI group of standards in future.

TCP/IP protocols defined

There are two reasons why TCP/IP standards are widely used in layers 3 and 4 to support the interconnection of LANs. One is that the standards were developed earlier than OSI ones. The other is that they were designed specifically for internetworking, that is, connecting LANs together. The protocols were developed largely for this purpose by the US Internet Engineering Task Force.

9

Architecture of TCP/IP

TCP/IP strictly speaking only addresses layers 3 and 4 of the OSI model, the internetworking and transport layers. It usually runs over Ethernet or token ring LANs, which fill layers 1 and 2. The IP part, corresponding to OSI layer 3, controls connections between LANs and the WAN connecting them, and routing through the WAN. The TCP is the transport protocol, responsible for providing end-to-end data transmission between applications. It coordinates the flow of data to ensure that devices are not swamped with data they cannot handle.

TCP/IP has been extended to provide facilities in upper application layers. These correspond to the top three OSI layers:

- ☐ Telnet, which allows PCs to log-in remotely to host systems running TCP/IP protocols, by emulating, that is, supporting, appropriate screen and keyboard functions.

- ☐ FTP file transfer protocol allows users to transfer files across TCP/IP networks.

- ☐ SMTP simple mail transfer protocol is an electronic mail utility. The word simple is apt, and SMTP has been widely criticized for failing to provide adequate email facilities. As a result, there have been moves to embrace the OSI X.400 messaging standards within TCP/IP.

- ☐ SNMP simple network management protocol for managing TCP/IP networks, which we describe in Chapter 10. In 1993 a more sophisticated version of these protocols, called SNMP II was introduced.

Future of TCP/IP

The future path of TCP/IP has clarified now that major network users around the world are insisting that it continues to be supported. The main part of TCP/IP, that is layers 3 and 4, will probably be subsumed into OSI as options. On the other hand some OSI protocols, such as X.400, may actually replace existing TCP/IP higher-layer options. Currently the X/Open group is developing software to bridge TCP/IP with OSI protocols. It therefore looks as if the two standards sets will converge, without users having to go through a painful conversion process.

Other *de facto* standards that you may encounter

So far we have only discussed standards developed by committees comprising a number of vendors, and in some cases larger user organizations as well. Many vendors of IT systems have abandoned proprietary protocols and based their products on open standards. But you will probably also encounter proprietary standards set by dominant companies in the field such as IBM and Novell that are then supported by other vendors as well.

We describe the two that are most relevant to LANs: Novell's IPX and IBM's SNA. Both these are based on the seven layer OSI model, but with some differences. The relevance for LANs is that apart from TCP/IP, these two are the most widespread protocol sets on LANs covering the layers above the first two. IPX is used on networks comprising Novell NetWare servers, while SNA is used on networks of IBM computers. For interconnecting LANs, both SNA and IPX are being ousted to some extent by TCP/IP, especially in networks that support a wide range of different systems. However, both SNA and IPX, especially the former, will be around for some years to come.

After describing SNA and IPX briefly, we will show that these four sets of LAN communications protocols are not mutually exclusive and often coexist in the same network.

SNA

The original structure of SNA is shown in Figure 9.6. As you can see, it is very similar to OSI, with the main difference being that SNA layers 4 and 5 together are equivalent to OSI layer 5, while OSI layers 3 and 4 are together equivalent to SNA layer 3. The differences largely follow from historical factors. SNA was originally developed for centralized hierarchical networks in which all communication was controlled by one or a few large mainframe computers.

These large computers were accessed by dumb terminals via point-to-point connections. This meant that there was no need for great sophistication in the lower network layers because in a sense there was not much of a network. However, in the early days of networking, telecommunication links were far less reliable than now. Therefore, a great deal of SNA was concerned with error control and recovery, to protect users and applications from the effects of poor communication links.

With the onset of LANs not much changed at first. As we saw in Chapter 6, IBM's preferred solution to interconnect LANs was via bridges which communicate essentially over point-to-point connections. To enable more complex networks of interconnected bridged LANs to be established, IBM developed the source routing protocols

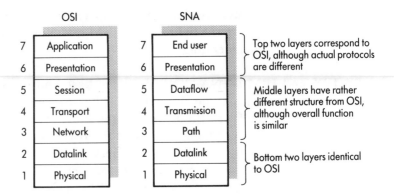

Figure 9.6   Structure of SNA.

that are described in Chapter 6. These became part of the SNA model, but despite pressure from IBM were never accepted by ISO as part of the OSI model.

Realizing that the LAN industry was moving away from bridging towards routing over wide area networks, IBM decided to refit SNA to give it a more distributed structure. New protocols called APPN (Advanced Peer-to-Peer Networking) that support intelligent routing were developed and brought into SNA. The difference between the new version, called SNA/APPN, and the old SNA is shown in Figure 9.7. The common transport interface introduced between layers 3 and 4 of the SNA model is designed to make SNA protocols more interchangeable with OSI and TCP/IP protocols. The interface supports mixing and matching of SNA protocols with others in the layers immediately above and below it.

SNA/APPN has been designed to suit the requirements of both LANs and the wide area networks connecting them, as well as catering for remaining traditional networks supporting dumb terminals.

IPX

The IPX protocol set was developed by Novell to facilitate communication between PCs and file servers across a NetWare LAN. IPX was subsequently used to route data over a network of interconnected NetWare LANs as well. On a large network, IPX may be one of a number of protocols being routed between LANs over local circuits or remotely over telecommunications links.

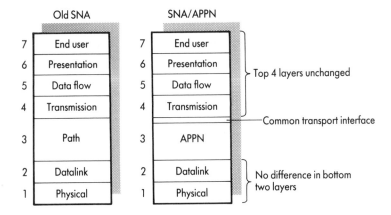

Figure 9.7   Comparison between new structure of SNA/APPN and old SNA. The main change is in layer 3, where APPN is introduced, with a common transport interface between SNA layer 3 and layer 4.

IPX in fact evolved from XNS (Xerox Network Systems), developed by Xerox. XNS is still used on another NOS, Banyan Vines. NetWare networks therefore use a very similar protocol set to Vines networks, which makes it possible with some tweaking to interoperate the two directly. Like other proprietary protocols, IPX (and XNS) is consistent with the OSI model. However, IPX was developed specifically for LAN operation, and therefore contains more functions in the bottom layers than OSI. The IPX protocols work very efficiently on LANs, having been designed for that purpose, providing faster response than TCP/IP or OSI protocols. TCP/IP on the other hand is efficient for inter-LAN traffic, as opposed to communication within each LAN. Figure 9.8 compares the fundamental structure of IPX with the OSI models.

9

How different standards groups fit together

It is important to emphasize that the four standards groups we have discussed (OSI, TCP/IP, SNA/APPN and IPX) are not mutually exclusive, and in fact are increasingly mixed and matched across a

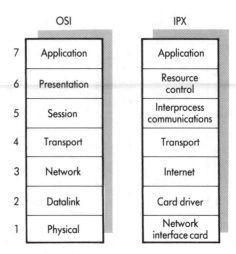

Figure 9.8   Showing structure of IPX. Note: the bottom two layers of IPX handle LAN-specific communications.

single network. This can be done as each is based on the same seven layer model, and it is possible to select individual layers from different groups, provided these layers interoperate. Increasingly they do. Novell, for example, has a product called LAN Workplace for DOS that allows PCs running the DOS operating system to access a TCP/IP network via a NetWare server.

The principle is illustrated in Figure 9.9. The top half of the diagram shows the network arrangement, while the bottom half illustrates the process schematically. PCs access the NetWare server using IPX for communication at layer 3 and above over the Ethernet LAN, which provides layers 1 and 2. The NetWare server then converts the IPX protocols into TCP/IP protocols. These are transmitted over the TCP/IP network to a host computer running TCP/IP protocols.

More generally, the way networks can be constructed logically (as opposed to the physical wires and hardware) from parts selected from all four models is shown in Figure 9.10. At the bottom, covering layers 1 and 2, you will see our popular LAN protocols and also frame relay, which operates in layer 2 over wide area circuits. All four of our protocol stacks are built on the same base of layer 1 and 2 standards. This demonstrates that there has been total agreement between vendors on a given set of standards in the bottom two layers.

In layers 3 and 4 we have, simplifying matters slightly, the choice between each of our four protocol groups. Then in between the

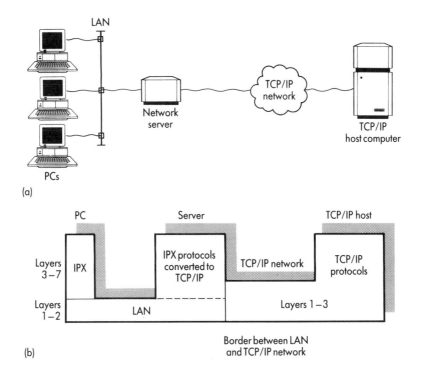

Figure 9.9   Showing how a TCP/IP network and a computer on it can be accessed from a Novell NetWare LAN via the server. (a) Outline of network. (b) How protocols are handled.

transport layer and the top three layers, we have what is sometimes called a transport layer interface, which connects the bottom layers with the top layers. Strictly speaking this interface is part of the transport layer itself. There has not yet been total agreement on how this interface should work, but it indicates the way the networking industry is moving.

Above the interface, we have again a choice from the major protocol sets up to the application layer. It is increasingly possible to mix and match from different protocol sets to build a network in this way, but as already emphasized it is as well to determine which elements do actually work together in order to construct a functional profile. We are now saying that this functional profile need not comprise just OSI standards, but also others such as SNA APPN. To an extent, however, the distinction between OSI standards, and well-established proprietary ones, is diminishing.

9

Describing the standards bodies

There is a hierarchy of bodies involved in developing OSI standards. Many of the standards were initially developed by national and European standards bodies, and in some cases by individual vendors, later to be adopted as international standards. There are three international standards bodies involved: the International Standards Organization (ISO), the International Electrotechnical Committee (IEC), and the International Consultative Committee for Telegraph and Telecommunications (CCITT). ISO originally formulated the OSI model, but IEC became involved with some LAN standards.

So to avoid conflict, ISO and IEC set up the ISO/IEC Joint Technical Committee (JTC1) to work together on OSI standards. CCITT developed some OSI standards that relate to communication over telecommunications links. Examples include X.25, and the V series standards for dial-up communication via modems, as well as ISDN. JTC1 and CCITT work closely together to avoid conflict and to ensure that the development of OSI standards follows a consistent path. CCITT is responsible for defining standards in layers 1–3 over

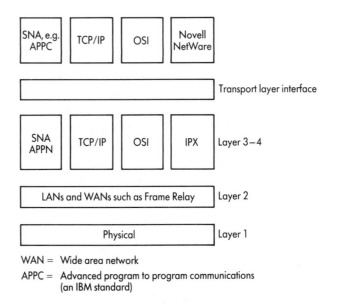

Figure 9.10   Schematic showing how protocol stacks can be constructed from different layers of more than one communication model.

public national and international telecommunications networks, while JTC1 is responsible for standards in layers 4–7 generally, and in layers 1–3 over private networks such as LANs.

ISO/IEC JTC1

This, the primary force behind OSI standards, particularly the more complex higher-layer ones, is a voluntary organization comprising various national standards bodies as voting members. JTC1 is split into various subgroups each of which deals with a particular area – for example SC6 deals with data communications.

CCITT

The principal members of the CCITT are national telecommunications carriers such as BT plc and AT&T. However computer and networking companies are allowed to belong as non-voting members. There are three types of CCITT standard. The V series refer to data communications over traditional analog dial-up telephone circuits. The X series refer to dedicated data network services, while the I and Q series relate to ISDN.

European and US standards bodies that feed into ISO/IEC and CCITT

9

European standards bodies

CEN/CENELEC

CEN and CENELEC are respectively the European groups of national members of ISO and IEC.

CEPT

This is the European Conference of Posts and Telecommunications. It is an association of European telecommunications and network operators and so to an extent is a subset of CCITT.

ETSI

This, the European Telecommunications Standards Institute, is part of CEPT responsible for formulating standards.

EWOS

The European Workshop for Open Systems (EWOS) develops and promotes OSI functional standards, which we described earlier in the chapter.

SPAG

The Standards Promotion and Application Group, formed in 1983 by 12 European IT firms to develop and promote conformance testing to OSI standards. Its role is similar to COS in the US.

ECMA

The European Computer Manufacturers Association, representing European IT companies, and also some US ones that trade in Europe. ECMA is involved in development of higher-layer OSI protocols.

US standards bodies

ANSI, the American National Standards Institute

ANSI coordinates the activities of various standards bodies in the US, and provides a forum for promoting US standards on the international front. The most relevant US bodies developing ANSI standards are CBEMA (Computer Business Equipment Manufacturers Association), which developed the FDDI standard, and IEEE (Institute of Electrical and Electronic Engineers), which introduced the famous 802 series LAN standards which are the cornerstone of this book. For example, Ethernet was known as IEEE 802.3 before being enshrined by ISO and given a different number. Token ring was IEEE 802.5.

NIST (National Institute for Standards and Technology)

Among many activities, NIST promotes OSI functional profiles, like EWOS in Europe.

COS (Corporation for Open Systems)

Comprises big US computer and networking companies, promoting acceptance and conformance testing of OSI standards, like SPAG in Europe.

Internet Engineering Task Force

Responsible for developing the TCP/IP protocols.

Other key body: X/Open

This is a group of vendors and users dedicated to creating and supporting the standards for complete IT environments, of which the network and OSI is just part. X/Open is particularly concerned with resolving differences between existing groups of standards. For example, it has been developing software to bridge TCP/IP and OSI protocols.

Key concept: Connection oriented and connectionless protocols

There are two fundamentally different types of network operation, which you may not need to understand, but which are worth explaining as a footnote in case you encounter them. These are connection oriented and connectionless operation, which are relevant to almost any communication process, not just computer networking. For communication to take place across a network, you either need to have a fixed path set up for the duration of a session or transmission, or you need to transmit packets of data each of which has addresses that can be recognized. The network can then route these packets to their destination.

The public telephone network is connection oriented, because you have to first dial a number to establish a path before you can speak. In fact communication over a connection oriented network involves three phases: set up, transmission, and release of the circuit.

The postal service on the other hand is connectionless, because you send individual packets that are addressed to their destination. LANs are also connectionless, requiring no call set-up, with all packets carrying addresses.

In general, connection oriented transmission is more efficient for sending small numbers of large batches of data, while connectionless is faster for many small items of data, where it saves by avoiding call set-up and release time.

10

How do I manage and maintain my network?

CHAPTER CONTENTS

CHAPTER OBJECTIVES

This chapter has been left so late partly to emphasize its
umbrella role, and not to imply that it is least important. In
fact its importance grows almost exponentially with network
size, so that it is only on the smallest LANs that it can be
disregarded. Even then it will soon become an issue if the
network grows.

Basic questions and issues tackled are:

Defining scope of network management

In this chapter we discuss not just strict day-to-day management of your network, but also security which although related is sometimes regarded as a separate area. And as well as considering network management products, we also look at actions you might take as a result of information gained from a management system. A good example of this is segmenting your network to maintain performance levels. This action might be taken when information from your management system indicates that traffic levels are increasing. We discuss segmentation later in the chapter.

First we define and discuss the areas that network management should cover. We explain how products for managing LANs have tended to focus on the physical network rather than on the computers, such as servers and particularly PCs, that are on the network. Yet a number of surveys indicate that problems relating to desktop systems are both more numerous and generally take longer to fix than those caused by faults on the physical network. Then looking at larger-scale networks comprising multiple inter-connected LANs, another problem is that there have been different incompatible management systems for the various elements. For example, there might be one management system for routers, another for dial-up modems, and another for each LAN's cabling system. We will discuss some standards and initiatives designed to tackle these problems. For example, the SNMP management protocols have been widely supported by vendors of networking systems, enabling a variety of products to be managed from a single system. However, until recently SNMP only extended as far as the network interface cards (NICs) in PCs. We look at other initiatives to develop comprehensive LAN management systems that fully embrace computers attached to the network and not just their NICs.

We look at the growing role of hubs as central points for network management. Essentially hubs make good management centres for two reasons. First, all data on a LAN passes through the hub which means that messages can be trapped there and measurements on traffic levels taken. Second, a growing number of LAN products such as routers are located within hubs, which means that they can be conveniently managed from that point.

Network management requires staff involvement, not just technical products

A point to bear in mind throughout this chapter is that the whole process of managing a network involves not just technical products but also staff. On a large network, one or more members of staff can be dedicated to the task of overall management. On a small network it may be best to make the task of management the responsibility of all users, who could be encouraged to report any minor faults or emerging performance problems.

Do all networks need management systems?

No. A two-user LAN linking a director and secretary, for example, hardly needs managing any more than a single-user PC does. The only form of management required would be a general awareness of impending problems, and as always careful backing up of critical data onto some removable storage media such as floppy disks. The only security needed would be physical in ensuring that the office is locked and that no unauthorized staff have access to the small network.

Even on slightly larger networks comprising five or six users, security may not be needed, provided the whole network is contained within a single room or open plan office area. There is no need for a sophisticated management system to report faults that will quickly become apparent anyway within a small closely knit workgroup.

10

Management begins to become essential when at least one of the following conditions applies.

(1)   The network is physically dispersed over more than one room or workgroup so that users are no longer within sight or earshot of each other.

(2)   Use of the network increases to the point when performance starts to degrade. Ideally network management will be introduced before this happens, which in general is unlikely when there are less than eight users.

(3)   When there is a need to discriminate between different users. For example, there might be sensitive information you want to restrict to just one or two people who need to access it.

(4)   When there is a need to access a wide area network or other computing facilities within your organization.

(5)   In general when the number of users exceeds 12, basic management to monitor the physical network and attached computers becomes desirable. As network size and complexity increase, the need for management tends to grow exponentially. A network of 100 users without any form of management would soon degenerate into chaos.

By the same token the sophistication required from a management system tends to increase with network size and complexity.

What elements need to be managed?

The management process can be viewed in terms of the distinct components that need to be managed, which can be split into three groups: the physical network; all hardware devices such as PCs attached to the network; and the software running across the network. These can then be subdivided further. For example, software can be split into client applications running in desktop PCs, and server components such as database management. Hardware can be split into desktop PCs, hubs, servers, printers, communications devices such as modems, routers and bridges, and other miscellaneous devices that can be attached to a LAN, which are described in Chapter 5.

However, there is a more structured way of viewing the management process in terms of the seven layer OSI model. The management process can then be broken down into seven distinct layers. This makes it easier to build up models of the information that needs to be conveyed from each device to a central management system. For example, the physical LAN is covered by layers 1 and 2. Therefore a management system only needs information from the bottom two layers regarding the LAN itself. The SNMP standards are constructed this way, as we shall see later in the chapter. Table 10.1 lists some of the elements that need to be managed and the corresponding OSI layers in which information is needed to manage them.

What functions should your network management system provide?

Eight main functions of network management can be identified, as cited in Table 10.2. However, not all of these are required on all networks. For example, there is no need for a map when you can see the whole network, and there is usually no need for cost accounting

Table 10.1   Some elements that need to be managed, and the OSI layers in which this is done.

Element	OSI layers
NIC (network interface card)	1–2
Physical cabling	1
PCs	3–7
Modems	1–2
Bridges	1–2
Routers	1–3

10

Table 10.2   Main functions of network management.

1 Performance analysis
2 Security
3 Fault monitoring
4 Configuration control
5 Network mapping
6 Inventory management
7 Network planning
8 Cost accounting

in a small business. The order in which these eight features often become necessary is the order in which they are listed in the table, with cost accounting only being required when there are several different departments on the same overall network.

We describe each of these functions in turn, and also where relevant the actions that can be taken based on information they provide. Under the general heading of fault management, we consider the crucial areas of backup for data and protection against power failures. These are not facilities provided within any single package, but are part of the overall task of managing a network.

Performance analysis

This involves monitoring the amount of data traffic on a LAN and the usage of resources such as a database server, keeping a historical record so that trends can be spotted and acted upon if necessary. The aim is to maintain adequate levels of performance in the face of evolving applications and often growing numbers of users. On a typical LAN, there might be 16 PCs, a database server and two printers. There might be two primary applications: word processing, for the production of standard letters, and processing of sales orders.

The management system should be able to produce statistics of traffic usage during each day to identify overall peaks and troughs that may occur at various times. It should be possible to break down the traffic figures to look at each user and device on the LAN individually. As far as the network is concerned, the relevant statistics relate to source–destination pairs, because this identifies the combinations of devices that are making most use of the LAN's capacity.

It can also be important to monitor usage of shared resources.

In our example above, the database server might start to be overloaded, or queues for one or both of the printers might become excessive. In the case of the printers the situation might be fairly obvious, but with the file server information about utilization might help action to be taken before performance deteriorates too much.

What actions to maintain or improve performance may be indicated?

Actions that may taken in response to network performance statistics include:

- Increasing the power and storage capacity of the server.
- Increasing the number of servers.
- Dividing the LAN into segments to restrict overall traffic levels.
- Changing the pattern of usage to avoid peak times.
- Moving to a faster network, such as from Ethernet to FDDI.

One or more of these remedies may be indicated depending on the shape of the statistics. For example, if the network as a whole performs adequately for 90 % of the day, but wilts under heavy loading during a short mid-morning peak, it may be possible to cope by changing working practices. Just as commuters can stagger their journeys to mitigate the impact of rush hours, so computer users may be able to spread out their activities without disrupting their work.

Another possibility is that network utilization levels remain low all the time but the server is getting overloaded, resulting in delays to database operations. Various remedies are possible. For example, if a server computer handles printing as well as a database, the problem may be solved by splitting the work of the server between two computers. However, if the load is mostly generated by the large number of database accesses and updates, the database server may need to be upgraded or replaced. The bottleneck is quite often in the disk drive, and may be remedied by installing a faster and higher-capacity drive. If the speed of access to the disk drive is a severe bottleneck, installing a new drive may not be sufficient. Then the required remedy may be to install solid state 'cache' memory, which acts as an intermediate level of storage between the disk drive and the server's main memory. Cache memory does not hold as much data as the rest of the drive, but access to data is much faster. The idea

10

is that the most frequently accessed data items are held in cache, which improves the overall access time.

Sometimes the physical network itself is the bottleneck. Then there are two possible remedies, depending on how serious the bottleneck is and on what kind of network it is. Usually if a single LAN serving a workgroup, department or a small company suffers from congestion, performance can be restored by dividing it into two or more segments, as we are about to describe. However, if a backbone LAN that is already linking a number of other LANs is congested, segmenting may not work. In this case, the best solution is to upgrade the backbone network to FDDI. If an existing FDDI network is itself becoming congested, then the only answer is to segment the FDDI rings. We shall identify more clearly the situations where segmenting a LAN is the right approach after describing the basic principle.

Segmenting explained

The use of bridges and routers to connect different LANs together, either locally or remotely, was described in Chapter 6. The LANs being connected are called LAN segments, to distinguish them from the network as a whole which functions very much like an enlarged LAN.

There are really two differences between an enlarged LAN comprising a number of segments interconnected by bridges or routers, and a single LAN segment. One is that an enlarged LAN may cover much greater distances, because the bridges or routers can connect two segments together over telecommunications links. The other is that some of the traffic on the enlarged LAN is restricted to local segments, because the bridges and routers act as traffic filters. Data packets that are sent from a device on one segment are only forwarded across the bridge or router if they are addressed to a device on the other side.

This principle is described in more detail in Chapter 6. Figure 10.1 will remind you of the basic principle of bridges, shown in Figure 10.1(a), and routers, in Figure 10.1(b). The main point for this chapter is that both bridges and routers keep data packets within the segment in which they were transmitted, unless they are actually addressed to a network node such as a PC outside that segment.

This function enables bridges and routers to restrict the overall traffic flow on a LAN. Although developed in the first instance to interconnect two previously isolated LANs, bridges and routers can

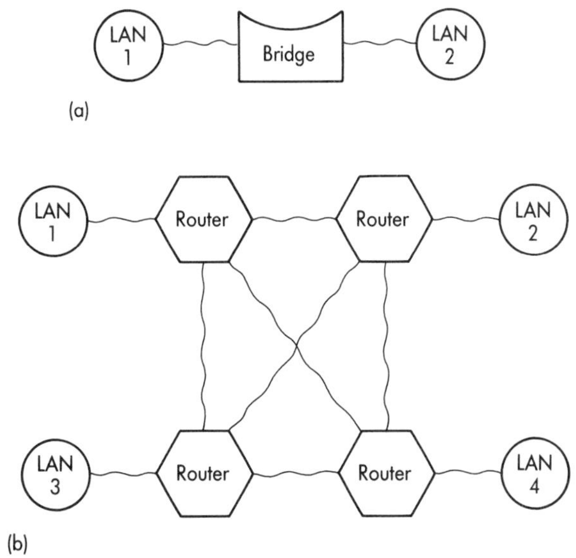

(a)

(b)

Figure 10.1   Recapping the basic principle of bridges and routers. (a) Bridge, for point-to-point links between LANs. (b) Routers enable LANs to be interconnected by more complex mesh networks.

equally well divide an existing LAN into more than one segment. It amounts to the same thing really, in that in both cases you end up with more than one interconnected LAN segment, except of course that LANs split up for performance reasons will comprise just locally attached segments. However, the motive is different, being to improve performance rather than to connect networks together.

The principle is illustrated in Figure 10.2. In Figure 10.2(a) we have a single LAN supporting two small workgroups, A and B, each with six PCs and a server. The workgroups are on a single LAN because, although they mostly access just their own server, they have occasional need to access the other workgroup's server. Users in workgroup A usually access server A, but occasionally access server B.

Suppose that after a while overall load on the network deteriorates to the point when response times on desktop applications that use the server become unacceptably slow. As shown in Figure 10.2(b), the situation can be remedied by installing a local bridge between the two workgroups, which would almost halve the total network traffic load.

Most of the LAN traffic will now be contained within each of the two segments, which each have the same total capacity as before. Only

10

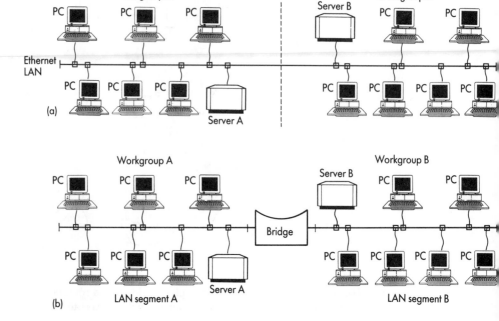

Figure 10.2 How a bridge can be used to segment a LAN. (a) LAN without bridge. (b) Use of bridge to divide LANs into two LAN segments, one for each workgroup.

when a user in one workgroup wants to access a server in the other workgroup would data have to cross the bridge and therefore occupy both segments of the network.

Routers can also be used to divide the segment in the network. The relative merits of bridges and routers as discussed in Chapter 6 mostly apply just as well to their use for segmenting LANs. Again it comes down to the size and complexity of the overall network, with bridges being preferred in small networks, but routers being better for large networks because of their support for multiple links and better use of alternate routes to avoid faults.

However, one advantage of routers, their more efficient use of available bandwidth in the network, is less relevant in onsite networks where there are no telecommunications links that have to be paid for on an ongoing basis. Therefore bridges are slightly more likely to be used for local segmentation than for interconnecting remote LANs.

Ethernet switching is an alternative to local routing and bridging

When an Ethernet LAN needs to be subdivided into segments for performance reasons, Ethernet switching is an alternative to local bridges and routers. The principle is similar to bridging, operating in the datalink layer of LAN addresses. However, it operates faster than bridges because it involves just a scan of the address header, whereas bridging requires the whole data packet to be picked up off the Ethernet LAN before making a decision on when to filter or forward it. This decreases the delay to the packet by about an order of magnitude. It also allows a number of Ethernet segments to be interconnected by a single Ethernet switch, whereas a bridge generally only interconnects two segments. In this sense it is more like a local router but again operates much faster. Furthermore, an Ethernet switch with five ports capable of supporting five segments costs approximately the same as a local bridge. It either comes as a stand-alone device or, like bridges and routers, it can be integrated into hubs. In many cases it is preferable to bridges and routers when an Ethernet LAN needs to be segmented for performance reasons.

So why would anyone ever want a local Ethernet bridge or router? Although an Ethernet switch is faster and more cost effective as a means of interconnecting locally attached LAN segments, it does not offer the same level of filtering control as a bridge, or especially a router. An Ethernet switch simply filters or forwards packets according to their destination address. It does not provide any control over which users can access which segments. So if, for example, it is desirable to prevent users in one workgroup from accessing information held on a server in another workgroup, then Ethernet switching is not the solution. A bridge, or more likely a router, is recommended, as they can make decisions based on more than just the destination address of the packet.

Another factor is that while Ethernet switching is a promising technology, unless and until standards are developed all implementations will be proprietary and dependent on the particular vendor. The range of products available in the field was still small at the end of 1992.

When should LANs be segmented?

Your network management system should indicate impending performance problems and whether the network itself is the bottleneck. Prompt action is particularly important for Ethernet LANs, because as explained in Chapter 2 its performance can drop spectacularly when loading reaches a certain critical point. Figure 10.3 plots response times of a fictitious application on a fictitious Ethernet network against loading on the network. Although the figures are not based on a real case, they give an accurate picture of the way performance can deteriorate quickly and the rate at which this would happen.

Segmentation will usually improve performance significantly. It is most effective where the LAN can be divided up into obvious workgroups that communicate mostly within themselves, as in the example shown in Figure 10.2. Where there is no such obvious division, the extent to which performance is improved depends on how well the segments are chosen. This is where good traffic statistics from the network management system are vital. These should help identify groups of users that, while they may not all belong to a particular department or workgroup, happen to transmit a lot of data to each other and rather less to users outside the group. The idea is to place a given set of bridges or routers in such a way that the total amount of traffic crossing between segments is minimized. It is also important of course that traffic is reduced to acceptable levels within every segment and not just some of them.

There are situations where segmentation is not suitable. Suppose a network in a 20-floor building comprises 10Base-T LANs on each floor – that is, Ethernet LANs running on unshielded twisted pair

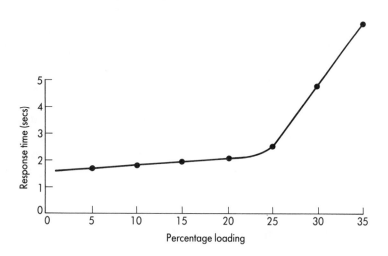

Figure 10.3 Plot of response times against percentage loading on a fictitious, but typical, Ethernet LAN. Note: response time is the time interval between a keyboard stroke and a response from a server on the LAN appearing on that user's PC.

(utp) cable linked in a star-shaped cable network into a hub. Suppose that each of these 10Base-T LAN segments is interconnected by a backbone network running vertically up the building, and that this is also Ethernet, but based on coaxial cable because the distance is too great for utp. It is quite likely that the backbone will at some time become a bottleneck restricting overall performance because its capacity is only the same as the segments it is connecting together. A theoretical option is to break the backbone up into two segments with a local bridge. But this is a cumbersome option, because it would involve breaking into the vertical riser of the building, and inserting a bridge into the backbone cable that is already attached to 20 bridges or routers linked to LAN segments on each floor. At some future point it may be necessary to insert a second local bridge into the backbone and then a third if traffic levels continue to increase.

A tidier solution, although considerably more costly in the short term, would be to replace the coax cable with optical fibre and install an FDDI backbone network. This could be done by linking all 20 LAN segments in a logical ring. Alternatively a routing hub, or Rub, could be used. Each of the 20 segments is then connected directly via fibre to the Rub, which provides an FDDI ring internally. The Rub is described in Chapter 8. This would not be practical for smaller businesses, but is worth considering when a number of LAN segments need to be interconnected, either in a large building comprising several floors or across more than one building.

Security

LAN security grew rapidly in importance as LANs began to be used for serious computer applications. Large LANs with powerful servers now process applications that used to require huge water-cooled mainframe computers. Some LANs therefore require levels of security equivalent to that of a mainframe computing environment in order to protect information from accidental or malicious destruction and from unauthorized access.

Even smaller businesses increasingly rely on LANs for 'lifeblood' applications. So they may need some security, although not to the same degree as large organizations.

The main security threats to LANs are listed in Table 10.3. Note that we do not include loss or corruption of data by accident, or as a result of faults, in this section. This is often regarded as being a function of security, because as far as users are concerned the outcome

Table 10.3 Main security threats to LAN.

1 Access by legitimate users to data they are not authorized to see.

2 Electronic eavesdropping, which could be by anyone within close range, even out-side the premises.

3 Hacking into the network from the public telephone network (only possible when dial-up access is allowed).

4 Tapping directly into the network to intercept or tamper with messages in transmission.

5 Computer viruses.

is often the same. But the measures taken to combat it are very different, so we discuss this under the general heading of fault management.

Traditionally computer operating systems have been responsible for protecting against many security threats. On LANs this responsibility has been transferred to the network operating system (NOS), which controls access to servers. Leading NOSs such as NetWare and LAN Manager provide sophisticated methods of controlling access to information and resources on the LAN. LAN Manager, for example, provides the ability to assign different security levels to print queues, directories and even files. This means that every file can be linked to each user of the network, but files can only be accessed by users authorized to do so.

The NOS cannot solve all security problems

The primary focus of the NOS is in controlling access by users from PCs or terminals attached to a LAN to resources located elsewhere on the network, such as servers and print queues. Control of access to print queues is important on larger networks mainly because it prevents users from jumping the queue by altering the priority of their print jobs – it avoids anarchy. Increasingly larger NOSs such as NetWare 3.11 and LAN Manager are also offering integrated security across a whole-enterprise network, in which users access not just facilities on their LAN but also a wide variety of remote facilities elsewhere in their organization.

Some offer single log-in, which means that users only have to go through one security procedure, in which they may enter a password and some other check, to access all the facilities for which they are authorized within their organization.

However, the NOSs do not in general tackle a major problem on LANs, which is eavesdropping on existing data transmissions on the network, as opposed to accessing a system from a terminal. Such eavesdropping can happen in two ways.

(1) By using electronic eavesdropping equipment to listen in to the electromagnetic signals radiated by copper cables during data transmissions.

(2) By attaching a terminal to the LAN to pick up directly data broadcasts from other users.

The second threat is only significant on larger networks not contained within single rooms of departments. But electronic eavesdropping can be effective against any network, because the equipment can be located outside the building. The principle is similar to the equipment used in the UK to detect whether there are televisions in houses that have not paid for a TV licence. However, for most very small networks the threat is not that serious because it is unlikely that anyone would take the trouble to 'listen in' to the data. But on larger networks carrying sensitive information relating to a company's business, such as designs of new products, electronic eavesdropping is a potential threat.

There are three possible solutions, only one of which covers both of the threats.

1. Use of data encryption addresses both threats, because it means that data on the network is scrambled until it is received by a legitimate user with the appropriate decryption key.

2. Use of optical fibre eliminates the electronic eavesdropping threat, because it carries light signals that do not emit electromagnetic radiation. It also makes it harder to tap into a network without this being detected because any unauthorized change to the network will have an effect on the transmission on the network. But it does not stop someone going to a terminal already on the network and listening in to data transmitted by other users. On both Ethernet and token ring, all data transmissions go to all attached devices, unless some filtering device is used. Therefore, a terminal or PC on the network could be used to intercept data transmitted onto the network by other devices, without this being detected. The way this works is shown in Figure 10.4, in which device B picks up data transmitted between PC A and server C.

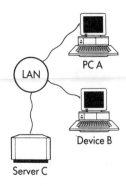

Figure 10.4   How a terminal or PC on the network could intercept data transmissions. Here we show a token ring LAN, but the principle could equally well apply to Ethernet.

3. Use of a hub which filters data in such a way that data is only transmitted to the destination device and is not broadcast to other devices. This is not an option on low-cost hubs for small networks, but is increasingly available on more expensive hubs in the middle and top part of the market, for networks of around 30 users and above. Of course there is nothing to stop such hubs being used on smaller networks, but at a price.

The way a filtering hub works for a 10Base-T Ethernet network is illustrated in Figure 10.5. Effectively the hub acts as a filtering bridge in the way described in the section on LAN segmentation earlier in this chapter. The difference is that whereas a normal bridge sits between just two LAN segments, on a 10Base-T hub the hub-based bridge can act as a filter between all attached devices. Technically each spur into the hub, at the end of which may be just one device such as a PC, is a LAN segment.

Viruses

The threat posed by computer viruses is often over-hyped, but exists nonetheless. Like their biological counterparts, these viruses are capable of invading their host, in this case a computer, and then inflicting damage as well as replicating themselves and spreading to other hosts. Also, like their biological counterparts, it is possible to protect host computers from invasion by viruses with special software packages. Such software acts rather like a vaccine in that it protects against certain targeted viruses, but not against new ones. It is also

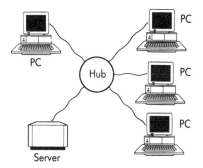

Figure 10.5   Operation of a filtering hub. Each PC and the server only receives data packets addressed to it.

possible to give computers some general protection against all viruses, like the immune system of the human body. Therefore the analogy with biological viruses is in some ways apt.

Viruses arrive in software programs that are loaded into a computer, usually a PC, either from a floppy disk or from a network to which the PC is attached. Most viruses are initially embedded in software of dubious source, which is loaded into PCs from a floppy disk. But having invaded the PC, they can then spread to other computers via the network.

The main effects of viruses can be summarized:

(1)   Harmless effects, like writing silly messages on the screen.

(2)   More serious, erasing or corrupting data files.

(3)   Most serious, destroying all data on a PC's hard disk, and spreading to other PCs.

Some viruses wait for a particular time to strike, like days that fall on Friday the 13th of a month.

10

Protecting against viruses

The primary protection is to reduce the risk of a virus invading a system in the first place. Users can be discouraged from loading floppy disks of uncertain origin into their PCs. New software can first be tested on an isolated PC not attached to the network to check that there are no viruses there before issuing it to users. Dial-up access into the network can be prevented, this being a potential source of viral invasion.

PCs can be protected by anti-virus software, but this is not guaranteed to work against all possible virus strains. So if infection has occurred, it is important to identify all affected devices, and this could conceivably include systems such as routers and bridges as well as PCs and servers. Then the virus should be purged from all affected systems, before an attempt is made to recover any data that has been lost or corrupted.

Perhaps the most effective protection against viruses infiltrating a LAN is the diskless PC. This is a PC without any disk drives, which can only function if it is connected to a network. Its central processing unit relies on the network to obtain data and applications software. One advantage is that such PCs are slightly cheaper, offsetting the cost of the central server which holds all data. But they tend to be installed primarily because they enable tighter control to be kept over usage of PCs. A major advantage they have is that because software cannot be loaded into them directly from floppy disks, they are highly immune to virus infection. Floppy disks are the usual route for viruses to reach PCs and ultimately the network.

Need for physical security

With so many security products around, the importance of physical security is sometimes forgotten. This is especially true of LANs, which tend to be located in open plan offices, as opposed to large mainframes, which for environmental reasons are located in specialist computer rooms. Such computer rooms are usually locked at night as a matter of course. Yet servers on large LANs are now in many cases storing and processing sensitive data and critical applications. Therefore, it is worth ensuring they are in secure areas that can be locked at night to prevent unauthorized physical access to the machine. Server security can be further enhanced by disabling the screen and keyboard. As servers are not running applications for end users, they do not need a screen and keyboard most of the time. By disabling them, direct access to data contained in them can be made difficult.

Fault monitoring

The single most effective way of combating faults is to take regular backups of data and maintain them in a secure place. As extensive support for backup facilities is provided by the NOS, we discussed this in Chapter 4, under the heading of Fault tolerance/recovery.

However, the actual monitoring of faults is down to the network management system itself. The roles of network management in this field are:

(1) To detect any faults that either have happened or are about to happen.

(2) To restrict the impact of such faults, for example by switching the network to an alternative route to bypass one that has failed. This is partly a matter of designing the network correctly in the first place, in such a way that it avoids single points of failure. Under this bracket come data backup procedures and uninterruptible power supplies.

(3) Troubleshooting, to fix the fault.

These roles apply not just to the network but also to the computers attached to it. Users are not generally interested in where the fault lies, but they do want it resolved as quickly as possible. Responsibility for the whole of fault management is beyond the scope of network management systems, which mainly address the first two roles listed above. Network management systems can detect faults, although it may require more than one management product to cover all potential faults on the network. The same is true with the bypassing of faults enabling networks to 'heal' themselves.

There are management products that can automatically reconfigure a network to avoid failed links or systems. But on networks of interconnected LANs, responsibility for bypassing faults on the links between LANs belongs to bridges or routers. We saw in Chapter 6 how the Spanning Tree algorithm enables Ethernet bridges to switch to an alternative route if the primary one fails. But Spanning Tree only supports one alternative route. We also explained how routers support more sophisticated use of more than one alternative link.

Within a LAN there are a variety of faults that can occur. These can be in the cable, in servers themselves, in PCs, in other attached devices such as printers, and in the network interface cards (NICs) linking devices to the network. LAN management systems should be able to detect that there is a cabling fault, but may not be able to locate it. It may not be immediately obvious where the fault is in larger networks where most of the cable is concealed under floors or behind walls. Locating the fault requires a LAN analyser, which is usually attached to the network only for troubleshooting when faults occur. They are too expensive to be permanently attached to every LAN.

Analysers are also used to locate higher-level protocol errors that

10

may be caused by data corruption or by errors in communication software. Network management systems may initially detect the presence of such faults, but are usually unable to pinpoint them precisely or resolve them.

Server reliability

With increasing dependence on servers for database management and printing in particular, increasing attention has been paid to server reliability. Various measures can be taken depending on how critical the applications are and on the size of the network. These are:

1. Read after write verification. This is a facility provided by some NOSs, in which data that has just been written onto the hard disk of the server is then compared with the data in the server's main memory from which it was written. If there is a discrepancy, an error has occurred, and the data is written to some other part of the disk, and checked again.

2. Transaction tracking. Again supported by some NOSs, this records in a file the whole sequence of database operations required for a complete transaction. An example of a transaction is drawing money from a bank's cash dispensing machine. This involves debiting a bank account, details of which may be held in one database, and also updating another database recording details of each cash withdrawal. If a transaction fails, it is important to ensure that all databases involved are rolled back to their original state. A transaction tracking file, which records details of each operation, enables this to be done. However, for best effect, the transaction tracking process needs to be supported by the application as well as the NOS. The application has control of the relevant databases and is responsible for updating them when transactions are successfully completed. Therefore it should also be up to the application to ensure that databases are rolled back if the transaction fails, making use of information held in the NOS transaction tracking file.

3. Disk mirroring and disk duplexing. Here data is written simultaneously to two separate disk drives attached to a file or database server, so that the network continues to operate without interruption even if one disk drive fails. The distinction between mirroring and duplexing is shown in Figure 10.6. With disk mirroring, both disk drives are attached to the same drive controller via a single channel

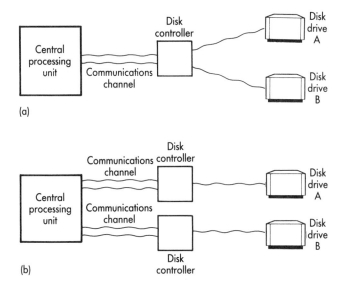

Figure 10.6 Distinction between disk mirroring and duplexing. (a) Disk mirroring. (b) Disk duplexing.

from the server's main processor. With disk duplexing, the two drives each have their own controllers that are being attached to the processor via parallel channels. Duplexing therefore protects against failure of the disk drive controller and channel as well as the drives themselves. These options are not particularly expensive compared to the overall cost of the network. More to the point they may seem positively cheap compared with the real cost of server failure. They are recommended on any LAN where heavy use is made of a single dedicated server. They are probably not relevant, however, for small peer-to-peer LANs, where careful organization of the network can reduce exposure to failure of any single non-dedicated server in any case.

4. Mirrored servers. This is the most expensive option, only just becoming available. It is recommended only on relatively large networks where failure of the server would have severe consequences for the business. It involves having two identically configured servers complete with disk drives, where one is dedicated just to tracking the operations of the other. The operation of mirrored servers is shown in Figure 10.7. An important point is that the link between the servers must be substantially faster than the LAN to which the servers are attached.

10

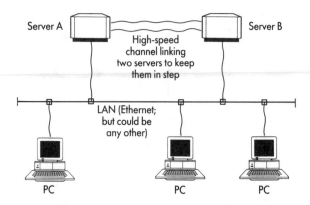

Figure 10.7   Operation of mirrored servers.

If this is not the case, then the second server will not be able to track the first one quickly enough to satisfy the timing requirements of the LAN. In Figure 10.7, the two servers are linked via a backbone FDDI network, while the LANs on which the server's clients are located is Ethernet. As FDDI is in practice more than ten times as quick as Ethernet, this ensures that the mirrored server operation is sufficiently fast. Another advantage of this arrangement is that it provides some protection against larger-scale disasters than a hardware or software fault. On an FDDI network the two servers could be located several kilometres apart, so that if one were destroyed by a fire, for example, the other would be unaffected. With some reconfiguration the part of the network not affected by the fire would be able to resume normal operation.

5. Uninterruptible power supplies (UPS). Large computer systems have long been protected against spikes (sudden surges in power), complete blackouts and brownouts (reductions in power) by uninterruptible power supplies, and in some cases by standby generators. Now that LANs run critical applications for a growing number of businesses, there is a similar need to protect them against power failure as well. Yet many LANs are not protected by a UPS, and therefore all processing would cease in the event of a power failure, with the added risk of serious data corruption during more minor brownouts. In many cases it takes a good power failure to make users aware that investment in a UPS, which is relatively modest compared with the overall cost of a LAN, is well worth making. The UPS is often an optional extra, but for any business where main

activities cease when the LAN is not available, it should be deemed essential.

Even where a UPS has been installed, protection is often not adequate. A mistake sometimes made is to assume that it is sufficient just to protect the server. But LANs differ from centralized systems in that a substantial amount of processing takes place on desktop PCs or workstations. Therefore to ensure that the network can be closed down smoothly without any loss of data in the event of a prolonged power cut, it is important that PCs are protected by a UPS as well as the server.

What sort of UPS solutions are available?

It is now possible to purchase small UPSs about the size of a single volume dictionary to protect individual PCs. These can conveniently sit under each desktop, with the server protected by a larger UPS. Alternatively all computing devices attached to the LAN, including PCs, servers and printers, can be protected by a single UPS. In this case the UPS obviously needs to be bigger, and the electricity cabling needs to be structured so that it fans out from the UPS to each device. This arrangement is worth considering when installing new LANs from scratch, particularly if the office is being rewired at the same time. Then electrical cabling can be laid in a structured way just like the data and telephone cabling, making it easy to manage in future. The advantage is that if the UPS has been chosen correctly, the network can be expanded easily without requiring additional investment in power supply equipment. It may be that at some point the existing UPS will need to be expanded, or even replaced, but this operation will be more straightforward if all mains cabling fans back to a central equipment closet along with the data cabling.

However, this arrangement may be too expensive and impractical for small networks, in which case the small stand-alone UPSs can be used. This may not require a UPS for every device. It may, for example, be possible to arrange PCs in pairs all fed off a single UPS.

10

Factors to consider when choosing a UPS

The first point to consider is whether to go for a central UPS feeding all devices, or for distributed UPSs for every PC, or some combination of the two. Then it comes down to deciding how big the UPS should be. Suppliers can advise you of precise technical specifications, but a basic consideration is how long you want the network to be kept running in the event of a complete power failure. UPS systems rely on rechargeable batteries to provide power, but they vary greatly in their capacity. A typical office UPS provides about 1500 VA (volt amps), and this would be capable of sustaining a network of about eight PCs, a printer and a server for about 20 minutes. But UPSs are typically rated by power capacity rather than by the number of devices they can handle. Calculations of UPS size therefore need to take account of the power input requirements of the devices on your network as well as the length of time you want to have guaranteed operation of the network in the event of a power failure.

Another point to consider is support of the UPS for network management facilities. For most networks it is not cost effective to provide sophisticated standby generators to cope with indefinite power failures. Instead the purpose of a UPS is to provide protection against short power outages or brownouts, and then to facilitate an orderly shutdown of the network. Key data can be backed up, and applications left in a state from which they can recover smoothly when power is restored. To do this it is necessary to know as soon as a power failure has occurred. Some UPSs support management facilities provided by NOSs such as NetWare.

UPS systems can also be distinguished according to whether they operate offline or online. Offline UPSs only come into action when there is a power failure; normally they simply channel the raw AC (alternating current) supply through to the computers, sometimes through a filter to smooth out minor fluctuations. Then when there is a power failure, they switch to the batteries, which provide a high quality uniform AC supply. This can lead to a damaging stutter in supply at the moment of cut-over to the batteries.

Online UPS systems on the other hand provide a continuous AC supply whether or not there is a power cut, so that there is no hitch at the point when a failure occurs. During normal operation, this AC supply is generated from the mains supply, then during a power failure they switch over to batteries, but this happens in the background transparently to the computers.

For larger networks, a standby generator may be worth considering, ensuring non-stop operation of the network in the event of power failure. In this case a UPS is still necessary both to generate a clean supply of electricity from the mains and to ensure a smooth cut-over to the generator after a power failure.

Configuration control

Like some other aspects of network management, the facilities required for configuration control can be viewed in terms of the seven layer OSI model. The overall need is to be able to reconfigure the network when changes are made. Possible changes include the addition or removal of devices from the network, the registration of new users, and the enhancement of the network, for example to increase capacity of particular links.

A general requirement when networks are reconfigured is not just to make any updates to tables and databases that are needed for the network to function properly, but also to update any management system so that correct information is available to administrators. For example, if there is a map of the network this needs to be updated. Network maps are described in the next section.

Physical layer

In offices where there is a structured cabling system, it should not be necessary to install any new cables to introduce a new user to the network. If the network does not have a manageable hub, the usual procedure is to make a connection at a central patch panel to provide a physical connection between the new PC or terminal and the rest of the LAN. However with a manageable hub, it should be possible to effect the connection from a management terminal without manual action.

Data link layer

The requirement here is to maintain up-to-date tables of addresses of devices on the network. Such addresses are typically held on the network interface cards attaching devices to the network, so that the device knows which address to attach to each packet before transmitting it onto the network. If, for example, a user wants to send an electronic mail message to someone else on the network, the user may enter the name of that person. This name would be matched with the correct layer 2 MAC (media access control) address by the NIC, which therefore needs to be updated if a new user is added to the network. Bridges and routers also need to be updated separately, because they maintain their own set of tables in order to filter and forward or route traffic correctly.

10

Network layer 3

Here the situation becomes more complex, because not all devices on a large network may support the same layer 3 network protocols. Routers need to be informed of configuration changes that affect layer 3 addresses as well as layer 2, because they operate in both layers. For example, suppose a whole new LAN segment is added to an existing network of LAN segments interconnected by routers. The router connecting the new segment to the network would need to be set with the layer 2 addresses of all devices on its segment and the layer 3 addresses of other routers on the overall network. On the other hand, all existing routers would only need their layer 3 address tables updated. As illustrated in Figure 10.8, this is because routers use layer 3 addresses to route traffic between LANs, over a wide area network, for example, but use layer 2 addresses for the final delivery of data within each LAN.

Higher layers

Implementations of higher-layer OSI, TCP/IP or other protocols will usually reside in computers on the LAN, or in some cases just in a LAN communications server. Again, tables need to be updated if users are added or removed from the network. In some cases applications themselves need to be updated. For example, security tables or a network mapping database may need to be updated, Another example is an electronic mail system, which may need to have a new user name added. Any directory of users would also need to be updated.

Network mapping

This really serves other network management functions rather than being an end in its own right. A map may look pretty, but unless it helps in managing configurations, faults and possibly some of the other functions, it serves no useful purpose.

There are two types of map: geographical and topological. The former provides a geographical map of the network. It is clearly not needed on single LANs which by their nature are contained within a small area. But on large national or even global networks of interconnected LANs, a geographical map provides a useful overview of network activity. Different colours can be used to identify a variety of conditions on the circuits and devices shown on the map. The use

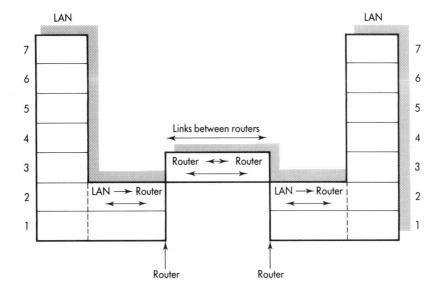

Figure 10.8 How routers use layer 2 for delivery of data within the LANs they are attached to, but layer 3 between themselves.

of graphical windowing systems can make it easy for administrators to obtain current or historical statistics relating to components or links shown on the map.

   A topological map shows the devices and links of a network in relation to each other without worrying if they are all in their correct geographical positions. This is clearly the most useful sort of map for small networks. For intermediate-scale maps, some combination of the geographical and topological approach may be best. This could be like maps of metropolitan underground trains, where the primary need is to show how each line and station relates to each other and to the overall network, but where it is also necessary for the map to bear at least a rough resemblance to geographical reality.

   On large networks, a hierarchy of maps is usually provided, so that administrators can obtain a basic overview map, and then home in on increasingly large-scale maps to obtain greater detail of current network performance in particular areas. Typically the small-scale overview maps of the whole network might be largely geographical, while the large-scale local maps would be more topological.

10

Inventory management

This is important even for small LANs, but becomes particularly significant on larger networks where it is harder to keep track of what items there are attached to the network. Inventory management is closely related to configuration management and also network mapping, because on a large network a crude list of contents is fairly useless unless it is related to locations, departments and individual users. It can help resolve problems, because if, say, a user phones up a help desk with a fault, support personnel can immediately obtain information about the hardware and software that user has. This information may be related to the network map showing where that user is in relation to other systems.

Network planning

This is the long-range function of the network management process. It is not covered specifically by standard network management systems, although there are software tools to assist with the task of longer-term planning. Whereas conventional network management is concerned with ensuring that the network serves its users well on a day-to-day basis, planning is about making sure it will still do so in the more distant future.

Many of the issues involved were covered in Chapter 8 which dealt with ways of ensuring that a network will last. Here it is worth pointing out that there are software modelling tools that allow you to mimic the effects of changes to your network without actually making those changes. There are also consultancies that can help you assess the impact of future changes and use such tools on your behalf.

On larger networks spanning many LANs, another option which has been applied successfully by some organizations is to pilot new applications on small portions of a network before extending it to all LANs. For example, a bank might want to introduce a new customer service that requires the implementation of additional application software in each branch. The new application would almost certainly increase overall network traffic as it would probably require access to centrally held data. The application could be tried out in just a few branches first, to gain some idea of its likely impact when extended to the whole network of perhaps 3000 branches. This may help anticipate future problems and decide how to extend the computer network in preparation for the new application.

Cost accounting

This is a feature that really only comes into its own on large networks spanning different departments. In some large organizations, each department is a cost centre that has to submit annual financial results almost like an independent company. For this to happen, costs have :d to each department on as fair a basis as possible. a resource that costs money.

zation has to calculate how much the network as a ·ear, by adding the annual telecommunications costs on new equipment and software licences, plus the existing hardware. The cost of running the network : added in.

department can be metered for use of network)sts allocated on some sort of pro rata basis. The exact ion will vary from company to company. But what-sed, there needs to be some form of network manage-measure usage. Network management systems often ...uaiied traffic statistics anyway, so cost accounting is a natural extension of their function. Another benefit of cost accounting is that it enables the productivity of individuals and groups of users to be compared with the network costs they incur.

How universal protocols – and hubs – are bringing network management systems under one umbrella

10

Until the early 1990s, network management was a very *ad hoc* process, relying on a number of systems that overlapped in function but were incompatible with each other. Typically there was a separate management system for each type of product on the network, such as modems and bridges. This meant that people responsible for controlling large networks would often have to examine several screens pertaining to different systems to monitor faults and track down problems. In many cases it obviously made sense if they could have a single screen, presenting not just a common map of the whole network but also a standard set of commands to interrogate all the different management elements.

The first step in this direction came with SNMP (simple network management protocol). At first this was too simple, providing only basic management information but it has been extended and has become the prevailing standard for managing LANs. It enables the network elements of the LAN to be managed from a single management station. This then raises the question of where to locate the management station. There are two main choices. It can be attached to a server, using management facilities provided by the NOS. Or it can be attached to a hub, using management facilities provided by the hub vendor. On a small network with hub cards located in a server, these two options amount to the same thing. In this case the hub card would itself be one element to be controlled from a server-based management system.

SNMP protocols have suffered from a major limitation in that their influence ends at the NICs. This means that SNMP-based systems have not been able to, and many still cannot, manage devices such as PCs, servers and printers. Another way of looking at it is that SNMP management has only embraced the bottom three layers of the OSI stack, while computers attached to the network are active in all seven layers. It is only communications systems such as modems, routers and ridges that are covered by lower-layer management.

CMIP (common management information protocol) was meant to provide the complete end-to-end management facilities originally lacking in SNMP, covering all seven OSI layers. But the complexity that such an ambitious management scheme entailed resulted in the complete CMIP model being very slow to arrive. Meanwhile a number of LAN vendors and the IEEE 802.x standards committees decided to develop a standard management scheme for LANs that would embrace desktop systems as well as the network itself.

The relevant IEEE standard is 802.1D, which is an extension of the 802.1 series of LAN management standards to embrace desktop systems. However, in a separate initiative, two vendors, IBM and 3 Com, collaborated on development of what they called a Heterogeneous LAN management standard. There have been discussions on including the IBM/3 Com work in the IEEE 802.1D standards.

So the final shape of LAN management standards is uncertain. What is clear, however, is that there will continue to be a substantial industry push behind SNMP. We therefore expect SNMP to continue improving, and would not be surprised to see it eventually merge into CMIP. It looks increasingly unlikely that CMIP will oust SNMP from its pole position in LAN management.

11

Case study, drawing together themes of book

Having described the various elements of LANs and how they fit together, along with a glimpse at potential alternative solutions such as minicomputers, we draw the themes together by looking at a case study. Although fictitious, it is based on a compendium of several real case studies investigated by the author in 1992. These were chosen because they illustrated particular aspects of LANs, and have been amalgamated to provide more comprehensive coverage of the points made in this book than each would on its own.

Our fictitious example is a public relations company that we will call ABC with 30 employees and annual turnover around £2.5 million ($5 million). Steady growth has been enjoyed, but this has recently been brought to a halt by the recession of the early 1990s. ABC's immediate objective is defensive: to hold onto existing clients while reducing costs. But at the same time in a competitive business where the potential rewards for success are substantial, the company wants to be well placed to exploit any upturn in the economy when it occurs.

Currently the company has 15 PCs of various types scattered around offices on which it owns the freehold just west of London, along with a laser printer and two dot matrix printers. Applications include word processing for the production of letters for distribution to clients and journalists; accounting; and marketing. But there is no network connecting the PCs, apart from a patching system enabling some of the PCs to connect to the laser printer when they need to. This lack of a network is leading to several problems:

(1) Users are increasingly unable to print their jobs when they want, because printers are busy.

(2) Handling accounting functions like billing clients is hampered by the fact that it is impossible with the current arrangement to give more than one person access to the

application at a time. The accounting system is based on a database package called dBase running on a single PC. If all accounts staff could have common access to a single system with just one source of data, time would be saved.

(3)   ABC wants to exploit synergy between different applications such as accounting and marketing, with exchange of data between the two, but this is impossible without some platform to support the relevant communication and interoperability.

(4)   Links between PCs, such as the printing patch panel, are beginning to accumulate in an *ad hoc* way. Chaos will gradually increase unless a clear plan is established and acted on soon.

(5)   Some of the PCs are running out of steam, being unable to support their current applications. The company is reluctant to replace them without considering more structured alternatives, such as a server-based LAN or a minicomputer.

(6)   Some form of electronic mail facility has become desirable, not so much for exchange of basic messages, but for documents such as feature articles for clients to be transmitted between different PCs so that several members of staff can work on them.

(7)   ABC had decided it was time to implement a consistent user interface such as Microsoft Windows 3.1 on all PCs, but to derive full benefit from this, existing applications should be integrated, with access to common data from all PCs.

Choosing consultant to help formulate RFP

ABC knew that some other companies in its field had installed LANs to tackle these problems, while one or two had minicomputers. But lacking the expertise to make intelligent buying decisions or even formulate a coherent request for proposals (RFP), it decided to hire a consultant to conduct an initial appraisal.

ABC was well versed in the art of hiring outside consultants in general for various parts of its business, such as hiring freelance designers to help prepare brochures. It was therefore able to provide a tight specification for a consultant. This was essentially first to evaluate the basic requirements, then prepare an RFP, and finally spend a day helping to evaluate the proposals.

Several consultancies quoted prices for this initial part of the work. In the end ABC did not go for the cheapest quote, but chose a consultancy with a strong reputation in the general field of networking.

The RFP

The consultancy quickly ruled out a minicomputer solution, partly because in this case it would cost more. Whereas a LAN would make use of existing PCs, a minicomputer would require either the installation of dumb terminals or the use of emulation software to make the PCs function as dumb terminals. There were other ways that PCs could be embraced by a minicomputer, but these would be too complex for the particular requirements. A LAN was therefore indicated.

Given that cost was a primary consideration in a year when profits had fallen by 50 %, it seemed likely that an Ethernet solution was preferable to token ring, which tends to be more expensive. Furthermore, the performance of Ethernet would be adequate, given that none of the applications were likely to make heavy use of network bandwidth. However, there was no point in ruling out token ring solutions in the RFP, provided it was stated clearly that cost would be a factor in the decision.

Another important consideration was that existing applications should be ported across successfully to the new network. It was decided that the same vendor should be responsible for the whole implementation, except for possible future developments such as integration of existing applications.

The RFP then read as follows:

1. The network will be based either on a token ring or Ethernet topology, with initial support for 16 PCs but with the potential to expand to 40 without requiring any software upgrades. The only

11

significant upgrades required should be memory and disk capacity in the central file server. The network should also be capable of supporting up to eight printers.

2. The network should be built around a central file server, but should be capable of operating if desired in peer-to-peer mode. This rules out network operating systems (NOSs) that cannot support peer-to-peer operation. The file server should be based on a 486 processor from Intel, and initially be configured with 16 Mbytes of main memory and a 600 Mbyte hard disk drive. Some backup storage device such as a tape unit should be provided, with capacity of at least 300 Mbytes.

3. The network must support 12 of the existing PCs (the other four being deemed either too old or incompatible) as clients on the network. These are a mixture of 286- and 386-based PCs from several vendors, all of the old IBM AT bus design. However, the vendor should evaluate these PCs and provide any memory upgrades that may be required for networked operation. The vendor should also provide appropriate network interface cards (NICs) for each PC, along with the necessary software components.

4. The vendor should provide four additional 386-based PCs each with 4 Mbytes main memory and 40 Mbyte disk drives, along with NICs.

5. On top of the basic networking features, there should be facilities for electronic mail. The network should also support remote access to a network via a dial-up telephone connection and modem. At this stage modems are not required as they are readily available commodity items, but the software to support this must be in place, so that the facility can be added just by reconfiguring the network at a later stage. Also, the network should be capable of being either segmented or expanded with bridges or routers, although this is not required at present.

6. The network should be built around a hub-based structured cabling system capable of expansion to support 40 PCs without requiring further cabling on the floor. ABC's offices where there are currently 30 staff could readily accommodate another ten people, although at present not all of them need PCs. The hub could be either a standalone box or implemented as cards for the server. Whatever configuration is proposed must be fully manageable from a single station.

Ideally the management system should be able to control and monitor users' PCs as well as the server and the network.

7. Existing applications should be reconfigured to work over the network, and any negotiations with software vendors over new versions or licences should be conducted. All data for accounting, marketing and mailing applications, including client and contact databases, will be moved to the central file server. This data will be organized in a relational database provided by the vendor. This database should support SQL access and come from a leading software supplier.

8. The vendor shall provide a day's training to three members of ABC staff who will in turn pass on their knowledge to other employees as appropriate. To follow up, the vendor will provide free telephone support and onsite warranty of all hardware and software components for six months. Cost of maintenance and support for three further years should be specified in the quote.

Other routine but vital points were included under the following headings:

- Implementation schedule, including testing and setting up of users with passwords to key data and applications.
- Point of contact within the company.
- Provision of references, usually at least two, from sites where the vendor has installed a similar network.
- Payment schedule. This might involve a deposit, further payment on final installation, and final settlement three months later.

Evaluation of quotes from vendors

11

The principles outlined in Chapter 7 were adhered to in evaluating the RFPs. Vendors of unknown or doubtful financial pedigree were eliminated, as were those whose proposals did not correspond to the specification. One proposal for a token ring network was ruled out on grounds of cost, being 25 % more expensive than a comparable one from another vendor.

In the end three proposals were short-listed, all based on Ethernet with 10Base-T structured cabling. The difference between the solutions lay in the NOS. Two were based on different versions of Novell NetWare, one on NetWare Lite, the other on NetWare 3.11. The third was based on a NOS not so well known in the UK, PowerLAN from Performance Technology.

The choice between the three was difficult in that none fulfilled every single requirement of the specification, while each had some arguments in its favour. The NetWare Lite solution incorporated DR-DOS, a powerful version of the DOS operating system now owned by Novell. The solution, based on the second release of NetWare Lite, provided several features missing in the first release, such as full consistency with commands in NetWare v3.1 and dynamic updating of print queue status information, allowing users to monitor progress of their print jobs more effectively. It also offered disk caching facilities that improved performance significantly over the previous release. However, NetWare Lite did not appear to offer the required range of backup facilities in its present version.

The solution based on NetWare v3.11 provided all the security, backup and management features required, but, unlike NetWare Lite, did not support peer-to-peer operation. Although printers could be attached to various PCs on the network, it was not possible to set up multiple non-dedicated file servers, which ABC wanted as an option. A future version of NetWare looked as if it would fulfil all conceivable requirements, but this was not yet available.

The solution based on PowerLAN fulfilled many of the requirements. It supported both central dedicated servers and non-dedicated servers in peer-to-peer mode. The PowerLAN NOS operated efficiently across a wide range of network sizes, and certainly would support any future growth at ABC. Furthermore, it came with a range of powerful options such as Powersave, which enables data to be backed up automatically from both servers and desktop PCs, and subsequently restored.

The only doubts about the PowerLAN solution concerned the stability of the supplier and future expansion of the product. Although PowerLAN was quite well known in the US where it had enjoyed rave reviews from magazines such as *LAN Times* and *Byte Magazine*, in the UK it was relatively unknown. However, there were several impressive reference sites where the product had apparently been very successful. Also, the dealer proposing the solution was able to convince ABC that it was fully committed to the product and would be firmly supported by the UK distributor, CMS Software.

Regarding future development of the product, the case for Novell appeared the strongest, given that the company had far greater resources and was also involved with other leading industry players like IBM and Unix International. Certainly the Novell route was the safest and most comfortable. On the other hand, for a company of ABC's size, many of the sophisticated management and integration features either available now or coming soon with NetWare would not be needed. PowerLAN had an option called Powerbridge meeting the requirement for possible future LAN-to-LAN connection.

Being less conservative than many businesses, ABC in the end plumped for the PowerLAN solution. The decision was swung not just by the NOS, but also by cabling considerations – the chosen solution appeared to provide the best support for growth.

One of the other proposals featured a hub without any management facilities. The successful proposal on the other hand featured the ExpressNet hub from David Systems, which provided the option of management based on SNMP. The relevance of SNMP is discussed in Chapter 10. Each individual hub supports just 12 attached devices, but up to four hubs can be strung together to cater for networks of up to 48 nodes. There was a price to be paid for the option of management at a later stage – managed hubs cost almost twice as much as simple unmanaged hubs. But ABC decided it was worth paying the extra price after talking to users of other networks that had initially gone for unmanaged hubs but subsequently regretted it and upgraded to a managed hub. In such cases it costs less, and is certainly less disruptive, to go for a managed hub in the first place.

Installation issues

Having made the choice, the installation at ABC proceeded smoothly. However, as it involved substantial cabling work with floors up and also the addition of panels to form an enclosed room for two hubs and a server, there was some disruption. ABC had hoped that the work could be done over a weekend, but some of it spilled over into the following week. The company's directors realized that they had been lax in not specifying in the RFP a precise timetable for installation work.

11

The central wiring closet was small, but would easily accommodate the four 12-port hubs that would be required if and when the network expanded to its maximum capacity of 40 PCs. Even if for some unforeseen reason the network had to expand further, this would be supported by both the NOS and the hub structure. For example, each hub could have its casing removed to become a module of a larger hub concentrator from the same vendor.

The main teething problems concerned application software rather than the physical network itself. As already mentioned, the company wanted to move to Windows 3.1. This in turn required new versions of the underlying DOS operating system, and of the applications software. In any case the applications programs had to be changed to support operation over a network. There were no insurmountable problems, but the process of ironing out incompatibilities and ensuring that each PC had the correct version of the various pieces of software needed proved more time consuming than expected.

Initially the network slowed users down in their day-to-day operations, but it was not long before almost everyone in the company began to appreciate the advantages such as consistency of data, access to applications from PCs throughout the offices, and more flexible and efficient printing.

There was soon pressure for more PCs, and there are now 20. At this stage the growing complexity of running the day-to-day network persuaded ABC to take up the option of SNMP management. This enables the network administrator to home in on individual ports on the network to see if there are any problems, and also to monitor usage of the network.

Now that the company has established a consistent source of data, it is beginning to exploit this by developing links between existing applications. For example, it is linking existing accounting records with a marketing system to assess the effectiveness of specific public relations campaigns, such as placing of feature articles about clients in particular magazines and journals. This information has two uses: it enables the company to identify the most effective methods of promoting its existing clients, and it is useful ammunition in attracting new clients, who it hopes will be impressed by this level of sophistication.

Therefore the LAN is already encouraging the development of new applications that help improve the quality of services and attract new business, as well as increasing the efficiency of internal computer applications.

APPENDIX 1

ISDN (integrated services digital network)

ISDN is the successor to the standard public switched telephone network (PSTN), providing digital rather than analog communications. This confers several advantages. It means that the network can transmit digital data between computers without needing a modem (although it still requires an ISDN terminal adaptor). It provides higher-quality voice transmission and more reliable data transmission, because digital signals arrive at their destination largely intact, without suffering the attenuation that befalls analog signals. Furthermore, ISDN offers the prospect of integrated voice/data services. A simple example is the ability to speak to somebody and exchange data or text messages between PCs over the same connection.

This is less likely to be a key feature for most small businesses at present, largely because the public ISDN service is not yet widely available on a worldwide basis. Different countries are proceeding at different rates, and services are not always compatible with each other. As a result ISDN is not yet a practical proposition for the typical small business, although it is likely to become so in future. Essentially, as with modems, ISDN links can be shared on a LAN.

The first generation of ISDN services operate at 64 kbit/s, which is substantially slower than LANs. This means ISDN is not suitable for carrying high traffic loads between LANs, except as a backup for permanent circuits. However, in future as ISDN speeds increase it may well reduce or even eliminate the need for permanent circuits at all. For LAN users this could cut telecommunication costs substantially by avoiding paying for permanent circuits that are only utilized part of the time. With ISDN you only pay while you are actually transmitting data over a dial-up link.

Future higher-speed broadband ISDN circuits accessed perhaps through Frame Relay interfaces may become the standard way of interconnecting LANs. Broadband is the name given to ISDN services planned for the future that will provide dial-up circuits with capacities of 2 Mbit/s or more.

Until that happens, however, the main use of ISDN will be either as a backup for existing leased services, or for overspill capacity. For the latter, a router or bridge dials up an ISDN connection in addition to the permanent leased circuit to cope with peak periods when there is heavy traffic between remote LANs. Many bridges and routers now provide ISDN connections for these purposes.

APPENDIX 2

Description of Ethernet and token ring technology

Ethernet

With Ethernet, the transmission speed supported is either one or ten Megabits (Mbits)/s. However the latter speed predominates, which means that ten million individual bits of data can be transmitted each second. A bit is a single binary digit of data, either a 'zero' or a 'one'. Character sets are represented by a number of bits, usually eight. Ethernet can therefore convey over a million characters a second, which seems plenty. And for most small business applications, Ethernet provides more than adequate capacity. But the response users obtain at their PCs is determined not so much by the absolute capacity of the network, but the method used to access it. For Ethernet, this method is called CSMA/CD (carrier sense multiple access with collision detection).

This method, illustrated in Figure A2.1, allows only one of the devices attached to the LAN cabling to transmit data at any time. All attached devices may contend for access when they want to transmit. When a device such as a PC wants to transmit data, it first monitors the network to determine whether there is any traffic on it. If there is, it continues to monitor the network and tries again as soon as the channel is free. Otherwise if all is clear it goes straight ahead with the transmission – this is the CSMA part of the method. The device then transmits a data packet, which can vary in size but must be in the range 64 bytes to about 1500 bytes. If, as would happen when sending a large document, for example, the device needs to send more data than 1500 bytes, the process of gaining access is repeated until all the data has been sent. The total transmission is therefore broken down into a series of packets each of which is transmitted independently across the LAN and reassembled by the receiving device.

The collision detection or CD part of the access method is required when two or more devices try to start transmitting data at virtually the same instant. The devices monitor the network for traffic at that time. If no other device is already sending data, they both, or all, then try to transmit data onto the LAN simultaneously, resulting in a collision. The collision is detected by the Ethernet hardware, and the devices are told to back off for randomly determined time intervals.

A random time interval is used to make it most unlikely that the collision is repeated. At first sight it might seem that a repeat collision can be avoided with total certainty by giving each device a different time interval to wait before trying to transmit data again. But this would involve an extra processing cycle to ensure that each device was given a different time. Two numbers would first have to be generated, and then compared to ascertain that they were different. This in turn would impose a further delay on the devices. In practice it is more efficient to carry a very small risk of a repeat collision than to make absolutely certain that the two devices will not collide next time.

Limitations of CSMA/CD

It is this method of contending for access by first monitoring the network, then attempting to transmit and backing off for a random time interval if there is a collision, that characterizes Ethernet. It also imposes a performance limitation on Ethernet quite separate from the actual bandwidth of 10 Mbit/s supported on the network. The total bandwidth only becomes a bottleneck when large files of data are

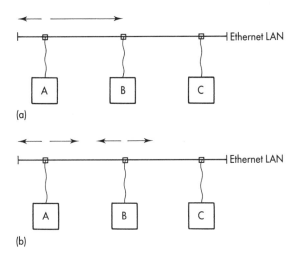

Figure A2.1 CSMA/CD method. (a) Device A starts to transmit, and the broadcast has just reached B. If B now wants to transmit, it knows it has to wait, because it can detect A's transmission. This is the CSMA part of the method. (b) Device A again has started to transmit data, but this time the transmission has not reached device B at the time our snapshot of the network was taken. If B decides it wants to transmit now, it will begin to do so, because it will not yet be able to detect A's transmission. Therefore a collision is imminent. However, when A's transmission reaches B, B will detect the collision and cease transmitting. The impact of the collision will propagate back to A, which will also cease transmitting. This is the CD part of the method.

transmitted. Although the growth in use of graphics and windowing systems on PCs is increasing the amount of data traffic on LANs, the 10 Mbit/s is still plenty for most users, especially within smaller companies.

But the CSMA/CD method can cause performance to degrade rapidly even when there is plenty of available bandwidth left – in other words when only part of the 10 Mbit/s is being utilized. This happens when a number of people are making heavy use of the LAN at a given time, which increases the incidence of collisions. Say, for example, the LAN itself is being used to 25 % of its theoretical maximum capacity, which means that 2.5 Mbit/s of the bandwidth is taken up. In theory this suggests there is plenty of spare capacity. But it means that any device will find the LAN busy for 25 % of the time, so that there is a one in four chance it will have to back off and try again. Furthermore, if other devices are also active on the LAN, there is an increased chance of a collision imposing further delay. The result is that users on their PCs will notice a delay on any applications that involve sending or receiving data across the network. For example, if they are retrieving records from a file server across the LAN, this will slow down.

The problem then with Ethernet is that performance degrades well before the network is saturated to its theoretical capacity. Furthermore, performance degrades in an unpredictable way.

Token ring does not suffer from a sudden fall off in performance, although it has a quite different limitation as we shall see. However we emphasize again that this limitation will not be a serious factor in choosing a LAN for most users. The main point is that where possible LANs should be chosen to keep future technology options open. It is increasingly important, and possible, to install cabling in such a way that both Ethernet and token ring can run on it, as well as any other type of LAN protocol that may emerge. The cabling issue is discussed in Chapter 3.

Ways of avoiding CSMA/CD limitations

There are ways to circumvent this weakness of Ethernet, its sudden collapse in performance when network loading exceeds a certain critical point. Increasingly, methods of avoiding the performance bottleneck are built into products such as cabling hubs that act as focal points for the wiring. Cabling hubs are discussed further in Chapter 3.

The main way of avoiding the performance bottleneck is to use local bridges or routers, or Ethernet switches, as discussed in Chapter 10. This applies to token ring as well as Ethernet, although in a slightly different way. Essentially these techniques work by dividing the total LAN into smaller segments, and restricting the flow of data between the segments. It is referred to as 'local' because it operates within a single physical LAN within an individual building or site. Remote bridging and routing, which are discussed in Chapter 6, interconnect distant LANs via telecommunications links.

Token ring

With token ring, access to the network is controlled by possession of a token. Unlike Ethernet, a wide range of transmission speeds are possible, but it so happens that the networking world standardized first on 4 Mbit/s, then extending it to 16 Mbit/s. FDDI (fibre distributed data interface), which is also based on token-passing technology implemented on a logical ring, operates at 100 Mbit/s, but this is not yet relevant for most small networks.

When a device wants to transmit on a token ring network, it takes hold of the token next time it comes round. Figure A2.2 shows two rings, the first where no device wants to transmit with the token circulating repeatedly, and the second where a device is seizing the token. After taking the token, the device then transmits a single packet of data across the LAN, and retains the token until it has finished. The data packet carries an address header identifying the destination device, which could be another PC, a file server or a printer, for example. When the packet reaches its destination, the address is recognized by that particular device. The destination node, which will usually be a network interface card (NIC), then takes a copy of the data packet and passes this to the PC or other device attached to it. At the same time it also inserts a message into the original version of the packet to indicate that it has been correctly received, and then replaces this onto the ring. The packet, now with the modified character indicating that it has been received correctly, continues to circulate round the ring until it returns to the device that sent it.

The sending device then strips the packet off the ring, noting that it has been received correctly – if it has not been, then it can have another try. If the data has been received correctly, the token is released back onto the ring, where it continues to circulate until another device wants to transmit and in turn takes hold of it.

Token ring's problems

This method avoids collisions, but it did introduce two new problems, one relating to performance, the other to reliability. However, both these problems have been resolved in some of the latest token ring systems, making it in many situations both more reliable and better performing than Ethernet.

The performance problem is called latency delay. This is the time taken to release the token by devices after they have finished transmitting. As we have already described, devices do not release the token immediately they have issued the data they want to transmit onto the network. Instead they wait for the data to return around the ring to them, complete with the acknowledgement of successful receipt. So just as an Ethernet LAN is standing idle while collisions are being resolved, so a token ring LAN is effectively idle while waiting for a device to release the token after transmission has already finished.

To tackle this, a method called early token ring release has been developed. With this amendment to the token ring method, devices transmitting data release the

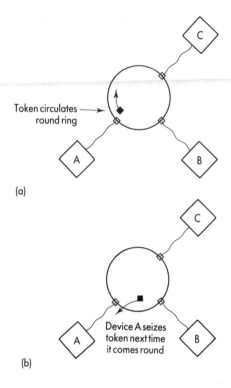

Figure A2.2   (a) Token ring in idle state. (b) Device A wants to transmit.

token back onto the ring immediately after finishing transmission of data, without waiting for the acknowledgement. This means that other devices can seize the token and be ready to transmit as soon as the previous device has finished transmitting data onto the ring. As a result the latency delay, or the time the network is idle waiting for a token to be released, is eliminated.

Early token release solves performance problem

With early token release, the token continues to travel round the network at the head of the data packet being transmitted, instead of being retained by a single sending device such as a PC. This allows other devices to join in and add their packets of data as the token passes by. So the token can now in effect be shared by two or more devices. Now it becomes possible for two or more devices to transmit at the same time, although each transmission is at a different stage of delivery. As before, a data packet is copied from the network by the receiving device, which inserts an acknowledgement. Then when the data returns to the sending device, it is stripped off, again as before. But this time there is no token to replace, because the token is already on the network.

The best analogy to explain early token release is with a train, where the ring is a circular track, the devices attached to it are stations, the token is the engine, and data packets to be transmitted are the carriages. Now when the network is idle, the engine circulates round the ring on its own without any carriages, and without stopping at any station. Then when a device wants to transmit, it halts the token or engine at its station and attaches one carriage, the data packet it wants to send, to it. Then the engine carries on round the ring, with the carriage attached. Another device may want to transmit, in which case it stops the train, and adds its carriage. There is no specific limit to how many devices can latch onto the train, except the obvious one that the train cannot be longer than the total length of track available. In other words, the number of data packets that can be in transit at any time is limited by the total circumference of the ring. This imposes a new physical constraint on the capacity of early release token rings, as can be seen in Figure A2.3.

The train then reaches its first destination, a station to which some of the carriages are destined. The train stops, the contents of the carriages are unloaded, and the train then continues. Each time the train returns to a station that on the previous circuit hitched some carriages onto it, those same carriages, having been unloaded at the destination, are now removed from the track – provided the contents of the carriages have been received correctly.

This as can be seen provides a much smoother and more fluid transmission mechanism than the first type of token ring. Early token release was not supported in the original token ring largely because the basic method was quite adequate for the small networks then envisaged. But as token ring networks expanded to include large numbers of attached devices, latency delay became a problem.

However, the early release token method is not implemented in systems based

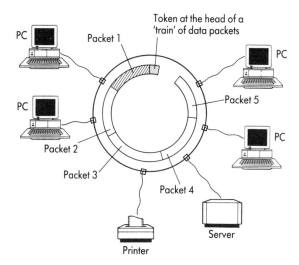

Figure A2.3   Showing how size of token ring LAN limits the amount of data it can transmit at a given time. The number of packets that can be hitched onto a train of data is restricted by the total circumference of the ring. In this example, any PC wanting to transmit data would have to wait until at least one of the packets is removed from the ring to create space.

on the 4 Mbit/s token ring. It is only implemented in the 16 Mbit/s token ring, and also in FDDI. As the cost of chip sets required to implement 16 Mbit/s token ring in network interface cards for PCs and other computers attaching to the LAN continues to fall, it will increasingly take over from the slower 4 Mbit/s version. But in the immediate future many smaller token ring LANs will continue to transmit at 4 Mbit/s without the benefit of early token release.

The latency delay is not so much of a problem on smaller networks with less than 25 users in any case. On larger networks, use of 16 Mbit/s token ring, with early token ring release, will ensure that satisfactory performance will be maintained.

Even with early token release, however, there is a small delay resulting from the fact that the token, and also data when being transmitted, has to pass through each device on the ring in sequence. Technically each device acts as a repeater, regenerating the signal as it passes through. As the data passes through one device at a time, this process is cumulative. On a large network with many devices, this could impair performance.

Ethernet does not suffer from this particular problem, because data is broadcast to all devices on the network, rather than passing serially from one to the next. With Ethernet, there is no delay while each device inspects an address to see if the associated data packet is destined for it, and of course there is no token to wait for. We can see now that performance of Ethernet and token ring are influenced by different factors. Comparative performance of Ethernet and token ring is discussed in Chapter 2.

APPENDIX 3

Cooperative processing

In Chapters 1 and 4 there is discussion of client/server computing on a LAN, in which applications are split between desktop PCs and central server machines. We have also shown that the server does not have to be 'central' – it can be just another desktop PC with a single user, but which also happens to serve data to other users across the LAN, in what is sometimes called 'peer-to-peer' networking. But it is really just another form of client/server computing, in which the server to the whole LAN community is also a client of just one user.

Client/server computing, then, is really just one way of splitting applications up to run on two different computers that are connected across the LAN (or indeed any kind of computer network). A growing number of computer applications are based on the client/server concept. And as we have already shown, many applications run more effectively in client/server mode than as stand-alone processes on a single computer. Then, for example, access to the required data can be handled by a computer designed for this task. A desire for client/server computing, as an extension to a basic requirement to share data, is therefore one reason for needing a LAN.

However, there is another possible reason for requiring a LAN, although it is less likely to be relevant for small businesses today. This is when different applications, as opposed to two parts of the same application, need to cooperate and exchange information across a LAN.

This participation of more than one application to achieve some overall task is sometimes called cooperative processing. The distinction between cooperative processing and client/server computing is a fine one, and needs to be made carefully with the help of an example.

Client/server computing tends to divide applications up into a specific part that handles a particular task, such as comparing the performance of a company's sales staff over a month, and a generic part relevant also to other applications, such as accessing the data. In this case the data to be accessed on the server would relate to the performance of each sales person. In other words, there is one client part that is specific to a particular task, and one server part that may be shared by other applications. It is really still a case of using the LAN to share a facility between a number of users.

Cooperative processing on the other hand involves the cooperation of more than one specific application. Whereas in client/server computing there is always exactly one client and one server, cooperative processing may involve two or three server computers, or it could involve several client machines, or both. The principle is that one application calls on another somewhere else on the LAN to perform some task.

Suppose, for example, a director wants a summary of his company's performance over the last year, including both overall financial results and the record of each individual salesperson. Furthermore, the director may then want to plot the salaries of each salesperson against their performance on a graph.

This could involve a total of four applications: one to calculate the financial results, another to obtain the total revenues of each salesperson, a third to access the salaries of each person, and then a fourth, on the director's PC, to match the salaries with revenues earned by each salesperson and plot this on a graph for display on the screen. The operations involved in this example and how a LAN could enable them all to be performed from a single PC is shown schematically in Figure A3.1. Note that the applications do not need to proceed sequentially one after the other.

In fact the end result – the graph – will be reached most quickly if the total revenues, the salaries and the sales performances are all obtained at the same time, with the results transmitted across the LAN to the director's PC as quickly as possible.

The ability to process different applications simultaneously is another factor distinguishing cooperative processing from straightforward client/server computing. With the latter, usually only one process is taking place at a time. First the client starts the application off, then the server takes over, perhaps to find some data and transmit it back to the client PC, then the client resumes. In complex networks, it is possible to combine client/server computing with cooperative processing, but this is beyond the scope of this book.

Three types of cooperative processing

Broadly there are three types of cooperative processing. One is where the primary application calls on a second one to perform a task, and waits for the task to be finished and any result to be returned to it before proceeding. Client/server computing will often be of this type, because the client will wait for the server to finish a task before carrying on.

The second type is where the primary application calls on another to perform some operation, but then continues without waiting for this to be completed. Then at some future time the application called on to perform the operation informs the primary task that it has finished, and if required passes over any result it has obtained.

The third type of cooperative processing is the loosest arrangement, and probably not so relevant for users of smaller LANs. It involves one application calling on another to perform some tasks, but not requiring any results and not being affected if the tasks are not completed at all.

There are various software standards to support development of cooperative applications. At the high level, there is a need for some technique enabling programs,

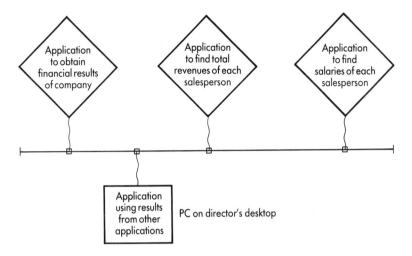

Figure A3.1   Example of cooperative processing on a LAN. Application on PC plots graphs of overall financial results, with a breakdown matching salaries of each salesperson with individual sales performance.

which may be on systems linked by a LAN or may be on geographically remote systems, to interact with each other. Such techniques have the generic name of remote procedure calls (RPCs). These enable a program running on one machine to make a call on one running on another.

APPENDIX 4

Costing of a low-end LAN solution

Here we glimpse at low-cost LAN solutions. We do not quote specific product prices, because these constantly change, but we can give a broad idea.

The first point to note is that the cost of a LAN depends not just on its size, but on what equipment you have already. The worst case is where you have to start from scratch, and buy everything, including computers and software. The best case is probably where you already have the PCs and a cabling system and need only to buy network interface cards (NICs) for the devices you need to attach to the network, and a network operating system.

Let us consider the ingredients of a LAN. The compulsory ingredients are: cabling; PCs and other computing devices such as a printer; NICs to connect the devices to the cable; and some sort of network operating system to run the LAN. In addition to this, many LANs now have a hub, which simplifies the cabling. Another important component for networks supporting more than about 12 users is a management system. This can be located in the hub to provide a central point for control, monitoring and configuration of the network. But small networks may not need a management system. Accordingly some vendors of LAN systems, such as Hewlett Packard, have introduced hubs for small networks without the management facilities, which reduces the cost.

Cost of LAN ingredients

For a small network the principal ingredients usually are: cabling; PCs, one of which may be configured to act as a dedicated file server; a printer; a hub; NICs; and a network operating system. A typical mid range PC complete with screen can be purchased for around £1000, or $1100, although some cost more, and it is possible to find one for less (note these figures are based on costs in the respective countries, which do not reflect the prevailing exchange rate). A modest laser printer costs around £700, or $900. A powerful PC capable of operating as a file server for a group of users costs around £2200, or $2400. A low-cost hub without management facilities capable of serving perhaps four or five users might cost £300, or $400. An NIC typically costs about £100 for Ethernet, or $110. A copy of a networking operating system such as Novell NetWare for up to five users costs around £500, or $600. The hardest element to cost is the cabling system, because this will probably involve paying for installation.

If unshielded twisted pair is used, and there are no particular installation problems, then a cabling system for a small office for up to, say, 12 users, leaving some scope for expansion, would cost about £1000 ($1500). Note that the difference between the dollar and sterling figures is greater for the cabling than for the other items. This is because cabling involves some labour costs. Commodity items such as hubs and PCs tend to be cheaper in the US, so that their dollar/pound price ratio is less than the exchange rate. But labour rates are roughly the same, if not rather higher in the US.

We can now estimate how much a small network would cost. If you already have the PCs and printer, as would sometimes be the case, a network for five users based on the above figures would cost about £2400, or $3160. If each user had a PC, but it was necessary to buy a more powerful server machine, which is also a fairly common situation, the cost would be £4400, or $5160. By shopping around, it might be possible to improve slightly on these prices. On the other hand, if you want the comfort of PCs from big name vendors, the cost would be more. It would also be more if you wanted to install an authorized structured cabling system from IBM or AT&T. Another item adding to the cost would be a network management system. If you wanted a hub with the potential for substantial network growth, this would also cost more.

However, where some growth is anticipated, but never beyond perhaps about 20 or 30 users, one solution worth considering is card-based hubs for PCs. For small networks, the hub does not have to be a self-standing box, but can become a function provided by a server computer. This solution has the virtue of compactness and elegance, in that the physical centre of the cabling system is also the logical centre of the LAN. Figure 3.6 shows a server functioning as a hub. Alternatively there are hubs that also function as servers.

Two caveats need to be made, however. Hubs based on standard servers that also perform file or database management will never support a large network, and they also present a single point of failure for both the cabling system and the higher-level operation of the LAN.

An alternative low-cost solution is to avoid use of a dedicated server and have a separate hub. In this solution there are no central computers shared by all users. Data and applications are distributed between PCs on users' desktops. The advantage of such a solution is that it avoids the cost of a dedicated server computer. The disadvantage is that it is limited in performance. However, some network operating systems allow you to start from a low-cost solution without a server, and then add a server at some future time. LANs without servers are sometimes called peer-to-peer networks, and can be appropriate for small business applications. Peer-to-peer networks are discussed further in Chapter 4.

Glossary

Alarm A warning of a fault or some pre-specified condition occurring on a network.

Alerts Messages sent out by network management systems, that may generate alarms.

Alternate routing Technique that allows communication to continue when one path or node fails or is unavailable.

American National Standards Institute (ANSI) Body responsible for defining US standards across the Information Technology (IT) field, also represented on international bodies.

Apple Filing Protocol (AFP) A protocol that allows the files of a server to be presented to users through the consistent Apple Macintosh graphical interface.

AppleTalk Seven layer protocol stack similar in structure to the OSI model used for communication between computers and other products in Apple Macintosh range.

Arcnet (Attached Resource Computer Network) LAN type developed by Datapoint operating initially at 2.5 Mbit/s using a token passing protocol. A new version now operates at 20 Mbit/s.

ASCII (American national standard code for interchange of information) Developed by ANSI to encode characters in units of seven digital bits.

Asynchronous communications Mode of data transmission in which each character has a definite end and beginning specified by stop bits and start bits respectively. This means each character can be transmitted independently, which can give greater flexibility than the alternative of synchronous transmission. On the other hand, each character is about 25 % longer which means that it is less efficient, particularly for sending large amounts of data.

Backbone network A network typically interconnecting individual LANs within a building or local site. Usually, but not always, the backbone is of higher capacity than the LANs being connected. However, a backbone network could also cover a wide area, interconnecting LANs at different sites. In this case the backbone will usually be of lower capacity than the LANs being connected.

Balun   A device for smoothing out impedance differences between different types of cable. A balun is required, for example, to connect unshielded twisted pair cable to coaxial cable within an Ethernet network.

Baseband   A method of data transmission where only one channel is provided on a medium, as in Ethernet.

Baud   The unit of signalling speed for transmission of digital data. It represents the number of distinct signalling events per second, which usually corresponds with the number of binary bits transmitted per second (bit/s).

Bit   A binary unit of information, either 0 or 1.

Bit error rate   The number of errors on a digital link, such as a LAN provides, expressed as the percentage of received bits that are in error.

Bits per second (Bit/s)   A measure of the raw speed of a digital link, being the rate at which individual binary bits of information are transmitted across it. For example, an Ethernet LAN provides a raw speed of 10 million bit/s (written 10 mega bit/s or 10 Mbit/s) between any two devices attached to it.

Bridge   A device for interconnecting different LANs. It operates at the media access control (MAC) level, which is part of OSI layer 2. A bridge makes the whole network function logically as a single enlarged LAN, but partitioning it into segments to prevent data being broadcast indiscriminately across the whole network.

British Standards Institute (BSI)   The UK standards body responsible for developing UK standards and also feeding into international standards bodies such as ISO.

Broadband   This is a system providing multiple channels across a medium.

Brouter   Has various definitions invented by vendors to suit their products, but refers usually to multiprotocol routers that also support bridging functions. But beware, because some so-called brouters are merely bridges that have more than two LAN connections. Really these should be called multiport bridges, not brouters.

Buffer   Temporary 'live' storage for data needed when data is transmitted between devices of different capabilities. Buffering is performed by LAN devices such as network interface cards (NICs) and routers.

Bus   A communications channel within a computer, also used to describe the topology of a tree-and-branch-shaped network such as Ethernet.

Byte   A unit of digital information, such as a character, usually comprising eight bits.

Carrier sense multiple access with collision detection (CSMA/CD)   The method used in Ethernet for controlling access to the physical cable. It is described in Chapter 2.

Carrier signal   The underlying signal used to carry information. This is electricity in the case of copper cable, and light for fibre optic cable. In either case the signal is transported in one or more frequencies, which are varied (modulated) to represent digital bits of information.

CCITT   An international body, made up of telephone companies and other players in the information technology field, responsible for setting global communication standards.

CEN/CENELEC   Combination of two committees, comprising European standards bodies, defining development of information technology standards.

Central processing unit (CPU)   The main processor at the heart of a computer such as a PC.

CEPT   The European Conference of Posts and Telecommunications Administrations. Comprising European telecommunications service providers, feeding into other standards bodies, such as CCITT and CEN/CENELEC.

Cheapernet   Otherwise known as thin Ethernet or 10Base-2. A version of Ethernet operating over thin coaxial cable.

Circuit switching   Transmission technique in which a fixed circuit is established across a switched network for the duration of a call or session. The public telephone network is circuit switched, but LANs are not.

Client/server computing   The division of an application into two parts, where one is processed on a shared server and the other on individual clients, which are often desktop PCs. The server usually handles tasks that require extensive processing power, memory and disk storage, such as database management, while clients handle tasks specific to the end user's application, such as screen presentation.

Coaxial cable   A cable comprising a central wire surrounded by plastic insulation and then a second shaft of fine wire screening.

Common management information protocol/common management information services (CMIP/CMIS)   OSI network management protocol and service.

Communications server   A server, which can be attached to a LAN, providing shared access to external communication facilities such as dial-up telephone links via modems.

Connection-oriented mode of communication   The transmission of data packets across an established path.

Connectionless mode of communication   Transmission of data where each packet is routed individually across the network using information contained in the packet's address header. The packets are reassembled at the receiving end to reconstitute the original data.

Connectivity   Ability of two systems to transmit information between themselves but not necessarily for applications running on the computers to understand it (compare interoperability)

Controlled access unit (CAU)   A souped-up and less dumb version of the media access unit (MAU), it can attach up to 80 devices (rather than eight for a MAU) in a token ring network. Like MAUs, CAUs can be concatenated to form a large inner ring supporting star clusters. However a single CAU is more likely than a MAU to form the hub of a token ring network in a star-shaped network, as explained in Chapter 3.

Copper distributed data interface (CDDI)   See FDDI.

Corporation for Open Systems (COS)   US organization comprising computer vendors and also some users focusing on issues such as conformance testing involved in applying OSI standards.

CSMA/CD   See carrier sense multiple access with collision detection (CSMA/CD).

Cyclic Redundancy Check (CRC)   A method of checking for errors in streams of data bits, often used in LANs.

Data compression   Reduction of total amount of data without affecting the information conveyed. There are various techniques, such as using short codes to represent commonly occurring characters like the letter 'e'.

Database server   A database management system implemented on a server, which can be accessed by applications running in desktop clients.

Datagram   A single packet or item of data, comprising a number of bytes. The packet contains information needed to route it across a network in connectionless mode.

Datalink layer   Layer 2 of the ISO OSI model, required for establishing a basic link for transmission of data packets between two points of a network over a physical link defined in OSI layer 1. Ethernet and token ring are essentially layer 2 standards.

DECnet   Digital Equipment's architecture for building computer networks (comparable to IBM's SNA).

Disaster recovery   Recovery from natural or man-made disasters that disable a network or computer system. High-speed links between LANs in different physical locations can be used to provide immediate backup of data for example, so that if one LAN is disabled, the other can continue running the same applications.

Diskless workstation   A PC attached to a LAN without any of its own magnetic disk storage, either floppy or hard. It relies entirely on the network to store files of data.

Duplex   Transmission of data in both directions. Full duplex is simultaneous transmission in both directions, while half duplex is transmission in both directions but only one at a time.

Dynamic routing   Process of selecting most appropriate route for each part of a transmission across a network 'on the fly' rather than always taking the same path. This requires information on current status of a network, such as availability of each individual link.

Early token release   A modified version of token ring where a sending device does not wait for the packet it has just transmitted to return to it after completing a circuit of the network before releasing the token.

EBCDIC (extended binary coded decimal interchange)   An eight-bit code for representing up to 256 characters, used mainly on IBM computer systems. Alternative character representation method to ASCII.

Electronic mail   Transmission and reception of messages and text-based information in general between computers or other electronic devices.

Encapsulation   Process of sending data encoded in one protocol across a network supporting another protocol. This is done where it is not practical actually to convert between the two protocols.

Ethernet   The most widely used LAN type operating at 10 Mbit/s. It requires a network arranged logically in a tree-and-branch structure (bus). However it can physically be a different structure, such as a star as in 10Base-T networks.

European Computer Manufacturers Association (ECMA)   Represents European IT companies, and also some US ones that trade in Europe. ECMA is involved in development of higher-layer OSI protocols.

European Telecommunications Standards Institute   This is part of CEPT and is responsible for formulating standards.

European Workshop for Open Systems (EWOS)   Develops and promotes OSI functional standards.

Fault tolerance   Ability of a computer or network to continue operating, although sometimes with reduced performance, in the event of faults. On LANs this can involve use of alternative physical transmission links between nodes, and also redundant disk drives on file servers.

Fibre distributed data interface (FDDI)   A LAN technology based on fibre optic cable, operating on dual counter-rotating rings at 100 Mbit/s. An extension of the standard called CDDI (copper distributed data interface) allows an FDDI network to deliver data at full FDDI speed direct to desktops over twisted pair copper segments up to 100 metres long, attached to a fibre backbone.

File server   A computer attached to a LAN, usually running a network operating system (NOS). The NOS controls operation of the file server, managing shared data and resources such as printers and controlling access to these from users' applications.

Frame   Synonymous with packet. A group of bytes sent over a link, including control and addressing information needed to reach its destination.

Frame Relay   A data communication method for wide area networks slowly replacing X.25. Like X.25, Frame Relay transmits variable length packets of data, but unlike X.25 does not incorporate any error detection or control, which makes it faster.

Functional profile   A specified subset of the OSI seven layer interconnection model, defined to ensure complete interoperability within a particular organization or industry grouping. The best known example is Gosip.

Gateway   Network interconnection device usually operating across the whole OSI protocol stack, often used to connect LANs to wide area networks such as X.25 or IBM SNA.

Government open systems interconnect profile (Gosip)   OSI profiles specific to individual countries, required by their national governments for public sector computer networks.

Graphical user interface (GUI)   Method of supporting user interaction with computer using windows, icons, menus and pointers (WIMP) rather than keyboard commands. Best-known example is Microsoft Windows.

Header   The control information, comprising typically source and destination address and routing instructions, inserted at start of transmitted messages.

Host   Term used to describe large computer, typically a mainframe or minicomputer, attached to a network providing services for a number of users.

Host server   Device connecting a host computer with a LAN, allowing it to communicate with terminals or PCs emulating dumb terminals that are also attached to a LAN.

Hub   The device at the centre of a physically star-shaped network. It provides the necessary electrical repeating or retiming to ensure that attached devices receive the appropriate network signals. Hubs come in various degrees of sophistication and size, ranging from simple products providing just the basic electrical functions for small networks of less than eight users, to focal points of control for large corporate networks.

IBM cabling system   Cabling system introduced by IBM in 1984, originally based just on shielded twisted pair, but now embracing unshielded twisted pair as well.

IEEE (Institute of Electrical and Electronic Engineers)   US standards group responsible for producing full internationally agreed definition of many LAN standards, including Ethernet and token ring.

IEEE 802.1   Group of standards and protocols for managing LANs.

IEEE 802.1D   Subset of the IEEE 802.1 LAN management standards, embracing just desktop systems, primarily PCs, attached to a LAN.

IEEE 802.3   The full Ethernet standard defined by the IEEE.

IEEE 802.5   The full token ring standard defined by IEEE.

Integrated services digital network (ISDN)   Digital successor to the analog public telephone network, capable of handling digital data without need for a modem. It provides higher-quality voice transmission and more reliable data transmission, because digital signals arrive at their destination largely intact, without suffering the attenuation that befalls analog signals. It also carries data significantly more quickly than is possible via modems over analog links.

International Standards Organization (ISO/IEC JTC1)   This, the primary force behind OSI standards, particularly the more complex higher-layer ones, is a voluntary organization comprising various national standards bodies as voting members. JTC1 is split into various subgroups each of which deals with a particular area – for example, SC6 deals with data communications.

Internet Engineering Task Force   Responsible for developing the TCP/IP protocols.

Internet protocol   The part of the TCP/IP protocol controlling transmission of data packets across a network.

Interoperability   Ability of applications on two computer systems to exchange information so that each can understand the other.

LAN analyser   Troubleshooting device for analysing data captured from a LAN to trace faults.

LAN Manager   Network operating system (NOS) developed by Microsoft. But confusingly IBM's network management system for token ring LANs was christened with the same name.

LAN monitor   Device or software that detects and records errors on a LAN. Can be part of a network management system.

LAN segment   Part of a larger LAN split off from other segments by bridges or routers.

LAN Server   IBM's version of LAN Manager.

LANtastic   Best known and most popular of the peer-to-peer network operating systems for small LANs. From Artisoft.

Lobe Attachment Module (LAM)   Device for attaching PCs to a concentrator in a token ring LAN.

Local area network (LAN)   Hopefully you know this by now! Network of computers governed by strict rules over distance, control of access, and structure (topology), enabling resources, data and applications to be shared between a number of end users.

Local Area Transport (LAT)   Digital Equipment's proprietary LAN communication protocol.

Local bridge   Bridge used to link two LANs in the same building or site. Typically divides a LAN up into segments for performance reasons – routers can fulfil similar function.

Logical link control (LLC)   The top half of OSI layer 2 for LANs, common to all IEEE LAN standards including Ethernet and token ring. It controls the transmission of data packets across the LAN. IEEE decided to split layer 2 up into a part common to all LANs (LLC), and a part specific to each LAN, the media access control layer, or MAC.

Media access control layer (MAC)   The bottom half of OSI layer 2, the datalink layer, responsible for control of access to the physical medium.

Each LAN type has its own MAC layer, an example being the CSMA/CD function of Ethernet.

Metropolitan area network (MAN) A fast network designed to interconnect different sites over an intermediate area corresponding to a large city.

Modem (modulator/demodulator) Device needed for computers to transmit digital data over an analog dial-up telephone link.

Multiplexer A device that enables multiple computers to transmit data over a single communications line. There are various techniques for achieving this, such as statistical multiplexing and time division multiplexing.

Multiport repeater Another name in effect for an Ethernet hub, allowing multiple devices to be attached at one physical point of an Ethernet network. This enables the bus structure of Ethernet to be transformed into a physical star without violating the Ethernet structure.

Multi-station access unit (MAU) A wiring concentrator for token ring LANS, supporting attachment of up to eight devices to a token ring LAN in a single star-shaped cluster. Alternatively a MAU can be used to form a single small token ring network. It allows a star-shaped network to function as a token ring network, fulfilling a function similar to the multiport repeater for Ethernet.

NetBIOS (network binary input output system) On a stand-alone PC, the BIOS (binary input output system) links the operating system with the input/output communications channel (bus) of the PC. This enables the operating system to control the movement of data within the PC, between the disk drive and central processing unit (CPU), for example. NetBIOS extends this, linking the PC's operating system with the network as well as the input/output bus. Developed by IBM, NetBIOS has become a *de facto* standard. It provides the basic software framework for PCs to operate on a LAN, and has been exploited by NOS developers, for example.

NetView IBM's network management system, used to monitor and manage SNA networks, but now supported by some other vendors, enabling their products to be managed from NetView.

NetWare The market-leading network operating system (NOS) from Novell. There are now two main versions: NetWare Lite for peer-to-peer operation on small networks, and NetWare 3.X (latest version NetWare 3.11) for larger networks comprising servers based on Intel's 80386 platform or higher (such as the 80486). There is also NetWare 2.X for servers based on Intel 80286 processors and higher, but this is gradually being phased out.

Network computing The distribution of applications across different computers interconnected by a network. Client/server computing is the most widespread example of network computing.

Network file system (NFS) A protocol developed by Sun Microsystems allowing computers to access each other's files as if they were locally attached. Uses the IP protocol of TCP/IP for routing across the network.

Network interface card (NIC)   The card that fits into an expansion slot at the back of a PC or other device such as a printer, containing the electronic circuitry needed to connect the device to the network. It cooperates with the NOS to transmit data to and receive it from the network.

Network layer   Layer 3 of the seven layer OSI model for computer networks. Layer 3 is responsible for providing an end-to-end connection between computers through a network, where choices of route need to be made.

Network management   The process of monitoring networks to detect faults, measuring traffic levels, metering usage of the network and controlling access to resources. Also used to configure the network.

Network operating system (NOS)   The software that controls operation of server and administers all functions of the network, as opposed to attached client computers such as desktop PCs that have their own operating systems and can run tasks independently of the network. Most NOSs have two components: a server part which is really a computer operating system in its own right, controlling access to disks, software, printers and other facilities shared across the network; and a client part which passes relevant requests from users' applications for networking resources to the server component.

Networked operating system   This differs from a traditional NOS in that it controls client computers as well as a server. It is then possible to have just one operating system controlling all aspects of a network, including desktop PCs as well as shared resources. Operating systems such as Unix, OS/2 and now Windows NT represent a move towards full networked operation by having inbuilt support for communication.

Node   A computing device, such as a PC, server, or in some cases a printer, attached directly to a network.

Open Software Foundation (OSF)   A consortium of computer vendors implementing common standards for operating systems and networking.

OS/2   An operating system developed originally by IBM and Microsoft for PCs based on Intel's 80286 and above. Unlike MS-DOS, it supports multitasking and programs that need more than 640 kbytes of memory. Microsoft subsequently abandoned OS/2 development to concentrate on Windows 3.1 and Windows NT. IBM, however, persevered, coming out first with OS/2 Extended Edition, and then OS/2 Version 2, providing progressively more inbuilt support for networking.

OSI model   Seven layer model developed by ISO (International Standards Organization) specifying how computers should communicate over a network. See Chapter 9 for full description.

OSPF (open shortest path first)   Dynamic routing protocol for networks of interconnected LANs. More sophisticated and therefore better suited to large networks than its predecessor, RIP (routing information protocol).

Packet   Synonymous with frame. A group of bytes sent over a link, including control and addressing information needed to reach its destination.

Packet switched network   Network in which data is transmitted as individual packets which are switched according to addressing information contained within them as they traverse the network. X.25 has been the main standard for packet switching, now being supplanted by Frame Relay.

Peer to peer   Communications between two devices where each has equal control over the session, as opposed to traditional master/slave communication where a central host (master) computer has full control.

Physical layer   Layer 1 of the seven layer OSI interconnection model, specifying characteristics of the physical medium of a network such as copper cable.

Polling   Method of controlling terminals or PCs emulating terminals in a master/slave relationship in which a host 'pools' each device in turn to see if it has any data or requests to send.

PowerLAN   A network operating system, from the US company Performance Technology, primarily for relatively small LANs operating in peer-to-peer mode.

PPP (point-to-point protocol)   An alternative routing protocol to OSPF and RIP, but aimed more specifically at exchanging routing information across simple point-to-point links such as dial-up telephone lines. It enables routers from different vendors to interoperate over such point-to-point circuits, which was not generally possible before.

Print driver   A program controlling printing and specifying relevant parameters such as paper size and print type.

Print server   Combination of a computer such as a dedicated LAN server and software allowing users on a LAN to share access to a printer. The print server acts as a buffer, holding data to be printed until the printer is free.

Protocol   Rules governing the flow of data across a network and interpretation of that data by end systems.

Protocol converter   A program that translates between two dissimilar protocols to enable applications in different systems to understand each other. Alternative method is protocol emulation.

Protocol emulation   This allows one computer to generate the protocols required by another, typically host, computer. Like protocol conversion, this facilitates communication between systems. See also terminal emulation.

Remote bridge   A bridge interconnecting geographically distant LANs via a telecommunications link.

Remote procedure call (RPC)   A method for applications or tasks running on different computers linked by a network to interoperate. RPCs are required as a basis of client/server computing across a LAN, for example.

Repeater   A device that increases either the span of a LAN or the distance between devices attached to the LAN, by reconstructing the signal.

RIP (routing information protocol)   Protocol used to exchange routing information between routers on a network of interconnected LANs. Unlike OSPF, it is suitable only for small networks.

RMON MIB (remote network monitoring management information base)   Part of the SNMP standard specifying the information required to manage remote devices in a distributed network.

SCSI (Small Computer Systems Interface)   A high performance standard interface for linking PCs with storage devices such as hard disk drives.

Segment   A continuous piece of cable within a network along which electrical signals travel without any amplification or retiming.

Server   A computer, usually a PC based on an Intel 80386 processor or higher, controlling access to resources on a LAN. A server may either be dedicated, in which case it has no other function, or non-dedicated, when it can also do other jobs, such as functioning as a desktop PC in a peer-to-peer network.

Shielded twisted pair (stp)   Twisted pair cable shielded from electrical interference by a wire gauze mesh, used widely for IBM token ring LANs, and in some larger networks for copper distributed data interface (CDDI).

Simple network management protocol (SNMP)   Originally called simple network management protocol (SNMP), it was developed to monitor TCP/IP networks running over Ethernet LANs. But now supports many more functions, and has become a standard for all LANs, including PCs and end systems. A key part of SMP is the MIB (management information base), which is a database management system for storing and retrieving key information about a network.

Smart hub   Intelligent hub with inbuilt computer capable of supporting different types of LAN and of managing the physical network.

SNA (System Network Architecture)   Like OSI, this comprises seven layers, but these do not all correspond exactly with OSI layers of the same number. Introduced by IBM in 1974, SNA was the world's first network architecture defining how computers should communicate. Its structure was originally hierarchical, but the latest version, SNA/APPN, is more suited to peer-to-peer communication across networks of LANs interconnected by routers.

SPAG (Standards Promotion and Application Group)   Formed in 1983 by 12 European IT firms to develop and promote conformance testing to OSI standards. Its role is similar to COS in the US.

Spooling (simultaneous peripheral operation online)   Process of controlling flow of data to an output device, usually a printer.

Start bit   Single bit delineating start of a byte in asynchronous communications.

Stop bit   Single bit delineating end of a byte in asynchronous communications.

Synchronous transmission   Communication of data in blocks within which bytes do not have start or stop bits. Blocks themselves have bits indicating their beginning, and a signal is transmitted to synchronize the devices at each end. This ensures that the receiving device knows when the transmission has finished. By avoiding the need for start and stop bits, volume of data is reduced by about 20 %. Furthermore, the need to identify each packet by looking at its start and stop bit is avoided, so that performance is improved.

System/7 Operating system for Apple Macintosh computers.

Systimax PDS Major *de facto* standard for structured cabling developed by AT&T.

TCP/IP Suite of protocols developed by the US Department of Defense, since adopted as an international standard, particularly for networks of interconnected Ethernet LANs.

Terminal emulation Process by which a PC mimics the attributes of a dumb terminal, so that its user can access an application on a host system in a master/slave relationship. The emulation software enables the PC to issue commands that the host expects to receive from a dumb terminal.

Terminal server A device attached to a LAN enabling a number of dumb terminals to communicate with a host computer also attached to the LAN.

Token ring The second most popular LAN type, in which access to the network is controlled by use of a token, possession of which is required to transmit data. The token, and data, travels sequentially from device to device in a logical ring structure, although with MAUs or CAUs the network may actually be star-shaped.

Topology Term for the structure of a network and how data flows within it. For example, in a ring topology, as used by token ring LANs, the data 'sees' the network as a ring and travels sequentially from device to device. With a ring topology there are two routes between any pair of nodes. On the other hand, with a bus or tree-and-branch network, like Ethernet, data need not travel sequentially from device to device. With Ethernet data is 'broadcast' in all directions simultaneously, to ensure that it reaches all attached nodes as quickly as possible.

Twisted pair Cable in which pairs of copper wire are twisted together to reduce electrical interference. There are two essential types, shielded and unshielded, and different grades within each of these groups.

Unshielded twisted pair (utp) Twisted pair cable without any form of shielding other than basic insulation.

UPS (uninterruptible power supply) A rechargeable battery sitting between the mains supply and one or more computing devices, providing backup power in the event of a power cut. Unless there is a standby generator as well, a UPS system is unable to maintain power for the duration of a sustained power cut – its role is typically to facilitate an orderly shut down of the network so that critical data can be backed up.

VINES (VIrtual NEtworking System) Banyan Systems' NOS based on the

Unix operating system. Designed for large networks comprising systems from a number of different vendors.

Wide area network (WAN)   A network spanning a greater distance than a LAN is capable of, usually making use of telecommunications links. These may be dial-up links, or permanent circuits leased from a telecommunications carrier.

Windows for Workgroups   A sequel to Microsoft's Windows 3.1 operating system, introducing peer-to-peer networking capabilities.

Wiring closet   A small room or recess providing the focal point for cabling on a floor.

Wiring frame   A frame on which cables are terminated and interconnected. Typically situated in a wiring closet.

X series   Recommendations specified by CCITT governing attachment of terminals and computers to a data network.

X.25   X series standard specifying interface between computers and packet switched network. Being supplanted by Frame Relay.

X.400   X standard for exchange of graphics or fax as well as textual data between users or applications.

X.500   Distributed directory services standard. It allows users or applications to obtain the address of intended recipients from directories distributed across a network.

X-Open   Body comprising computer vendors and some users responsible for promoting and applying open systems standards such as OSI.

X-Windows   Standard for creating graphical user interfaces (GUI) on PC or intelligent terminals called Xterminals.

XNS (Xerox network systems)   A protocol stack designed by Xerox for LAN communication, forming the basis of Novell's IPX.

10Base-2   Version of Ethernet using thin coaxial cable, colloquially referred to as Cheapernet. The name describes the speed, 10 Mbit/s, the transmission type (Baseband), and the maximum cable length, almost 200 metres (actually 185 metres).

10Base-5   Version of Ethernet using thick coaxial cable. The name describes the speed, 10 Mbit/s, the transmission type (Baseband), and the maximum cable length, 500 metres.

10Base-T   Version of Ethernet using unshielded twisted pair cabling. The name describes the speed, 10 Mbit/s, the transmission type (Baseband), and the cable type, twisted pair. Network is arranged in star shape around a hub, with recommended maximum length of each segment 100 metres.

10Net   A peer-to-peer network operating system from Sitka.

Index

O

P

129341